The Sound Of Water

Valerie Davies

ArrowGate

Published by Arrow Gate Publishing
London
Copyright © 2013 Valerie Davies

13 12 10 9 8 7 6 5 4 3

Arrow ...   eases
creativ...   l pro-

Than...   for
comp...   , or

You ar...   ng to

A CIP...   tish

978-0-9575930-5-3

Printed in the United Kingdom
Set in Theano Didot
Designed by Arrow Gate

www.arrowgatepublishing.com
Arrow Gate Publishing Ltd Reg. No. 8376606

Editors
Chloe Pilsbury, Sandra David

INTRODUCTION

This isn't so much a diary of a nobody, as a well stuffed Gladstone bag, crammed with the pleasures of books, food, music, memories, stories of war and peace, events and people in far-flung countries, fragments of life and experiences which emerged from their sleep and forgetting into the light of common day, as the date in the diary jogged the memory. Though it began as a diary and a confidant, it became a journal, a memoir, a nature diary, a journey, all 'the earnings and gleanings of a busy life'.

It's also about the inner life, lived in a tiny fishing village of just over 400 souls on a remote harbour – almost at the ends of the earth. And always there are the seasons, the sea, storms, sunshine, birds and butterflies.

Though yet another traveller's tale from a person like me is of small account in the history of the world, maybe I'm speaking to some who walk the same path, since all stories are the maps and spiritual logbooks of the human race. And maybe some people will find themselves amused and entertained by the detours, deviations, wrong turnings and resting places on the winding path of an easily distracted wayfarer.

The poet Antonio Machado said: *'Travellers, there is no path, paths are made by walk.'* This is my walk.

GITANJALI 90

*On the day when death will knock at thy door what
wilt thou offer him?*

*Oh, I will set before my guest the full vessel of my life-I
will never let him go with empty hands.*

*All the sweet vintage of my autumn days and summer
nights, all the earnings and gleanings of my busy life
will I place before him at the close of my days when
death will knock at my door.*

-
                                    RABINDRANATH TAGOR

CONTENTS

1

Oct/Dec 2007

October 10

The death of the dolphin was a mystery – still is. And now the magic, tragic dolphin has entered the mythology of this distant place.

Jane and I stood with our hands on the sun-warmed sculpture of Opo, not far from her burial place, and tried to imagine what that summer had been like. To this tiny settlement on the edge of the remote Hokianga harbour, thousands of people flocked that summer.

They came to see Opo the dolphin playing with the children on the water's edge. They came from all over the country, driving along dusty unsealed gravel roads through empty endless countryside. They came in their hundreds, day after day, in that long summer from December 1956 to March 1957. The country was in love with Opo.

Valerie Davies

Too many people came to Opononi, a tiny fishing settlement, hardly even a village – a few hundred houses, a handsome two-storied verandahed Victorian pub, some Victorian shop fronts and a wharf where the fishing boats tied up. The people of Opononi became increasingly concerned for the welfare of Opo, as well as for their village, as the crowds kept on coming, and the people lined the sands and the narrow road along the edge of the sea, and grown men tried to climb on the little dolphin's back. On 8 March, they achieved official protection status for Opo. The next day she was found dead, wedged in the rocks. No one knows who, how, or why, but her death shocked the country, leading the news. The local Maori people gave her a full ceremonial tangi.

Over forty-five years later, Jane and I paid our respects to her memory, and were caught by surprise at how strong the memory of Opo still is. We are not the only ones. People still make the pilgrimage that we had made to visit Opononi, which looks out across the blue Hokianga harbour to gold sand dunes the other side. It's still the home of the fabled dolphin, and there still seems a lingering ineradicable sadness at her absence.

Rather subdued, we retraced our footsteps back to Rawene, where the ferry shuttles across the harbour to Kohukohu. We had lunch in the Boat-Shed, sitting over the edge of the water in the sun, looking across to

Kohukohu a pretty Victorian village so untouched by progress that it's like stepping back in time to walk there. The pastel-coloured Victorian villas with their wide verandas and porches decorated with lacy carving, clustered on the hillside by the water, have survived unmodernised, dreaming in the sunshine. Few places in New Zealand are romantic, but Kohukohu is.

The Boat-Shed, however, had its own atmosphere, and smoked salmon fettuccine and almond chocolate cake with good coffee were an unexpected treat in this forgotten settlement.

The owners are travellers too. Every winter for a month or so in August, they take off to Italy and pick up more culinary inspiration before returning to this idyllic place. Fortified with such good cheer, we took the long drive back home.

October 16

Knowing that epileptics don't swallow their tongues was really useful first-aid this morning. Having been lent the book A Recipe for Bees by Gail Anderson-Dargatz a few weeks ago,

I finally forced myself to read it yesterday. Novels are rarely my thing, and I'm not keen on that atavistic Canadian Gothic genre – it even made me realise what dungeons of despair were implied in Anne of Green Gables, when you know what you're looking for! But loving facts, I found all the information about bees the most interesting part of the whole book.

And then, today, I came out of the dentist's and found a man lying on the pavement with two women, looking helpless, crouched down beside him. As I reached them I said, 'Is there anything I can do?' By then I could see it was an epileptic fit. The Pakeha woman squatting beside him said, 'We're worried that he'll swallow his tongue.'

And because I'd read A Recipe for Bees, with this information in it, I said very firmly, 'No, you don't have to worry about that. That's an old-fashioned theory.' I knelt down, so thankful to know this, and put my hand on his burning heart. Someone came running from the doctor's surgery nearby saying the doctor was coming, so I left.

October 18

Driving along the road, I passed the somewhat disheveled gang of men gathering up all the tacky remains of the inorganic rubbish collection, strewn along the roadside. This was my big opportunity. I stopped by one of the men, wound down the window, leaned across from the driver's seat, and called to him. He bent down to peer in the window, and I saw a figure from the Old Testament or maybe St John the Baptist. He was probably Maori, with waist-length dreadlocks, stripped down to a pair of shorts and tattered running shoes, and was deeply browned from the sun. He looked at me with piercing, deep-set dark eyes.

I thanked him for the wonderful job he was doing. He leant into the car and reached across the seat, and I took his hand – the hands that were picking up the filthy rubbish.

The touch of his on mine was exquisite. It was one of the most perfect and memorable moments in my life. Pure, peaceful energy flowed from him, and his radiant presence took me by surprise.

'Thank you, lady,' he smiled, 'you've made my day.'

The words were banal, but they felt like a blessing. I drove off euphorically, feeling I had had an encounter with a Master, or one of those great Bodhisattvas who come back to earth to assist mankind.

October 28

I've been reading Abraham Maslow's 'hierarchy of needs', going from the survival needs of water, food, and oxygen, on to warmth, shelter, safety, clothing, and love, going up to esteem and social status, and top of the list: self-actualisation and enlightenment. But it doesn't mention the need for beauty, and yet for me, and many of my friends, it's an absolute necessity, and always has been. More than that, beauty has an intrinsically spiritual quality, I feel. A life without beauty would be a life of deepest deprivation. Quaker Caroline Graveson wrote: 'there is a daily round for beauty as for goodness'.

I remember moments of beauty right back to my earliest childhood, when I was two, gazing up at the sweet smelling honeysuckle in the hedge above me, outlined against the blue sky. That moment was just one of many in that enchanted Dorset, countryside of 1940 when long blue dragonflies still flitted above the clear water of the River Frome, and emerald green waterweed flowed in long streamers with the current. On long summer nights, wisps of hay were strung horizontally along the high hawthorn and hazel hedges at dusk, when tired dray horses dragged the overloaded hay wagons down the narrow lane past our cottage, bringing the scent of summer with them.

And I remember the misery I felt at thirteen, after leaving the Yorkshire dales, and finding myself in an ugly town like Aldershot. We lived outside Crookham, and I caught the bus to school in Aldershot. One morning, as we left the bus to walk the mile or so to school, past the ugly railway yards, I saw the cranes and rooflines outlined black against a blazing red sun-rise, and still remember the gratitude for that beauty in the middle of the industrial mess.

Beauty is still an absolute necessity. This is the joy of living here, in this place with trees and views and sea, in a house with beautiful music, good books, pictures, flowers, birdsong, with food as tasty as I can make it, on china as pretty as I want, in an atmosphere of peace and harmony. I must be one of the most fortunate people in the world, to have my needs met so perfectly.

And I go to sleep each night to the words of that haiku by the twentieth century Japanese poet Yoshii Isamu:

> *Even in my sleep*
> > *the sound of water*
> > > *flows beneath my pillow.*

I wrote it on paper, which I stained with weak tea, and had it framed for Patrick to hang on his wall. It's also carved on a boulder beside the river in Kyoto.

November 12

We went to a farewell party where we met many old acquaintances. After twenty years, some had changed, and some had not. Our hosts, Cuthbert as charming and as good as ever, Ginnie as earnest as ever – 'planted 3,000 trees all on my own...' Evelyn the same as ever at eighty. I hadn't made much effort to seek her out in the throng, but as we were leaving, she rushed up to me, pushing and bobbing around other people, gabbling everything she wanted me to know; how busy she was... her writing... the parish magazine... the vicar gave her a big pat on the back... busy working all day in her study... Dick next door, busy with his painting. Several messages there, 'what a wonderful old couple we are, and also, mummy, aren't I clever, and daddy (the vicar) thinks so too.' Cuthbert was the only one to ask us what we were doing! Exhausted when we got home.

The following day Hilde came for lunch. With old age, she has become much gruffer, and has lost her joie de vivre, and enjoyment of people and little things.

Conversation had become rather laboured. I said, apropos of some remark, 'Did you ever see the film Death in Venice?'

Hilde looks baffled so I try to explain who Thomas Mann was. More bafflement, so I say, 'Oh well, I won't go on, because it won't mean anything to you.'

So then, Hilde says:

'Was Thomas Mann a writer who was popular during my mother's forties?' Being seventy-eight herself.

'Yes', I reply, at which she tells me in a ruminative fashion, that she once saw a film of his, called Death in Venice.

At this point, I have forgotten what I was originally going to say in the first place, and I abandon the subject! Our old friendship seems now a duty, which cannot be neglected. Old age is when we really do need our community, I realise as I watch Hilde's resistance to its frailty.

I'm reading aloud to Patrick, Robert Byron's classic, *The Road to Oxiana*, since he had so enjoyed Charles Glass's *Tribes with Flags*. Even though Byron's worldview seems completely lacking in compassion or nice women, his writing moves me. Paragraphs like:

There was no furniture in the room. In the middle of the floor stood a tall brass lamp, casting a cold white blaze over the red carpets and bare white walls. It stood between two pewter bowls, one filled with branches of pink fruit blossom, the other with a posy of big yellow jonquils wrapped round a bunch of violets. By the jonquils sat the Governor, with his legs crossed and his hands folded in his sleeves; by the blossom sat his young son, whose oval face, black eyes and curving lashes were the ideal beauty of the Persian miniaturist. They had nothing to occupy them, neither book nor pen, nor food. Father and son were lost in the sight and smell of spring.

Again, at Persepolis:

In the old days you arrived by horse. You rode up the steps on to the platform. You made a camp there, while

Valerie Davies

the columns and winged beasts kept their solitude beneath the stars, and not a sound or movement disturbed the empty plain. You thought of Darius, and Xerxes and Alexander. You were alone with the ancient world. You saw Asia as the Greeks saw it, and you felt their magic breath stretching out towards China itself...

These words keep me reading.

November 22

We went to see Hilde and her garden. Her corner is so sheltered that already the profusion in the garden makes it look and feel like high summer. It's crammed with examples of just about every summer flower, including rampant golden day lilies, regal lilies, roses everywhere, irises still in bloom, and daisies of every description. The pink valerian and marigolds she's sown along the crack between her fence and the pavement look enchanting, with climbing roses, Buff Beauty and Wedding Day, waving from the high trellis fence overhead.

Her front garden was described by a passer-by as 'like Provence,' and so it is. Flowers and creepers, including geraniums, weave in and out of each other, Queen Anne's lace jostles with poppies and pinks, vines and roses clamber up the banisters and along her veranda, orange orchids and purple lavender tip out of a border, and pansies and daisies sprawl across the path. Self-seeded marigolds and violas inhabit cracks in the pavement beyond her gate, pots of flowers crowd the steps, and the flaming colours, gold, orange, purple, violet and crimson are quite unlike a cool English garden. We had one of those conversations, which consisted solely of the names of plants and flowers for a whole hour, and then I left with seeds and cuttings.

This house was sprayed for insects.

A big, gentle man arrived, and in very broken English told me he loved spraying my house because it was so peaceful and beautiful.

I asked him where he came from, and he said he was Armenian.

I have a passion for Armenian history, and I exclaimed to him about his country's tragic past (some aspects of it remind me of Poland). He said I was the first person he'd met here who had heard of Armenia (incredible), and told me that he'd come from Iraq, where they were treated as second class citizens (no doubt).

Something about his energy reminded me of the Persian who used to serve petrol at the garage in town. This man was always immaculately groomed, exquisitely courteous, and I always wondered if he was a Sufi, because his service was like a gift to God. When I asked, he said no, Baha'I – both Muslim.

November 23

Feeling flat and cut off from myself... not actively unhappy, but as though life is grey and has lost its savour. I feel very out of touch with God. Is this the barren desert the mystics talk of? I know in my head that the feeling is not what matters, that the journey, the washing up and the stopping at traffic lights, the making of the bed, and smiling at a child are as much part of the journey as the soaring spiritual highs. And that it is the doing of them consciously that matters. But somehow, when I feel like this, even the remembrance of the name of God is difficult.

I found a poem by Rabindranath Tagore, which seemed to match my mood...

When the heart is hard and parched up, come upon me with a shower of mercy.

When grace is lost from life, come with a burst of song.

When tumultuous work raises its din on all sides, shutting me out from beyond, come to me, my lord of silence, with thy peace and rest...

At least gave myself a belly laugh on reading a remark about Jeffrey Archer: 'Is there no beginning to his talents?' Envy grips me when I think of him celebrating at The-Old Vicarage at Grantchester. Rupert Brooke must be revolving in his grave in foreign fields along with the shades of many a rural dean... it's enough to make strong men weep, in Rupert's words.

November 25

I took a trip over to Kawau Island on the ferry, feeling like a dose of sea, fresh air, and different pastures. Wandered round elegant Mansion House, which had once been the governor's house, and up the walk through the trees. The white peacock mooching around the house was looking a bit mangy, I thought. I find the restoration rather dated and overly correct, but how I would have loved to live in it; a white porticoed Georgian house with Victorian additions, dreaming on the edge of a turquoise sea that looked like glass that day, with the trees and hills behind. No cars, no phone, no TV, no pollution, no people, no noise, nuffink.

On the way back, it was cold and overcast, so I went inside and read my book, Sanditon. More particularly, just the fragment Jane Austen wrote.

It fascinates me. Austen's opening speared me; her gaiety and wit seemed to have been frozen into disillusionment and acidity. It's as though in these chapters written before she became too ill to write any more, her observations had become cynical, unleavened with the humour which always made her acute perceptions bearable.

So Lady Denham is a harsher and less ridiculous figure than her literary predecessor, Lady Catherine de Bourgh. Lady Catherine was rather a delicious joke. Lady Denham is a thoroughly unpleasant old woman – she, *'like a true great lady, talked and talked of her own concerns.'* When silly Sir Edward, one of Austen's most unattractive anti-heroes, quotes the poet Burns inaccurately and inappropriately, she bitingly makes Charlotte, the heroine, say of Burns: *'I have no faith in the sincerity of the affections of a man of his description. He felt and he wrote and he forgot.'*

Yet, when I got home and re-read the letters she wrote at that very time from January to 18 March 1817, the day when she finally laid down her pen, she sounds as gay and caressing as ever to her correspondents.

To her beloved niece Fanny Knight, she wrote on 13 March,

'Women have a dreadful propensity for being poor – which is one very strong argument in favour of matrimony.'

I could write a long essay on how that remark has been turned on its head by feminism and careers, and yet it often still holds good for the once married, or divorced, with children.

14

Through staying with my brother Robert at Branscombe, and shopping at Sidmouth, I now know what Sanditon and Brinscombe were like... Austen was writing a gentle (I think) mockery of the new fashion for novelty, change and seaside holidays.

Three years after Austen had poked fun at Sidmouth/Sanditon, the Duke and Duchess of Kent and their seven-month-old daughter, the future Queen Victoria, went to live in 'gilded poverty' at Sidmouth. The Duke caught a cold and, within four weeks of arriving, died on 23 January 1820 having lost more than six pints of blood, as prescribed by the best doctors in the country.

December 14

I fell down the garden steps and broke my wrist after the last entry. My right wrist and I am right-handed. Tough. I'm getting used to it now. Tonight as I write, I'm listening to Dietrich Buxtehude's *cantate Jubilate Domino,* sung by Alfred Deller.

I've loved it ever since I sang it in the choir for the Christmas concert. And I also love the idea of nineteen-year-old Bach trudging two hundred and thirty miles to Lubeck to hear the great Buxtehude play the organ there. Probably his famous Advent concerts, since Bach stayed over from October 1705 to January 1706, getting back late and in trouble to Arnstadt where he was organist himself. Buxtehude died the following year.

The longing in those lines, adapted to our carol In dulce Jubilo, which go, '*Oh, that we were there, oh that we were there*' always moves me. The words throb with the deep love and devotion of those old Protestants who wished to the bottom of their hearts that they had been there in Bethlehem. I have never been sure. Would I have been so sure as those who worshipped then? Would I have recognised the moment as those shepherds did?

I made the Christmas cake today, from the recipe given to me by a reader of my column nearly thirty years ago. It is fail safe, needs only some stirring which can be done with a left hand, and is hideously fattening, stuffed with fruit, nuts, butter, sugar, brandy and topped off, of course, with marzipan and icing. Since no one else in the family actually likes it, Patrick and I eat it, and it goes far too quickly for the good of our waistlines...

We finished The Road to... and the last pages made me nearly weep.

We keep seeing on the TV news, and in the newspapers, the scenes of war in Afghanistan, the ruins of towns and villages, people living in heaps of rubble, which were once their homes. Surrounded by a barren land, deserts of grey stone or dusty sand. Not a tree or a blade of grass. No women, except the rare sight of a figure hidden beneath a full-length veil, accompanied by the statutory man...

Byron had written:

Dar al Aman is joined to Kabul by one of the most beautiful avenues in the world, four miles long, dead straight, as broad as the Great West Road, and lined with tall white-stemmed poplars. In front of the poplars run streams confined by grass margins. Behind them are shady footwalks and a tangle of yellow and white roses, now in full flower and richly scented.

While Bruce Chatwin's poetic introduction told us:

On the streets of Herat, you saw men in mountainous turbans, strolling hand in hand, with roses in their mouths and rifles wrapped in flowered chintz...

Between the Mujahideen and the Russians, the Taliban and the US, a world of beauty has disappeared, and it will never be seen again.

15 December

It is so still and silent that I hear as each foxglove bell slips from its stem onto the table beneath. I hear the petals drop from the roses Christine gave me, and each stray yellow leaf that falls from the puriri tree and lands with a rustle outside the French windows. A thrush is singing. A white butterfly is hovering above the white hydrangeas. Occasionally a lazy wave washes onto the rocks down below. If I could live every moment of my life at this level of sweetness and awareness, and did nothing else but sit here in this peace and solitude, it feels as though it would be enough.

December 17

Since I can't do much gardening or housework with my plastered arm, I don't feel guilty about reading half the day. I've just finished re-reading John Evelyn's Diaries. I'd forgotten his dreadful descriptions of a kidney stone operation without anaesthetic – amazing that they had enough medical knowledge to do it – the passage about a man being racked, simply on suspicion of being a thief, and the account of galley slaves' terrible conditions. He also records, without any apparent consciousness of the agony involved, all his wife's eight childbirths in a simple sentence: *'This day was my wife delivered of her first, second, third etc child.'*

On the other hand, at the death of his eldest son at five years old, he wrote *'Here ends the joy of my life, for which I go mourning to the grave.'* The day before the child died so suddenly, when he was still fit and well, he told his father that though he *'loved him dearly, he would leave his house and lands and all his fine things to his brother Jack.'*

18

Jack did inherit, but died at the age of forty-five, Evelyn's only child to live that long. I shall think of John Evelyn every time I wash my hair in my herbal shampoo after reading that on 13 August 1653: *'I first began a course of yearly washing my head with warm water mingled with a decoction of sweet herbs.'*

I treasure too the picture of Evelyn and his wife stopping to examine Stonehenge on a fine summer's day, in an empty landscape, and Evelyn striding up to the stones, and after marvelling at them, trying with a hammer to dent them, and failing. How come he had a hammer?

Did he have a carriage first aid kit tucked under their seat?

Pepys wrote of John Evelyn: *'The more I know him, the more I love him'.*

December 23

Yesterday was peerless – in the words of an ancient family joke – cloudless sky, turquoise sea, and scarlet pohutukawa trees outlined against the blues.

As we sat outside the strawberry place licking our ice-creams in the sun, I heard a lark singing, notes tumbling endlessly around and above us, and search though I might, I couldn't find the black dot sending this torrent of sound round the sky and down into distant hills and green fields.

Engrossed in Ulysses Grant and the Civil War though I am, I was torn between reading and poring over battlefield maps, and just sitting savouring the glorious day. The evening was crystal bright, and the duck egg blue sky hardly defined against the pale still waters of the sea.

Cara, our tiny black cat, and I did our nightly ramble round the cemetery, she scampering across crumbling tombstones, me reading the inscriptions... 'Sleep on Grumpy', on one, and 'Together at last' on a stone which recorded a marriage which had lasted seventy years. Considering that the belief today is that we live longer than our forebears, the number of old gaffers and Victorian dames here, who lived well into their seventies, eighties and beyond, is remarkable.

During my nightly perusal of the stone tablets, I learn something new about the past inhabitants of this place every night – last night I came across the inscription of a lady who had included both her OBE and her WRACNZ number. Then, a family, the parents of whom had been born in Scotland, and their daughter, buried with them, who had been born in Nova Scotia. This told me that they had done the great trek from place to place around the world with the astonishing Scots of Waipu, searching for a better life and a promised land. They were Highlanders, who left Scotland in 1817 with their leader, the Rev. Norman McLeod.

They lived in Nova Scotia until 1853 when potato blight and other plagues struck them. So they built some ships and upped sticks, and sailed off around the world to remote, unmapped, unpopulated New Zealand. 800 of them came, led by their charismatic Presbyterian minister, who by then was seventy-one. A handful of them came to this empty bay.

On our way round, we pause to sit and contemplate the harbour below, fishing boats at anchor, and tonight, being holiday time, hearing bumps and voices, as a handful of holidaymakers in yachts below prepare their evening meals, and relax in the most perfectly beautiful harbour in the world.

We sit on a green marble bench dedicated to a father by his large family of Dutch sons and daughters, and, if we're lucky, and it's been a warm, sunny day like today, the seat is warm, holding the heat for several hours and hard to leave.

Slowly we meander past white china angels, and pots of flowers freshly replenished for Christmas by visiting relatives, including a flat stone in the grass with just the name and dates. This man came to rest here in 1951, over fifty years ago and yet, tonight, someone has placed red and yellow hibiscus flowers in a ring around the stone.

December 26

Christmas Day was a good one. The feast was as good as ever. I made huge amounts of the famous potatoes, cream and garlic, which disappeared in the same huge amounts. Ever since the Christmas six years ago, when the grandchildren discovered this grown-ups' treat, and gobbled it all up under the distressed, greedy eyes of the adults, I've made it regularly whenever the children come. They even eat the left-overs for breakfast. Elizabeth David, 'the onlie begetter,' would be pleased.

Because my wrist was still in plaster (purple and I bought a purple top to wear with it) after my fall down the garden steps, the boys came over and took away the big bags of potatoes, and they and their father had a great potato peeling bee, returning them for the anointing of cream and garlic in three casseroles.

After lunch, we played charades, laughing dementedly. And after supper, Piers begged for charades again.

We played for hours, Julian nobly humbling himself to be jeered at by his children, as well as Eugenie, who has a genius for mimicry and the total absorption of a child.

So the day ended with much shrieking and hysterical laughter.

I laughed so much I couldn't talk and the tears ran down my cheeks.

2

Jan/Feb 2008

New Year's Day, January 1

Fireworks at midnight, with me outside calling for Cara in case she was panicked by all the bangs, whistling and lights. Found her crouching by one of the large pots. Then continued reading Shelby Foote's account of the end of the American Civil war, the surrender at Appomattox ... very pale compared with the insights and symbolism of Bruce Catton's account.

I'm also searching in both accounts for Lincoln's visit to Mrs Pickett when he did his walk through the abandoned city of Richmond, Mrs Pickett being the wife of General Pickett of the Charge at Gettysburg. At that moment, Pickett himself was busy elsewhere doing as much damage as he could to Lincoln's soldiers. When Mrs Pickett entered the room with her baby in her arms, Lincoln took him from her, and spoke to both babe and mother, before continuing on his tour.

Neither Bruce Catton nor Shelby Foote mentions this attractive and typically human story about the president. So I went to Jesse Bowman Young's eyewitness account of Gettysburg. And yes, there was the story, in an account taken from Mrs Pickett's book, Pickett and his Men. Shelby Foote doesn't list his sources, and Mrs. Pickett isn't listed in Bruce Catton's account, so these men obviously didn't bother with a mere woman's book. To my mind, they missed some fascinating information, including the fact that Lincoln found the young man a place at West Point, and so set him on his way to what was known as Pickett's Charge at Gettysburg, which rivalled the Charge of the Light Brigade, nine years before, in bravery and pointlessness.

Didn't get much sleep, and was up in good time to prepare lunch for Caroline and Jane. Cauliflower and pea curry, followed by a lemon cream pudding – nothing but cream, yoghurt, lemon curd and crushed meringue. Divine. We ate on the veranda, with the sound of the sea crashing on the rocks below, and the colours as sharp and bright as yesterday, with glacial-green water and ice-white foam swirling over the rocks. To my amazement, Caroline solemnly picked out all the peas and ringed them around the edge of her plate before beginning to eat the rest. So much for the maturity of late middle age...

The family went home today. Lots of laughter this Christmas, including reading Alan Bennett's The Uncommon Reader, a clever little tour de force about the Queen's imaginary discovery of books.

January 7

We don't often go to dinner parties, and this one confirmed my slight resistance to such occasions, unless I know the people. One woman gaunt, groomed, vain, dogmatic, silly, and yet sweet; the other tiny, tragic, and emotionally exhausted by the endless strain of trying to hold her family together in the ruins of their disaster. One man gentle, kind, and rather lost in the harsh cynical world in which he was stranded; the other, tough, arrogant and clever. Our host clever and friendly, but stuck between the toughie and the softie at the same time, and our hostess trying to control chaos. Patrick and I only catching one word in ten, in the general hubbub and chat about people we didn't know. No real conversation, just sallies and ripostes, and in-jokes and in-gossip. One of the lower levels of hell.

I've begun sorting through drawers of loads of recipes collected since the early sixties. I frequently can't find the one I want and though I try to keep my favourites all together, they still stray into other collections of 'intending to try,' and 'must try'. After hours spent sorting them into piles, and several rubbish bags full of the unwanted trimmings of yellowing newsprint and magazine borders, I knew that this truly was what is called a backbreaking job. I hadn't even handled a quarter of the clippings.

Method: sort through the whole lot, putting them into piles: cake, pudding, pasta, rice, chicken, fish, soups, salads, suppers, savouries, sauces and so on. Then sort the piles, throw out the duplicates, and trim yet again, to fit into scrapbooks, and stick them in. The cake book was huge, almond, fruit, lemon, plum, rhubarb, apple, madeira, chocolate, coffee, the whole nine yards. It has taken me days to get this far.

January 10

Charles Stevens and Rosalie came for dinner and to stay the night – in a bed! I think it was a treat for them after being coiled up in their tiny camper van touring the North Island – they're both tall. The last time they came to see us was at Howick, and Charles had just given up trading in antique Japanese swords, and become a sort of rover in the style of Richard Burton, travelling to remote and unexplored places on his own.

He had with him to show us, his portfolio of photos of Bedouin women, ravishing and mysterious, of gau-

chos in South America, and beautiful African and So-
mali women and children. He had also taken pictures of
the Cambodian hill tribal people, the Mong, who
hailed, aeons ago, from Mongolia, and are shamanistic
and animistic. He won't write about these people for
travel magazines, because he feels it would accelerate
the destruction of their culture if tourism were to enter
their lives.

Rosalie had done a seven-year apprenticeship in ge-
omancy, and was on the same 'New Age Nutter' wavelength (Patrick's description) as me. Patrick said he
could hardly believe his ears when he overheard our
conversation while he was listening to the endangered
species talk with Charles! She practises Feng Shui, and
said it was no good people just changing the house
around to remove blocks; you have to work with people
to help them move past their emotional blocks, which
are what are reflected in the house. Listening to her
talk was meat and drink to me.

I had asked her what she had felt when she came into the house we lived in back then.

'Humble face – gem within,' she instantly replied. I
laughed delightedly at this spontaneous koanlike answer, it was so apt and accurate. The house looked so
little and cottagey from the front, and then you walked
through into a soaring room with huge windows, ga-
bled ceiling and filled with treasures.

So I was looking forward to a similar enriching encounter this time. It was not to be. Charles has now
discovered he has diabetes, and feels he will only have a
short lifespan, and thinks his mother could outlive him.
I think he's still coming to terms with all the implica-
tions for his life. Rosalie rather withdrawn. They live
in a country house in Dorset and now deal in Georgian
antiques, and bring up their two golden retriever pup-
pies. Rather an enviable lifestyle.

January 12

Still at my self-imposed chore with all the recipes.
It's satisfying, but the hours spent on a hard chair at
the dining table, sorting, cutting and sticking, are bad
for my back. Being the summer holidays, with no duties, chauffeuring to board meetings for Patrick, or
trips to specialists etc, I have long stretches of time to
myself, spent on sticking in and reading. The interesting thing is that I recognise most of the recipes, know
where we were living then, and even remember with
many of them, how and when I tore or cut them out,
right back to 1964, when we were living at Newney
Hall in the hidden countryside of Essex.

I can remember many of the dinner parties and the
people who were there and the menus. Croquembouche
in the height of a Hong Kong summer, with no air-
conditioning then, dripping with sweat, as I baked

choux pastry balls, whipped up cream with cointreau, and made the caramel to dribble over the pyramid of puff pastry balls. Biscotten torte, a Danish coffee and walnut confection which could be made a week beforehand, given to me when I was engaged by my stepmother's best friend, vol-au-vent, one of my father's favourites, and mint and orange salad, a Robert Carrier special from the then new Sunday Times colour supplement.

Then there were the handwritten ones, salmon slice from Jenny, fruit cake from some people who read my columns, and who delivered a cake personally – then a recipe which the children still hanker after – a vegetarian meat loaf, made principally from peanuts, garlic, carrots and herbs, this sent by a reader in Tauranga, after a column on vegetarianism – Marianne's beetroot relish, Frances's apple cake, Evelyn's strawberry jam. So the whole exercise raked over old memories, stretching back for fifty years.

I became interested in cooking at twenty-two, when I offered to look after a friend's toddler when she went into hospital to have her second child. The idea was that I would look after her hungry husband too. So I mugged up on recipe books, never having had any interest in food before, living in an officers' mess and having food put in front of me. But Shirley had her baby before my leave from the army was due, and I ended up looking after the toddler at her grandparents' rather stately Queen Anne house in Hertfordshire, an experience I enjoyed. They were so relieved that I took their fretting grandchild off their hands, that they petted and spoiled me.

The cooking never happened then, so the day my new husband and I arrived in our first home after our honeymoon, I couldn't wait to get stuck into the business of food. We arrived at the flat outside Salisbury at about five o'clock, having crawled from Twickenham with a large bookcase lashed to the roof of the tiny MG, and the inside crammed with wedding presents. Once inside the door, out came my Cookery in Colour, and the ingredients for making moussaka a la Marguerite Patten. Not even having made a cheese sauce before, the process took a long, long time. My newly-wed, hungry husband finally got his meal four hours and many sherries later, at nine o'clock, and then we made up the beds, and collapsed.

My next culinary triumph, or disaster, depending how you look this imposter in the face, was my first dinner party. Marguerite Patten had a seductive picture of some small stuffed lamb roasts, and I thought it looked interesting and delicious. I was a bit surprised when I bought what she called 'lamb flaps' from the butcher to find that they were only sixpence each, but it certainly fitted our miniscule under-army-marryingage budget. So I rolled, stuffed and roasted them, and they turned out to be fatty, tough, and tiny. Hardly enough for my best friend and her rich, gourmet lawyer husband. It was only when I mentioned this to my stepmother shortly after, that I learned that lamb flaps were the cheapest cut of all, and certainly not dinner party fodder.

I'm alternating between a biography of Mary Todd Lincoln, a much misunderstood woman, and re-reading, yet again, the tranquillising, little-known diaries of Mrs Millburn, a middle-aged, middle-class woman living in a country village in Warwickshire. They cover the five years of war, and what is so attractive about this utterly prosaic account of the cost of tomatoes, the man who ruins matins every week with coughing, the planting of onions, the sitting by the fire knitting on a dark winter's afternoon, is the feeling of a quiet routine, in a life without great dramas, and the precious ordinariness of it.

Her diaries bring back memories like my grandmother's knitting bag – everyone had one (except my non-knitting stepmother) – a wide shallow bag with handles, long enough to take a pair of long knitting needles and a ball of wool. Mrs Millburn described picking bunches of primroses, tying them with strands of wool, sitting on the tartan rug in the woods having a cup of tea from the thermos, and then going home to wrap the primroses in damp cotton wool and post them to friends in town. I remember doing the same as a child, and the post was so efficient then, that they arrived next day, fresh and fragrant.

She talked of the postman coming on Christmas Day – cheerfully! And of snow, reminding me too of the glorious surprise of waking up to that still, white, silent world which arrived so secretly and unexpectedly... the muted colours of snowscapes, sometimes a blue light, sometimes crystal sunshine... memories awakened by reading one woman's account of her very ordinary life.

She wrote of the weather, cups of tea, shopping and planting, a new hat, the price of vests, set against the backdrop of bombs and blackout, long damp nights in the air raid shelter during the bombing of nearby Coventry, the deaths of friends and family. There's the concerts at the Mothers' Union, work with the Women's Voluntary Service, and looking after the girls in the Women's Land Army, ringing the police to report apples stolen from the orchard, and darning ladders in her stockings, the hopes, the courage and the simple goodness.

January 15

Had an appointment with a numerologist, one of my secret vices. I'd met him briefly before, and his slightly distant manner had made me feel that he had written me off as a spoiled, middle-class lady. This time, with my numbers in front of him, with the proof that that is what I am not, he was entirely different. Friendly, fun, and fascinating, he confirmed for me when I asked, what I've always felt, that I'll die when I'm eighty-two. And that's as far as I want to go... he said my life energy will begin to run down when I'm eighty, which is fine by me. Bring on the hemlock!

Now I know that, I must savour each spring, each autumn, each summer and every winter. There are twelve moons in a year, so I have a hundred and twenty full moons if the nights are clear! But only ten cherry trees in bloom, ten more summers when the Queen of the Night perfumes the garden, ten more autumns when the leaves flame on the liquid ambers, and the poplars turn the countryside into a golden blaze. Ten more winters of enjoying sitting by the fire, wearing snug, richly-coloured winter clothes, and eating hot, wintry casseroles and porridge with cream and brown sugar!

Ten more years to watch my grandchildren grow up. Ten more years to explore discover new books, new places, new people, new ideas and new enjoyments. Ten more years to make the most of myself, untying all my knots, living on good terms with myself, learning to be more loving, more tolerant, more confident. Ten more years to do my best, to practice courage and kindness, and to do everything with my whole heart. Is there time? But if I was told that next week is the time to go, I would be ready. My only regret, not being here if any of the family needed me... but the next great adventure would be waiting!

While I waited in the café for Peter to arrive, I met Pat who I've been to on and off for years for psychotherapy. We had a quick coffee together. To my surprise, the powerful and perceptive counsellor I had always experienced in her room was a rather anxious, diffident person putting on a brave, bright front and coping with an insoluble problem today... insoluble until she sees what is really happening! It didn't seem the time or place to counsel her!

On one of my visits to her she had told me about a past life experience she had had.

She experienced a life as a little boy in a French chateau, and being utterly spoiled and pandered to, she was an orphan and had inherited a grand title and estate. She told of standing on the steps of the château looking down at her carriage as a seven-year-old, and the feelings of pride and arrogance, as she looked at the playmate who had been brought to keep the lonely child company. The playmate was a girl, and though he was diverted by having someone his own age to play with, he despised her.

As a young man, he went to an academy for young officers, and graduated into a crack regiment, which ended up fighting in Spain. He revelled in wearing a magnificent powder-blue uniform encrusted with gold tassels and braid. Still insufferably proud and arrogant, the young aristocrat plunged into his first battle with delight, and was struck down almost immediately. His last conscious thought was of lying on the battlefield and seeing a couple of foreign officers in dark blue uniforms walking among the fallen soldiers, checking the bodies. When they reached him, one said to the other:

'This one's dead,' and he knew nothing more.

Pat's answers to my questions suggested that it may have been the battle of Salamanca.

The officers in navy uniforms were probably Wellington's staff officers inspecting the battlefield.

And had she not heard them pronounce her dead, she would probably have become one of those spirits that haunt battlefields, that we call ghosts... it sounded a very convincing story from someone who knew very little history.

In this lifetime, she was born the youngest of ten children to a poor country labourer in Kent, and knew nothing but poverty and humiliation.

My father always used to worry about soldiers killed in battle so instantaneously that they didn't have time to know that they were dying, and so prepare themselves.

I've finished *Indian Summer* by Alex von Tunzelmann about Indian Independence in 1947. The most intriguing aspect of the book to my trivial, gossipy mind was the very detailed account of the love affair between Lady Mountbatten and Nehru. In the many public and private photos in the book, they made no attempt to hide their love for each other, which continued until Edwina's death in 1960. She had just stayed with Nehru, before going on to tour Malaya and Borneo for St John Ambulance.

In Borneo, she was found dead in bed, with Nehru's letters on the bedside table, and some on the bed. She had been reading them as she died. Her body was taken back to England, where she was buried at sea. Nehru sent a frigate to escort her, and to drop marigolds into the waves as Edwina's coffin subsided into the deep.

(The Queen Mother, who had a somewhat barbed wit, is reputed to have commented that 'Dear Edwina always liked to make a splash.')

The most charming story I've heard of her was immediately after the war when she landed unexpectedly in Sumatra. A battered and emaciated ex-prisoner of war rushed over to the plane to warn the pilot to stop any others landing on the unfinished airstrip, and his loin cloth dropped off as the door opened. An elegant figure in uniform appeared at the top of the gangway. 'I do apologise,' said the naked figure as she came down the steps. 'Not at all,' she replied, 'what you need is a cigarette,' holding out a gold cigarette case. As he puffed on his first cigarette for over three years, he asked her name. 'I'm Lady Mountbatten,' she replied.

February 11

My brother, Derek's birthday is today. So it's sixty years since the day we awoke and found our stepmother had been taken to hospital at Hanover, in the night. Hanover, because it was the nearest hospital to Belsen where my father was stationed. He told us he didn't know why she had gone. So my sister and I went to school feeling incredibly important that our mother was in hospital, and everyone conjectured as to why. Then someone said, well, p'raps she was having a baby, because she was getting fat. I coldly replied that she was not getting fat, and of course, it wasn't a baby, or they would have told us, and we went home, as we did in those days, for lunch prepared by the maid.

My father was waiting, beaming all over. 'You've got a baby brother,' he said. I acted in all the appropriate ways of being delighted. And I was. But underneath was a stab of pain, the hurt that they hadn't wanted to share it with us. And, inevitably, we slid back into second place with everyone. There was no more time to play games with us, or go for walks with us, or do anything with us anymore. Bread and jam for afternoon tea, never the chocolate biscuits!

During that cold snowy week in February 1948, my father drove back and forth from Belsen to Hanover every night. The combination of snow, ice, and hostile German drivers, who seized the opportunity to harass a lone British Army vehicle, resulted in several accidents and visits to the emergency department for my father. One of these nights, he said to me as usual, on leaving: 'Now don't forget to be a good hostess if Dr Muller calls.'

Dr Muller was the local vet who lived a few miles away at Bergen, the nearest village to Belsen. During a distemper epidemic, our dogs inevitably caught the dreaded disease and succumbed, but during that time we got to know Dr Muller very well indeed. He made house calls. My father courteously gave him a glass of gin and tonic, unobtainable in civilian post-war Germany, and from then on the doctor got in the habit of calling, even when we had no dogs with distemper.

He would bring for my stepmother one of the rare orchids, which he reared in hothouses. I hated them, mostly in wild psychedelic colours before the word was known, shocking magentas and shrieking pinks, acrid yellows and acid green, strangely be-petalled and unfurling long stamens and unexpected quiffs of curling leaves. He handed them over with much bowing and clicking of heels, a Prussian reflex it never occurred to him that anyone would find unattractive in post-Hitler months.

His elder daughter Susannah then began to come on Sunday afternoons to teach German to my sister and me, and we exchanged afternoon tea visits. When we went to their house, Frau Muller, a pale, washed-out, blonde woman, told me, when I admired their beautiful Meissen china, that they had dug a deep hole in the cellar to hide it from the invaders. Were we the invaders, I wondered? They had no flour to bake cakes, so we children ate sour apples dipped in sugar instead.

On our way home, I heard my stepmother say apropos of Susannah and her mother telling them about seeing their poor, wounded soldiers in bloodied bandages trundling past in the hospital trains: 'If they saw those trains, how come they didn't know about the others?' But since I hadn't been told about the horrors of Belsen's past, I didn't understand what she was talking about. So the remark stuck, as so often when one doesn't understand.

At ten o'clock on that night, being stitched up in accident and emergency after another accident on unlit, icy, hostile roads, my father received a frantic phone call from his nine year old daughter: 'Daddy, please come home, the doctor's in the corner, all funny.' I don't know how I struggled through the impenetrable military telephone network to reach him, but I did. Where the German housekeeper and maid were I don't know.

When my father returned, he found me huddled apprehensively in a corner of the sitting room, as far away as possible from Dr Muller who was stretched out on the sofa in front of the fire, roaring drunk, with an empty gin bottle, and the new puppy lying on the hearth rug, chewing all my father's crossword rubbers to crumbs. I'm not sure whether the loss of the gin, or the rubbers hurt more. And I've never been able to stand the smell of gin since.

I never forget my brother's birthday, because a year later, my sister and I were sent to a convent in Yorkshire, and February 11 was the feast day of Our Lady of Lourdes.

Though not Catholics, we were required to participate, though our parents dug their toes in at providing us with the de rigueur white dresses and veils for these innumerable feast days, to our great mortification, of course.

They thought it was bad enough spending all their money just for us to process around the grounds singing hymns on these regularly recurring feast days, instead of getting on with long division, French verbs and parsing sentences.

When I was paying school fees myself some thirty years later, I could see their point.

February 20

After my trip to Whangarei to see Johnny, the homeopath this week, I drifted into an op-shop on the way to my parking spot after lunch, and did a quick survey of the dog-eared rubbishy books on their shelves. I came home with the pick of the bunch, a historical novel by Joanna Trollope set in the Crimean War, and a book on winds by Lyall Watson. Devoured the Trollope in bed that night, a good read, and then got stuck into Lyall Watson's Heaven's Breath.

What intrigued me most were the ocean currents, especially in the Pacific. The Islanders sail their great outrigger canoes by the currents rather than the stars, reading the different currents through the soles of their feet on the decks. The currents had names like the Humboldt Current, East Australian Current, and Southern Equatorial Current.

Presumably, these are the currents which sweep all the dreaded plastic rubbish along to destinations where there are now huge islands reputed to be the size of countries, composed of plastic bags and other plastic rubbish. They trap fish, dolphins and birds, and decompose into tiny plastic shards, which enter our food chain via the fish. One woman, a scientist was so

41

shocked that she went back to her hometown and started the first plastic-free town in England. When will we all do the same?

February 24
Sunshine and the sound of a mother blackbird bathing and flapping its wings in the birdbath. It sounds like applause with gloves on. Found this remark from William James. It seems like the hopes of my life these days:

I am done with great things and big plans, great institutions and big success. I am for those tiny, invisible loving human forces that work from individual to individual, creeping through the crannies of the world like so many rootlets

In a remainder bookshop, I found a biography of Irina Baronova, one of my favourite ballerinas when I was a ballet-mad child.

I had always wondered what had happened to her. I now learned that she had married Cecil Tennant, the London impresario, who swept her off her feet in three weeks, and married her on condition she never danced again. It sounded cruel, but it was probably the only way to make their marriage work. They were very happy, and he died far too soon in a car accident, leaving her with three young children. The circumstances were strange.

Some years before, Laurence Olivier, a close friend, had asked them to come over and help calm down his unstable wife, Vivien Leigh. She was going to Paris, and wanted money from Olivier to buy a wardrobe of Dior clothes, breaking the strict customs conditions about the amount of money that post-war, cash-strapped Britain would allow travellers to take out of the country. She had worked herself into a frenzy of rage. And when Tennant did his best to convince her of the impossibility and illegality of what she was planning, she turned on him.

When she had finished cursing him, she sank back on a sofa and went into a silence that the horrified onlookers thought was a doze. Suddenly, she opened her astonishing green eyes, fixed them on Tennant, and said, 'When I die I'll take you with me.' Cecil Tennant went yellow, Olivier was rocking himself to and fro, his head buried in his hands, and Baronova said there was a sense of evil in the room. They left immediately, and shortly after, Olivier himself left for good, unable to cope with Vivien's mental condition.

Some years later in 1967, after seven years spent with John Merivale, Vivien Leigh, suffering from TB, collapsed, and was found dead on the floor of their flat.

Cecil Tennant went to her funeral. But when they were dressing, he stopped Baronova putting on her funeral clothes, and said he didn't want her to come. To her surprise, a few minutes later, he said that he wanted her to have a session with their accountant very soon, so she knew what their situation was.

He then said: 'If anything happens to me, I want you to marry again.'

He came back from the funeral looking ill and tired, and then drove over in his Jaguar to pick up their children from friends. He crashed on the way home and died instantly. The children were unharmed.

Baronova never married again.

3

Mar/Apr 2008

March 10

Jim and Stella came for lunch on a blazing hot summer's day. I kneecapped myself by constantly harking back in my mind to the sumptuous dinner we had had with them before Christmas, so couldn't think of anything worthwhile to give them. My summer standby of chicken mayonnaise, Stella had asked for the recipe years ago, and I kept changing my mind about an alternative. Rather bombed out, I feel, and also dropped one of the lemon puddings, just avoiding Stella's lap, and smashed the glass coupe.

Stella is intelligent, good, well-read and beautiful. Her refinement is reflected in her voice, which reminds me of my stepmother's beautiful, low, well-modulated voice. And I relish Jim's wry sense of humour and irony. We laughed a lot, particularly over an ancient joke, photocopied either from the Guardian or from the

Spectator a good twenty years ago: the Tory Atlas of the World, full of politically incorrect place names and inglorious ignorance. They included terms such as: 'Greasy Gaucho Land', 'Filthy Shoplifting Arabville', 'Slanty-eyed Chinky takeaway Land', 'The very Wonderful Hardworking Japanese', 'Frog Land', 'Wop Land', and huge distortions, like 'Gib', which takes up the whole of Spain or great gaping holes of ignorance. Australia is labelled 'Singapore (now that I do know)', 'Can't remember', for the whole of Indo–China, and another large area: 'Used to be British but gone to the dogs now.' There's *Plucky Little Poland*, and probably the most wickedly politically incorrect of all: '*The much-maligned South Africa.*'

March 17

The guava tree is laden with fruit this year. I hear the pigeons whirring in to perch on a heavily laden branch to rob us of our fruit – it makes delicious tangy eating, and tangy red jelly. The plum tree is in a state of confusion and covered in sprigs of pale pink spring blossom.

Cara has been at her worst the last few days, catching mice to play with, and even climbing the puriri tree to terrorise the fan-tails. I always know when she's up there menacing them, because they start screeching in panic and circling round the top of the tree. I was driven to spraying her with the hose to get her down last night.

Thanks to Amazon, I possess at last a copy of Helen Waddell's book *The Desert Fathers*, which I've always wanted. What struck me about the genuine Desert Fathers, as opposed to an eccentric – like Simon Stylites, who gives piety a bad name, and was expelled from his monastery – was their courtesy and good manners to each other. Helen Waddell called it 'heartbreaking courtesy,' and she was right. Like the little group who got lost as darkness fell, and who had to spend the night on the mountain because their monk guide lost the way. The others wanted to direct him to the right path, but their leader, Abbas John, wouldn't hear of it, because he said it would hurt and humiliate their guide.

He said: *'He will be desolated and ashamed... I'm going to pretend to be ill and say I must rest until dawn...'* The others said they couldn't go on without Abbas John, so they all sat and waited until dawn so as not to hurt the feelings of the brother who had lost the way.

The monks were taking care, in the Chinese phraseology, not to let their brother lose face. On the other hand, to care about losing face oneself would be spiritual pride... reminding me of the Tao verse: *'He who would be humble, remains entire.'*

I felt the same delicate courtesy in Peter France's book, Hermits in which he discussed the Russian starets, or saintly hermits (NOT like Rasputin). Their courtesy was also humbling. I wonder if the holier people become, the more thoughtful and courteous they become... maybe yes, maybe no! They were also intensely practical... living out that cliché that it's no good being heavenly, if you're no earthly good.

I came on an eleventh century monk, Marbod, Bishop of Rennes, who said it was bad–mannered to go around looking as if you need comfort, and that, *'in a world where there are so many lovely things... if a man looks on them and his mood is not softened, nor a smile on his face, an intractable clod is he.'*

What impressed me about the hermits and anchorites of the desert, and the Russian holy men too, was their sound common sense, as well as courtesy. According to Peter France, discernment was considered one of the chief spiritual virtues, so no wonder the craziness of Simon Stylites, so-called because he lived on top of a pillar in the desert, would not have been condoned by the sensible, down-to-earth Desert Fathers.

Courtesy and discernment are virtues, which make it, seem easier to walk a spiritual path. Courtesy in this context, being absolute respect and reverence for life, whatever the category. Discernment, the ability to recognise truth, keeps a sense of proportion, and uses one's intelligence, common sense and a sense of humour. I do believe God/the universe is practical.

April 10

Glorious autumn weather, golden, mild, and deliciously chilly at night. The trees are starting to turn, including our liquid ambers. They are beginning to give the impression that the roadside is a blaze of colour, and with another few years of the growth they've been doing this year, they'll be a real spectacle.

I feel nostalgic for our garden at Howick at this time of year, when we looked across the valley through a curtain of yellowing grape vines, to the copper beech fading to russet rose, and the Lombardy poplar on the other slope streaked with yellow. The silver birches in the garden would turn, and the purple salvia surrounding them looked wonderful against the orange and gold of the falling leaves. There were crab apple trees laden with red fruit. The towering poplars in Patrick's Japanese garden covered the ground with a thick yellow carpet, making a cathedral of gold, above and below.

One of the glories of that hidden town garden was the textures of all the different trees and foliage, from the dark, shiny leaves of the magnolia grandiflora juxtaposed against the sharp reds and oranges of the crab apples, the tender ferny fronds of the Chinese swamp pine growing next to the yellowing fretted leaves of the gleditsia, gold poplars and browning oaks outlined against dark green natives, the grey-blues of the eucalyptus, and shades of purple, crimson and tangerine on the liquid amber next to the pepper tree.

Our tiny garden now has a different order of texture, with puriri trees and loquats, purple plum and scarlet bottle brush, shiny camellias and spiky flax... a more random and haphazard collection of texture and shape.

I set off in fine fettle to a factory sale of my favourite clothes. Driving down the north-west motorway, not one of my usual haunts, a car careered past me in the middle lane, weaved and cut in front of someone in the fast lane, and then dived back into the middle and then the slow lane. That is an accident definitely going to happen, I thought to myself as we all braked, and then found myself surrounded by police cars hurtling past, lights flashing, sirens screaming, and the police helicopter overhead.

I saw the fleeing car suddenly cut across all the lanes, and turn down the off-ramp I was about to take. I pulled off into it myself, and noticed in my rear vision mirror, a police car trying to cut down the off-road lane, so I pulled as far right as possible into the driving lane to give him plenty of room to pass. Suddenly, there was the speeding car, having done a U-turn, hurling itself back up the off ramp, heading straight for me. I jerked back to the left again, and he was gone, straight back down the motorway, carving a swathe in the path of all the oncoming traffic.

I heard later that he was caught somewhere in the eastern suburbs, for an attempted burglary in a jeweller's shop. If he had cleaned me up, or crashed into another car on the motorway, I don't think a life in exchange for an unsuccessful burglary was worth it. I think the police should examine this equation! Despite this experience, I had a successful visit to the sale, and emerged several pairs of trousers and jumpers better off. Nothing to set my heart on fire, but useful work horses.

April 12

Shopping in Warkworth, I browsed in an op-shop, and came out with a copy of Fitzroy Maclean's *Eastern Approaches,* still in its old, familiar, fifties book-club wrapper. His chilling account of one of the big, but secret Moscow show trials of the thirties, described thuggery as skilled as Gestapo trials a decade later, while his attempts as a diplomat to travel to the forbidden eastern parts of the Soviet Empire were both tragic and hilarious.

He finally made it to Bokhara/Bukhara, and the photographs he managed to take, and descriptions of a place, which was first inhabited five thousand years ago, are magic – his word. Sleeping rough, he was entranced by the magnificent architecture, before being hauled back to the British Embassy in Moscow by two secret service men who had been tailing him.

The Russian determination to prevent his travels and keep tabs on him, reminded me of the poet Anna Akhmatova's story. Like all Russians, she longed to travel, and dreamed of the freedom of England. Telling a friend how you could just book a train ticket and travel anywhere in England, the friend replied that this could not be true, for if it was, how could the authorities keep track of everyone's movements?

During a somewhat unorthodox war service which included kidnapping a Persian general from his home (kidnapping enemy generals seemed a popular British wartime hobby), Maclean ended up in Yugoslavia, assisting Tito. After experiencing Communism in Russia he was worried that Tito would cement Communism in yet another country, and consulting the inimitable Churchill during the latter's visit to Cairo, the following conversation ensued:

Churchill: *'Do you intend to make Yugoslavia your home after the war?'*

Maclean: *'No, sir.'*

Churchill: *'Neither do I, and that being so, the less you and I worry about the form of government they set up, the better. That is for them to decide. What inter-*

ests us, is which of them is doing the most harm to Germany?'

April 15

I went to see Lear with Eugenie.

The Royal Shakespeare Company, with Sir Ian Mckellen and beautiful young Romola Garai. I know I should have enjoyed it but to my regret, I didn't. I found Sir Ian McKellen cold, going through the motions of being a great Shakespearean actor, while dropping his trousers was really rather unnecessary except as a piece of exhibitionism. Romola Garai's Cordelia was too fiery for my liking – I've always felt Cordelia was the calm centre of the play – but not here. There was no calm centre. The theatre was too big, I couldn't hear very well, and the actors seemed to talk too fast... I'm getting old!

So I left the theatre unmoved by one of the great events of dramatic life in Auckland. Am I a philistine or just plain middlebrow?

April 25 Anzac Day

Typical Anzac day, chilly, grey, threatening to rain. We gathered outside to watch the ceremony at the cemetery, waiting to see the Volunteer Fire Brigade march down the road accompanied by any veterans still capable of doing so, and by the various dignitaries of the village, like the chairman of the Residents' Association, who was Jack, our friendly builder.

As they were all marshalling at the end of the road, the fire alarm wailed, and the poor firemen had to rush off to change from their best uniforms into fire-fighting gear, while the ceremony went ahead without them. Just as it was all finishing, a few of them straggled in, pissed off at missing their great annual moment of glory, which they fully deserve, since they are not paid for their heroic and time-consuming efforts. The unkindest cut of all was that it was just a nuisance call; merely a stolen car caught fire, rather than a full-blown emergency.

We had invited Harry for coffee afterwards, and Mike and Annie. I made hot scones to eat with my last jar of homemade strawberry jam from the summer. Harry had trouble coping with his paralysed side but he is always courageous and full of plans. Everyone was very gentle and tender with him.

Amazon produced for me Alanbrooke's diaries covering World War Two, edited by Arthur Bryant. I was fascinated to discover at last, why my father didn't leave France until several weeks after everyone else at Dunkirk.

His tank regiment had been fighting on the Somme trying to cooperate with the French and hold back the Germans from the Dunkirk evacuation. But the French never turned up to be supported, and the Fifth Tanks had to withdraw in considerable danger.

Some of it I had already pieced together, from what my father (who's been dead for more than forty years) had told me when I was young, and from reading regimental histories. Reading the diary, I discovered that Lord Alanbrooke, as he became, had been recalled from Dunkirk early in the piece, leaving General Alexander to complete the Dunkirk evacuation. Alanbrooke had a week's leave, was then summoned to London, and given orders to return to France to work with the French government in Bordeaux and support the French armies.

As soon as he got there, Alanbrooke could see his mission was hopeless, and that the top French officers had no intention of fighting. He then spent two weeks trying to convince England of this, and fend off insinuations of cowardice from Churchill. During this time, he was quietly getting the remnants of the British Army into position near the coast, so they wouldn't be cut off, since the French were not supporting them.

The French failed to tell him when they did capitulate, which would have meant about 150,000 British troops automatically being surrendered to the Germans. But, at that the minute, Alanbrooke finally got permission to withdraw, and my father's regiment, Fifth Royal Tanks at the time, scrambled onto a little ship, SS Manx at Brest. 2,000 exhausted men were crammed onto the decks, and took the perilous cross-channel voyage, managing to avoid both mines and the Luftwaffe, and land at Plymouth early on the morning of the 17 June. Their commander, Alanbrooke, arrived in Plymouth at about the same time, and hastened to London.

At Plymouth docks, women of the WVS were waiting for the soldiers with mugs of hot tea. My father told me – *'I will never forget them.'* The regiment then travelled, unfed and disconsolate, to several different barracks until room and rations were found for them. They were lucky. The 51st Highland Division was captured fighting to the last bit of ammunition, surrendered to Rommel, and then spent five long years as POWs. Like the other prisoners captured during the Retreat, they were marched all over France, Belgium and Germany, spat on and jeered at in German towns, sleeping in the open, and shot if they fell out from exhaustion and starvation. So much for the Geneva Convention.

I find the thought of General Alexander, standing in a little motor boat at 2 a.m., touring the empty, smoking beaches of Dunkirk, calling through a megaphone to check that no one was left behind, rather moving. As also, a little-known story I read in Frances Partridge's A Pacifist's War. Her brother-in-law was staying with them, and he had been stationed at Dover, responsible for the men arriving back from Dunkirk, many of them wounded or dead from air attacks at sea.

He described the dogs' cage on the beach. He told his astounded listeners, that all the dogs the soldiers had rescued and brought back with them from Dunkirk, were taken to this cage, carefully labelled and registered, and kept in quarantine until they could be sent to the men's home addresses. Only a British army would do that!

On the other hand, many of the 26,000 French soldiers rescued from Dunkirk, caused lots of trouble and even riots, so were given the option of staying in England as Free French, or returning to Vichy France. Many opted to return, and were solemnly conveyed back, with all their weapons and equipment to join the enemy and then use these weapons against us! I sometimes think chivalry can go too far.

My brother Derek told me my other favourite Dunkirk story. The Colonel-in-Chief of his regiment, by then a general, told them how, when he was a young subaltern at Dunkirk, exhausted, wet, dirty, having made it to a civilian ship, and got his men stowed safely away, he staggered up the gangway from the lower decks. He discovered the ship's bar, in full working order, with a steward nonchalantly polishing glasses behind the counter. On his last legs, the young man dragged himself exhaustedly to the bar, leant his elbows on the counter and asked, 'Any chance of a drink?'

'Good heavens, no, sir,' said the steward righteously, with bombs dropping all round, explosions going off, guns firing, sirens screaming, 'we're still within the three mile limit, sir!'.

4

May/Jun 2008

May 14

Yesterday I went to Whangarei to meet Jane for lunch, and also visit Johnny, the homeopath. I'm tired all the time. I began with a trip to one of the second-hand bookshops, which owed me $45 for some books I'd sold to them months ago. I did a great raid, but left feeling I'd picked the eyes out of the place over the months – already had all the good biographies, nothing worth having in the limited literature section, no diaries or good autobiographies and nothing good on American history.

So I ended up with some good factual books, Cosmos, Arthur Guirdham and the Cathars, and a couple of historic Georgette Heyer's, The Spanish Bride, about Juanita and Harry Smith in the Peninsula wars, plus An Infamous Army. I'd once read that this was so accurate on Waterloo that it was used as an army text at Sandhurst – then over the road to the other second-hand bookshop. Not very good either, except in the literature section which included a heap of P.G. Wodehouse. Never having actually read any of his, though I've always felt I had, and certainly loved the TV series, I bought one – I thought one would do as well as a dozen!

Rendezvoused with Jane, found a new café, and talked non-stop till it was time to get back to Johnny. At my first visit, there was a one-legged lady in a wheelchair, whose need was obviously greater than mine. Johnny told me that she'd gone to Auckland for a stent to improve circulation to help heal a leg ulcer, and the surgeon found gangrene in the ulcer, and refused to do anything till he'd taken her whole leg off. Now a devastated, angry, helpless old woman.

So tired when I got back home that I went to bed early and started An Infamous Army. It was brilliant, and I couldn't stop, so finished it at 1.30 am, feeling I could treat myself to a late night with nowhere to go in the morning for once. The days are cold and bright and sparkling, my favourite time of the year. I'm a bit worried about Cara who has been tearing great chunks of fur off her back legs, which she only does when she is stressed.

May 17

Read The Spanish Bride. Found the accounts of campaigns and battles utterly absorbing, bringing to life all the histories I'd read of the same period. The South African town of Ladysmith was named after the fascinating Juanita Smith, the aristocratic Spanish fourteen-year-old Harry Smith rescued, and married after the siege of Badajos. Today I went for a long walk at Omaha. The beach and the dunes were empty, just me and the rabbits, the birds and the builders' hammers. At the weekend, we had dinner with Mike and Annie, having pre-dinner drinks watching sunset over the water, and then the light-house shining across the harbour. Dinner by candlelight, delicious duck, and good conversation.

May 25

On the strength of reading An Infamous Army, I re-read all my books on Waterloo, Wellington and the Peninsula Wars and am now so familiar with them, that at last I can follow what Wellington was up to in Spain, and how Waterloo came to be fought where it was. And now I understand just what 'a damn close-run thing' it was too. I was also pleased to discover that Major the Hon Henry Percy from the 14th Dragoons, one half of the 14/20th Hussars, my father's regiment, took the news back to the Secretary of State in London. It took him two days to get there.

And I discovered why Wellington thought it was such an 'infamous army' made up of rag tag and bob-tails from different regiments and countries. All the best regiments were either in America, or disbanded after the Peninsular wars and Napoleon's exile, the way the British Government still always economises on the army once it's done its job. So, all the out-of-work vet-erans and wounded remnants were scattered. Very dif-ferent to the Prussian veneration of its army ...

Only 7,000 of Wellington's British soldiers in this new army had ever heard a shot fired in anger, as the saying goes, the rest had only been on domestic duties in Britain. In one British regiment, there was no sol-dier over the age of twenty-two. They all fought heroi-cally when the time came.

Rosemary, a friend who had married an officer from one of the regiments, which fought at Waterloo, at-tended the ball in Brussels held on the 150th anniver-sary of the Duchess of Richmond's Ball on 19 June, the eve of the battle. Rosemary's ball was held in 1965. I envied her. I was just coping with my second baby born three weeks earlier.

And at last I have worked out where Brigid and I stayed the night when we stopped by chance at Water-loo. We'd been driving all day from Bonn, stopping at Aix for delectable coffee and rum babas, which set a bench mark for all rum babas eaten since.

The Sound Of Water

We sat outside the café in the sun, by a bridge and a river, with that childhood poem ringing in my ears: How They Brought the Good News from Aix to Ghent, and then we'd been on the road ever since.

We felt too tired to go on into Brussels, to cope with city traffic and find somewhere to stay, so when we found a little inn on the roadside we pulled in and asked for a bed for the night. The innkeeper seemed grumpy and we definitely didn't get a welcome, but we stayed anyway.

The next morning, I met Brigid in the hall on our way to the dining room for breakfast, and she looked as heavy-eyed and unrefreshed as I felt. We confessed to each other that we'd had an awful night, full of bloody dreams and hideous nightmares.

And then we saw a raised contour map on the wall in the hall. The map of the battlefield. Until that moment, we hadn't registered that we were anywhere near Waterloo. La Belle Alliance, where we had been sleeping, had been in the thick of the battle, and heavy fighting had raged all round it. It had been Napoleon's headquarters for a while, and Wellington and Blucher finally met up here victoriously. Old Marshall Blucher had said they would call the battle, symbolically, 'La Belle Alliance', while Wellington, somewhat churlishly, stuck to his custom of calling his battles after the place where he had spent the night before, hence Waterloo.

May 31

After this welter of Wellingtonia, biographies, battles etc, I decided to tackle the Greville Memoirs I'd found in Whangarei months ago, covering the same period, though I only have two of the eight volumes. Tantalising, knowing that Mike and Frances Partridge had done an unexpurgated version, and wondering what Henry Reeve, the original transcriber, had suppressed in my copies. It took the Partridges nine years, working off the originals at the British Museum. They produced eight volumes with notes, biographies and index. Apart from awe at their amazing industry and stickability, I find it awesome too, that a publisher should commission and pay for such a monumental enterprise. Can't imagine any publisher even thinking about such a project these days. Alas.

I was so intrigued by several quotes from Count Ciano's diaries in Arthur Bryant's The Turn of the Tide, that I ordered some biographies of Ciano and Mussolini from Amazon, and also Count Ciano's diaries.

The story of the diaries, – which were dynamite to the Axis powers – being smuggled out of Italy, was like reading a thriller. Edda Ciano disguised herself as a pregnant woman and hid the diaries under her dress, as she escaped from her father Mussolini across the border into Switzerland. And the chap who helped her escape after Mussolini had had her husband Ciano shot was Count Pucci, the famous post-war dress designer.

Ciano was not very attractive, and prone to the over-sentimentality of some Italian men, but he had moments of greatness and nobility too. His end was that of a very brave man. He and the others condemned with him were not allowed to face the firing squad, because they had been sentenced as traitors. At the last minute, he slewed round in his chair to face the bullets.

It was his moral courage, which had brought him to this end. When the vote was being taken against Mussolini in the Grand Council, they had plenty of numbers and didn't need Ciano's vote.

But Ciano, formerly Mussolini's foreign minister, as well as his son-in-law, put his money where his mouth was, and voted according to his conscience.

It brought him to the firing squad in Verona, a victim of both Mussolini and Hitler, who had double-crossed him, kidnapped him, and handed him over to Mussolini.

From early on, Ciano had seen through Hitler and the Germans, and did not believe that they could beat the English. But as fast as he thought he'd convinced the Duce, Mussolini would be seduced by Hitler again. Mussolini sounded a rather nasty serial rapist. I even wonder if his daughter had been a victim of his violent attentions, since Edda was so terrified of sex that she tried to climb out of a window on the first night of her honeymoon with Ciano.

Took Cara to the vet. He couldn't find anything wrong.

June 7

A happy week looking after the boys while Julian and Eugenie went to a conference at Blenheim. But tiring! Get up much earlier than I usually do, in order to cook their breakfast and get them off to school before eight o'clock. I am then dragged round the streets, or across the park, by Lucy, who is now so big that if she wasn't crossed from a Great Dane, she was certainly crossed from an athletic Rhodesian ridgeback. At the other end of the day there's meals to cook, and sometimes games to play, but mostly, staying up late to pries them off their computers, PlayStations or TV serials late at night. So I'm permanently exhausted – and embarrassed – after backing into the car belonging to the grandfather of neighbours across the road.

It's easier to walk Lucy round the streets, rather than to the park, since there are so many smells to halt her in her tracks that she doesn't get up speed to drag me off my feet. It worked most of the time, until we began meeting an elderly chap, struggling along on crutches each morning. Lucy felt his crutches were a menace to everyone's peace of mind, and tried to disable them, lunging towards the poor man and jerking her caregiver after her. The second or third time this happened, I took a wide berth of him, right out onto the road, and called out: '*Boisterous, undisciplined, too big, and my daughter's.*' He roared with laughter, and replied, 'And she allows you to take her for a walk!'

I got to catch up with Cynthia for lunch, shopping, exploring and lunch with Marianne, and enjoyed an inspection of Frances's Tuscan farmhouse building project, and coffee. It's a work of art, like everything she does. I have to rely on charm to get by in my houses, while she can only create perfection.

Decided after reading Ciano, which I wanted to really understand how the Second World War came about, and I read William Shirer very carefully, all through *The Rise and Fall of the Third Reich*, and his Berlin Diary, and End of the Berlin Diary. I also found the German Ambassador Count Lichnowsky's memoirs and diaries at the Northern Club, right down to the last telegrams from London before First World War began. In his memoirs, he described how Germany was subverted by militarism from the time of Bismarck, resulting in World War One – engrossing.

My appetite whetted, I found The Kings Depart by Richard Watt, another authoritative American, about the Versailles treaty, the German revolution and Weimar Republic. This was a revelation, particularly his assessment of righteous, arrogant President Wilson with his messiah complex. I was amazed to realise that Wilson, after coming into the war at the last minute, was so insensitive that he negotiated with the Germans without consulting the Allies who'd been bled of men, money and morale for four years. Also, that at Versailles, Wilson, exhausted and at the end of his tether, refused to soften the proposals, when at the end of it all, Lloyd George realised it would perpetuate the European conflicts.

It was sad to read of honest German Socialists trying to establish democratic government and being undermined by the military, who secretly re-established a military domination, which led to the next war. Just as sad, was to discover that violent anti-Semitism was nothing new in Germany (or in Paris or Vienna, or Russia, come to that). It had been flourishing since before Bismarck. No Jew was ever allowed at the Kaiser's court, unlike Edward VII's, and however rich a Jew might be, no German would dance with his daughter, even at her own dance.

Reading these books has convinced me that everything that happened in Nazi Germany was a logical conclusion to German history. The obedient, unquestioning, law-abiding citizenry, who had always supported authority and the military – which were synonymous in Germany – inevitably supported Hitler, who was successful in leading them to world domination till it all turned to custard. Many of the plotters, like Stauffenburg, seemed less concerned about the Jews and human rights than about Hitler's military defeats. While Hitler was winning, only a few very brave people resisted him, and the price of resisting as an individual was the concentration camp. On the other hand, in some accounts, where a few individual officers refused to obey their brutal orders, they seem to have got away with it.

Shelley's lines say it all:

...obedience,
Bane of all genius, virtue, freedom, truth,
Makes slaves of men, and of the human frame
A mechanized automaton.

It seems miraculous now that the traditional German militarism seems to have been completely obliterated, and that new generations of young Germans have the same peacemaking ideals and world view as their contemporaries. So the world does make progress.

June 10
Our new wood burning fire, though not good-looking, is a little treasure. It lights first pop, and responds to the very simple mechanism for regulating

heat, unlike the old one. It's clean, efficient, and when the power went off, played the part of a range. I boiled water, and fried bacon and eggs, and heated up pumpkin soup on it. It was a huge comfort in the middle of the storm.

When I got home from Auckland, I took Cara back to the vet, as she seemed to be getting worse, and mewed piteously all the time. I tried everything to work out what she wanted. I actually felt I might not be bringing her back from the vet, things seemed so wrong with her. But he gave her a steroid injection, and she came home much calmer, and the vet gave me some pills to get into her. Easier said than done.

I was given a voucher for a facial at a well-known beauty salon.

Full of anticipation I arrived, and then sat in reception, while staff chatted and greeted various customers, some glamorous, some not, but all favoured regulars. I had that familiar feeling of being an outsider, and worse, of being old, plain and boring.

Finally, the girl who had drawn the short straw ushered me into a tiny room, and began cleansing, steaming, mopping and massaging. During the half hour or so of steam cleaning my face, she worked on my neck and shoulders, fondly believing, I think, that she was giving me a massage. Every time my head thumped back on the table after she'd poked around my neck, I thought fearfully of the girl in Australia who is now completely paralysed after an inexpert neck massage. I left eagerly, my eyes so blurred and sore with cream that had run into them that I could hardly see to drive home.

June 16

After several days of misery and pain, I knew I would have to get my neck fixed as a result of the famous massage. I drove up to Kiri in Whangarei, who was appalled at the state of my neck and shoulders, swollen, as well as needing re-aligning. Back home, I rang the salon the next day, but they didn't want to know. I can only suppose that there are dozens of unfortunate women wandering around Remuera with their necks out, and feeling all the misery of such a condition, both physical and emotional.

June 18

Cara has continued to be a nightmare, mewing, almost screaming all the time. Frantic. She also wants me to stand by her every time she has her food. This is sometimes in the middle of the night, and it's been going on for a while. I didn't add it into the equation of her strange behaviour until today. The mewing is beginning to die down now, her fur is beginning to fuzz back on her legs, but she still wants me to stand guard over her while she's eating. I now realise that the escorting to food has been part of all that's been going on for her, and perhaps the vet was right when he suggested that she had been attacked and had had a fright. Fetching me to guard her while she eats, may be part of the fear of being attacked again...

June 22
My birthday on the 19th. My seventieth. I heard from all my friends and family, here and overseas. Lunch and red roses with Patrick at Ascension Winery, lunch with Lily and Eugenie at The Maple Room, and a celebration dinner at the Northern Club with the whole family, including grandchildren, organised by Eugenie and Roland. The pianist played Happy Birthday, the incredible cake given me by Eugenie, and covered in layers of white iced roses, was served with a great flourish, with a secondary, one in case the cake inside the splendid iced one was not fresh enough! I left huge slices for the kitchen staff, since we had cake for Africa.

The next day was my special treat, lunch at Roland's house with my grandchildren – no other adults. They hadn't all been together for a while, and it was a bit stiff to start with. Then Raymond jumped the gun by pulling one of the crackers straight away instead of at the end of the meal. There was a bang, and streamers from the cracker flew up and landed plum in the

chandelier hanging over the dining table. With a delighted shriek, the others grabbed theirs and aimed for
the chandelier. They continued to smother it with
streamers till we ran out, and then Raymond said: 'I
know where Daddy keeps them,' and brought through
a box half full of them.

After lunch, we played games like pik-a-stick and
ate the highly coloured iced cupcakes, which Eugenie
had donated. Each time we have a time together like
that, with all the old fun and silliness, I think to myself,
this may be the last time, for I'm so conscious of how
fast they are all growing.

They've grown out of my annual Christmas party,
including the year when Piers, at fourteen, said he
wouldn't come that year. And then he arrived, and became the most energetic competitor in the blowing of
bubbles off the deck into the bush, in the traditional
games of hunt the thimble, hide and seek, and the ritual of getting out their notebooks, and recording how
much they'd grown that year, the colour of their hair,
eyes, weight, size of shoes, favourite foods, animals,
books, etc. Then the list of favourite animals, which
stretched interminably as they remembered yet another one that they'd forgotten.

The feast included de rigueur chocolate mousse,
crackers, mottoes, hats and giggles, squawking whistles and trumpets that reached a crescendo of hideous

cacophony. Holidays included seven-year-old Charlie feeding the eels in the river at the bottom of the garden, and his chubby hand coming out of the water, with a long eel hanging onto his juicy little forefinger for a nibble. Both brothers spent hours making boats out of flax, launching them over the waterfall, and then tearing down the road back to our garden to watch them sail past. They rarely did. At Pah Road, another river, and this time a bridge, and hours spent on pooh-sticks, dams and more boats to float in the current. They'd come home wet, muddy and rosy, and ask me to come down to the river to see the dam, or the boats, or the pooh-sticks, and to stay and watch them.

I wonder how much they remember, like saying goodbye to three-year-old Annabel at the airport, when they moved to Melbourne. She gave me her hand and said very formally (she must have rehearsed it): 'Goodbye, Grandmother, I will never forget you.' She must have thought Melbourne was forever.

On this day, I also looked back to my tenth birthday, sixty years ago, and the other memorable birthdays of my life. The first one I had spent with my father, and the first birthday I remember celebrating. It was at Belsen. The night before, he was as excited as I, and couldn't wait until the next morning. My new stepmother called me out into the garden before bedtime at seven, where they were sitting in wicker chairs enjoying their gin and tonics in the summer evening. He gave me two presents; a gold-nibbed black fountain pen, and a string of pearls. I still wear pearls all the time. By the time the next birthday came around things were very different. My baby brother had been born, we were back in post-war miserable England and the cracks in all our lives had begun to appear.

June 28

Roland gave me a big cheque for my birthday, which I am having great fun spending. The first thing I treated myself to was a little bachelor's set of silver teapot, jug and sugar bowl. My other little silver teapot is In need of repair, and knowing what it cost to repair the handle on my big silver teapot, it's actually cheaper to buy another antique pot for my lapsang souchong. It is the prettiest thing, and gives me pleasure every time I lay the tray to make a pot of tea, which I have with my pretty old flowered teacup, and rose-patterned hot water and milk jugs. I blew the rest of the money on a pearl, agate and lapis lazuli pendant hinged in a most unusual way onto a fine silver chain.

June 29

I'm reading Charles Glass's sequel to *Tribes With Flags*, which had ended when he was kidnapped in Lebanon. I had particularly enjoyed his descriptions of

Damascus and Aleppo. In this book, The Tribes Triumphant, he resumes the interrupted journey fourteen years later. It was a painful read as he talked to the dispossessed Arab families who had lived in Jerusalem for over a 1,000 years, collecting ancient manuscripts, creating libraries and gardens, building villas and living the civilised Arab way of life that had endured for centuries. Now destroyed. They talked not just of dispossession and exile, but of unbelievable torture perpetrated on them by a people who had themselves endured terror and torture in Nazi Germany, Russia, Poland and elsewhere.

Balfour never visualised ethnic cleansing of the Arabs, but rather, a chance for Jews to create a homeland and live alongside the Arabs.

The 1917 Balfour Declaration guaranteed that nothing would be done to prejudice the political and religious rights of everyone already living in Palestine. Non-Jewish communities were then 90 per cent of the population.

And I had no idea that when the Jews sat down by the waters of Babylon and wept, Nebuchadnezzar had taken the Jewish elite to Babylon, to help him build an empire.

When they were allowed to return to Israel, few did. The Jewish community in the land, which finally became known as Iraq, lived there for over two 2,000.

They felt they had been there for thirteen centuries longer than the Arabs.

However, when Israel re-created itself in the twentieth century, the backlash in the Arab world, caused by Israeli treatment of Palestinian Arabs, resulted in the expulsion of Jews from all over the Middle East. This included the Iraqi Jews from Baghdad where Jews were nearly 40 per cent of the population, Jews who actually felt they were more Iraqi than the Iraqi Arabs. And in the European land of Israel, they felt unwanted, strangers in a strange land, who spoke a different language and had a different history. To read Charles Glass's book is to read 400 pages of historic heartbreak.

5

Jul/Aug 2008

July 10

I went to a sculpture exhibition with Eugenie who seems to know everyone these days, and she introduced me to a minister of the crown, who said on hearing my name, 'Oh, the woman who brought us all up,' a flattering reference to my family columns years ago.

I was grateful. When one is a has-been, any little crumb of recognition is like a large freshly baked loaf! At seventy, one is a has-been in so many ways – has been slim, has been dark haired, has been good at tennis, has been a good swimmer, has been a reasonable singer, has been a reasonable calligrapher, has been full of fun – now perhaps half-full ... has been sought after – now invisible... has been a successful career woman – now an obsolete homebody, has been agile – now stiff, has been a dog owner, now a cat owner... As I said to Cynthia when she said a man I was trying to avoid would have recognised me: 'No, men never even notice grey-haired women, much less remember them!' She has managed to go on looking blonde, but she knew what I meant.

July 12

We've been having really rough weather, but in the gaps in the storm, the resident thrush and blackbird have been singing with great consistency. Their song is piercingly sweet, sometimes rapturous, and sometimes meditative. They are the most melodious of songbirds, and yet to many New Zealanders they are unseen and unheard because they are not natives. Tuis are the only songbird many people seem to be aware of here.

The lovely thing about winter is all the winter things... winter clothes, warm wool, rich colours, scarves, coats, boots, winter food, soups and casseroles, porridge for breakfast on a cold morning, hot scones for afternoon tea, hot chocolate as a treat on a cold day... and the other things, lighting fires and lighting candles, drawing the curtains to shut out the dark and the cold, warm beds and electric blankets, that feeling of drawing the house around me like a snail in its shell.

I love listening to the wind blowing round the house at night, and the sound of the sea crashing on the rocks below. I love winter trees stripped of their leaves, outlined against the sky, the touch of white frost on the grass in the morning, the wispy white mist which reminds me of chill English mornings, when only the tops of the trees can be seen above the line of fog, and blue spires of smoke rise from scattered farm houses.

July 15

Wet and wintry still, good to be indoors. Heard by chance on the concert programme, a Vaughan Williams piece based on those magnificent words of Captain Scott's, before he died in the snow: 'We took risks, we knew we took them: things have come out against us and therefore we have no cause for complaint, but bow to the will of Providence, determined to do our best to the last.'

In contrast to that stoicism, I've been struggling to read Thomas Merton's early journals, repelled by his rigid Catholic masochistic thinking, that God demands constant misery and crosses to bring us into subjection to His will (always a He), lighting candles by the finger-bone of some dead (one hopes) saint, celebrating the feast of St John, who was boiled in oil, and venerating Christ's victimhood.

He moans on, month in and month out, about not being able to be a contemplative because he's so busy writing and praying. He revels in this suffering as being the cross that God demands, presumptuously haranguing God, Jesus and Mary about not yet being at one with them, not being a saint yet, and writes of: *'so many limitations to opportunities for real intimate union with God'* – in a Trappist monastery! I'd have sent Merton a copy of Brother Lawrence's The Practice of the Presence of God, if he hadn't been dead for thirty years! It makes me feel quite nervous to run counter to so many enlightened people's opinions of Merton. But I cringe, reading his manipulative letter to Aldous Huxley – *'I approach you with none of the crudities or prejudices which I am sure annoy you in other clerics'* – and so on.

He was taking Huxley to task for suggesting that mystical experiences caused by taking certain drugs could be genuine mystical experiences. He ended this letter: *'My dear Mr. Huxley, it is a joy to write to you of these things. I hope you can reply. God bless you'...* i.e. I am a man of God who loves his fellowmen (unless they are other clerics), which struck me as both fawning and patronising at the same time. Huxley replied courteously but unresponsively. When Merton writes straight from the heart, he is attractive, but when he writes as a devout Catholic, he uses religious clichés and impenetrable language.

I also watched an old film Tom & Viv. I say I, because Patrick lasted only a short time, during which things began falling off the table, he dropped things, blundered off to get some ice-cream, and in the doing tipped all the coffee in the deep freeze onto the kitchen carpet, swore long and deeply, and finally trundled off next door to get away from the film. I had been getting brassed off at not being able to concentrate on the film while all this was going on. It turned out that it was pressing all his buttons over his first marriage.

The film highlighted what I've always felt, that spiritual people like Tom (T.S. Eliot) are not necessarily well-integrated people, and that spirituality without parallel emotional growth doesn't seem to help a human being behave any better than anyone else. We live our lives at our emotional level of maturity, not at our spiritual level. The trick is to develop emotional maturity at the same time as spiritual maturity. This is what the personal growth movement is about, I treasured Viv's mother's withering comment to T.S. after he'd had her daughter consigned to a mental home, to the effect that English people are not like the Bloomsbury circles he moved in, and that they do not 'make art out of gossip, or write nasty novels about their friends.'

I have had Thomas Traherne's words on my mind: 'When we do dote upon the perfections of one creature, we do not dote upon that one too much, but all others too little.' I have no idea where I read it. I dote on details, like the bloom of sun on a child's cheek, the colour of a Jersey cow and her black eyelashes, the smell of coffee, the silence that falls among friends, flowers in the rain.

And there are sounds from childhood too, that I miss here – the chiming of church bells, the silence of snow, the incessant soft cooing of wood pigeons on a summer's day, and a sound that no one ever hears now, but I remember it well. It woke me every morning when I went to stay with my step-grandmother in London in the late forties. The sound of the milkman, the hooves of his horse clattering on the road, the jingling of the horse's harness, and the clinking of the milk bottles, are linked forever in my mind with shafts of early sunlight beaming through the crack between the long, green velvet bedroom curtains, at six thirty in the morning.

July 24

We couldn't resist the Russian ballet, though we've agreed that we can't really afford these stupendous ticket prices any more. We've given up concerts, but the ballet is always irresistible. It was one of the loveliest Swan Lakes I've seen, and worth the money and the trouble finding parking, organising meals and getting Patrick to and fro. I drove back the same night, empty roads, but hard driving through the rain. Luckily, not too many dazzling lights coming the other way at that time of night.

July 27

Last night was the last weekly meeting of our small group until the next 'term'. We've come to know each other well. Someone who has great difficulty grappling with the idea of God, having grown up with missionary parents, was expressing her discomfort with the concept. Rachel said that at Al-Anon they substituted the word 'Good' for 'God', and it made the concept more acceptable to those who didn't relate to the idea of God.

Helena is good at guiding the group along the lines of the readings of the course, and yet skilfully letting the discussion follow a thread. She keeps her own beliefs to herself and yet is so articulate, whether discussing Einstein or the BBC World News! I'm constantly surprised at the range of her interests. I also brought my King James Bible. Last time we met, we had a reading from Matthew, from one of the new-fangled colloquial translations. It referred to Jesus calling himself 'our slave'. I was revolted by this, and checked up in the King James. He says he is our servant, which in the context, sounded much more likely, and a hell of a lot more dignified than being a slave! Service is rather different to slavery.

I had made an almond lemon cake with lashings of thick icing, which was received with groans of despair, and intentions to have just a tiny bit, and then a rash of second helpings.

I went to see The Painted Veil. I came out wrecked. The unhappy marriage, trapped in a narrow colonial society, the horror of being with someone you can't stand and who can't stand you, the sad, unfulfilling extra-marital love affair and betrayal, her blind groping towards a spiritual awakening, brought back the whole nightmare of Hong Kong, which I thought I had buried years ago. I cried my eyes out all the way home. It was also such a visually beautiful film; it pressed all the nostalgia buttons for the unspoilt, unpolluted, unpeopled world of my childhood. Even Hong Kong, nearly fifty years ago, still had that lost peace and silence up in the hills, away from the hell of the filthy, noisy, chaotic streets and slums.

It was while walking those lonely paths in the hills (and stepping over the odd cobra) that I churned my way through the death of my marriage, the death of my father, the misery of a dead-end love affair, through despair and hopelessness, and tried to wrench peace of mind from the beauty of the hills, the sea and the radiant atmosphere. The shining air seemed to hold some rapturous secret that I couldn't find the meaning of. But you could almost see and feel the love-stuff that mystics, and sometimes scientists, talk of being the glue that holds each particle of matter together. Later, lying in hospital in Kowloon with hepatitis, I began to feel my way towards some sort of misty understanding of that different order of reality.

But back then, leaving my solitary walk, I would return to the ancient, parked Morris Minor, with screws too rusty to raise the hood in rainy weather, and the rusty floor so broken that I had a layer of cardboard in the back for the children's feet. They had instructions not to put their feet down when it was raining. And so back to the puzzle of how to make ends meet in my bank account and in my life, the constant teetering on the edge of disaster.

Here in New Zealand as I walked up the garden path this morning, I froze, and tiptoed silently backward down the steps without taking my eyes off the dogs' water bowl at the top of the path.

A big, fat wood pigeon was perched on the rim, having a long drink.

How his weight didn't tip the bowl over I'll never know.

August 3

The Painted Veil shook me up, so I went back to see it again today and Patrick came too. Neither of us could understand why it had had such mediocre local reviews. The only false note was Diana Rigg as the holy mother superior. She does not project spirituality.

In the meantime, I had found a copy of the book in a second hand bookshop. I had forgotten what an interesting writer Somerset Maugham was. He described with such acuteness and perception that surface life of colonial and military society which I knew so well from living in Malaya and Hong Kong. It was a life high and dry in an alien environment, displaced people trying to hold on to the customs and cultures of their homeland, and the poignancy of real people trying to suppress their truth, and stick to the unspoken rules of hierarchical colonial communities. It was a lonely life with plenty of social occasions, but with few real connections.

Maugham knew too, the tragedy of people who had forgotten they were real, going through the motions, living the meaningless days of their life in Shakespeare's terrifying words:

Tomorrow, and tomorrow and tomorrow,
Creeps in this petty pace from day to day...

How often I felt like that then, and sometimes even now, when I have lost my way yet again, facing the grinding inevitability of all the days ahead... Maugham has Waddington say to Kitty, in answer to her question: 'Tao. Some of us look for the Way in opium and some in God, some of us in whisky and some in love. It is all the same Way and it leads nowhither.' As an atheist, Maugham writes with some insight about the Search.

Wonderful stormy weather. I go to sleep with the sound of the waves crashing onto the rocks below, and awake to the same sound. Every morning I look out to sea and to the rim of land on the horizon that is Omaha, and gauge what the weather will be today. Sometimes the sun is already turning the tops of the trees gold in the valley leading down to the sea.

August 4

A small, cream-coloured pigeon began wandering round the garden in a lost way a few days ago. On the second day, seeing it perched on the veranda, I put out some porridge oats for it. They disappeared fast. After a few days, sparrows began turning up for breakfast too.

Lunch at Pigeon's Perch. I like going there for the ambience, but find their menu rather heavily meaty, and even the fish dishes rather hefty. However, on the way out, I bought some bottles of quince ratafia, and became involved in a stimulating discussion with Andy who makes it. The vineyard is his dream, and he's specialised in Italian wines. Before he and his wife built this custom-designed restaurant, we used to dine on the terrace at their home, and had to pass through their library on the way to the terrace. I was immobilised by the bookshelves, reading his wonderful collection of titles, ranging from Aristophanes and Euripides, Horace and Terence, to Freud and Tolstoy, Chekov and Hardy, and everyone in between. I preferred the charm of eating there in their home to the sophistication of the new restaurant.

Andy hadn't realised that ratafia was the innocuous drink Regency bucks used to give shy young (rep?) maidens too young for a glass of wine or champagne. The pages of Georgette Heyer are littered with the word. However, Andy's quince ratafia would be very unsuitable for young maidens since he uses brandy as a base, and sells it as a dessert wine. It is a glorious pinky-apricot shade, and I bought three in their long, thin elegant bottles with a cork topped in emerald green wax. It looks like a jewelled stopper...good with lemon puddings and creamy blue cheeses, he said. I have just the lemon pudding!

The results for the testing of my hairs for allergies have come back and I had a session with the naturopath. Pretty depressing. A life of deprivation stares me in the face. No dairy. No wheat. No potatoes, tomatoes, peppers, aubergines. No onions, garlic or spring onions. No monosodium glutamate. No soya. No fun.

August 5

As a paid-up member of the Colin Firth fan club, I went to see him in Helen Hunt's film, *She Found Me*. For most of it, I was wondering why I was there, doing what I don't enjoy – watching other people's pain and seeing them make a hash of their lives. Her Jewish prayer in the hospital: *'I am the god of love and I am the god of fear'* caught my heart, but the thing that really caught my eye was Salman Rushdie in a cameo appearance, acting as a charming Indian consultant. The first time I thought I was imagining it. The second time he appeared I was sure, and at the end stayed to watch the credits until his name came up. Curiouser and Curiouser, to quote Alice. Charming indeed, I could well understand how he came to have so many beautiful wives. Move over Colin Firth!

I couldn't put Malcolm Gladwell's *The Tipping Point down*. Swallowed it in one sitting and discovered that Eugenie already acts on the broken window theory, and tackled a tagger outside her house the other day. We agreed that that was how it used to be with the village bobby walking the streets, and jumping on small misdemeanours straight away. It reminded me of Mrs Millbank's Diaries, and her account of ringing the police station when someone was stealing apples from her garden in 1943. She heard one police officer at the other end of the phone say to another, *'Doesn't she re-alise there's a war on?'*

August 7

I rang round various people who might like pigeons, be missing one, or wanted one... no luck, so I put a notice on the board at the village store, lost pigeon etc, and someone replied, quite shirty about her naughty pigeon and people who fed him.

By a strange coincidence, the pigeon stopped coming after that... I hope she went back home to her disapproving owner. But, and a big but, we now had a hungry sparrow population, and a few silvereyes, expecting regular meals.

Patrick made me one of the bird tables like we had at Howick, where I fed literally hundreds of town sparrows. But in those days we didn't have a cat. Nor was there a large mynah population. Here, I made a rod for my own back by feeding the birds early and getting back into bed to watch them from the bedroom window.

I then spent the next half hour leaping out of bed, banging on the window, opening it and clapping my hands and shouting, to shoo the mynahs away, and succeeding in shooing everyone else away too. So today, I went to Matakana and bought a piece of trellis slightly bigger than the bird table, and got Patrick to nail it a few inches above the table, so the sparrows could still nip in.

We went to see a cult film, 'Rain of the Children,' about the Tuhoi/Tūhoe tribe. I never got to see Once Were Warriors, finally saw Whale Rider on TV, so thought I'd make an effort to be up with the play on Maori matters. Patrick and I stuck it out to the end, thinking there must be some reason or resolution to what was, in effect, a grim documentary. It was the true story of a tragic old woman who, after several husbands (including one who brought his brother along, so they never knew whose child she was carrying) lost most of them to disease and social welfare. A brave Pakeha teacher adopted four of the children but got no credit for it. Several wife-beating husbands later, and after about ten children, when the last of her husbands had been killed in a drunken stoush over beating her up in the pub, she was left with a fat, middle-aged, autistic son.

The broken and demented old woman, (who wouldn't be after such a life?) posed a puzzle to the sympathetic Pakeha filmmaker who didn't seem to understand what her problem was. And when she finally died, her desperate son got drunk, was beaten up in the pub, and left lying stripped naked in the main street of the remote Maori settlement where he eventually died. For several days he lay outside where he fell, according to a well-known, tattooed and apparently heartless Maori activist, who watched it all, and who also watched the dead man's two loyal cats come to sit by the body and keep him company. Did anyone then take responsibility for those two loyal and homeless cats?

If you want to see a film about early colonial racism, tribal violence, arranged marriages, wife beating, child abuse, poverty, deprivation on every count, drunkenness, heartlessness, and utter despair, then this is the one. There wasn't one instance of the much-vaunted aroha, cultural pride, or even a simple European word like kindness.

I can't imagine how a film-maker, who obviously admired the tangata whenua, could make such an indictment of what seemed like a Stone Age community, the way it was portrayed, in spite of the many apparently normal Maori storytellers he talked to. These Maori relatives and kinsfolk seemed to have no psychological understanding of the true story. There was no love, respect, or kindness for the poor old woman.

After this, I felt overwhelmed with the immensity of trying to an end to the torture and murder of so many Maori children, compared with the rest of the population. To read the childhoods and life histories of the tragic men like those who tortured and killed the little girl Nia Glassie was to realise that they were transferring their own emotional deprivation and pain on to another helpless victim. Never having experienced gentleness and love themselves, how could they have any to give to another?

I still remember the shock and the hopelessness I felt when our Maori neighbours returned from another neighbour's party at the same time as we did. The great-grandmother (sixty) and the grandmother (forty) were holding the daughter's two-month-old baby, and they were obviously upset. When I asked what the matter was, they said the baby had been naughty, and they were taking her home as a punishment.

They then proceeded to strap the tiny girl into the car seat, which was upside down and had no support for the baby's head and spine. Nothing I could say would convince them a: that the baby was not naughty, but probably hungry, and certainly tired and upset by the crowds, noise, smoke, fumes etc. of the party, and b: that the car seat was upside down.

A few years later, when I was sitting in a hospital waiting room, a spiritual-looking Maori grandmother was holding her six-week-old twin grandson, while the mother took the other in to the specialist. I admired him, and she became excited and began playing with him. She obviously adored him, but her only vocabulary was insults. '*You little liar,*' she would intone lovingly, *'I'm going to punch you in the face.*' Repeatedly she crooned her sweet nothings to him, but the words were all threats and violence. She had obviously never had a kind word said to her in her life, and though she oozed aroha, she had no appropriate vocabulary.

If I said this publicly, I would be accused of being racist. What is racism? It is intolerance.

To me it's the same as sexism, anti-Semitism, speciesism (treating animals badly). It is seeing others as inferior, and not worthy of the same treatment and status as oneself.

It goes on between Jew and Arab, and Arab and Jew, between Chinese and Indian, it goes on between Christian and all other religions, it's the same intolerance that causes persecution between Shi'a and Sunni, between Muslim and Hindu, between Muslim and Baha'i, between Iraqi and Kurd.

It is not respecting the other person, and not accepting that they, their beliefs, their culture, have the same value as one's own. I like the Maori Party's *manaakitanga* – principles. The concept of *'manaakitanga'* is defined as *'behaviour that acknowledges the mana of others as having equal or greater importance than one's own',* demonstrated by 'the expression of aroha, hospitality, generosity and mutual respect'.

Coming back down to earth, petty pace, the daily round and common task, I'm coming to terms with my deprived diet, and finding ways round. Using leeks instead of onions and garlic means that risottos, for example, taste so much subtler and more refined. Kate says I can reintroduce some things after a month or so. Top of my list will be dairy. I can actually get used to the rest.

August 21

Still occupied with the bird situation. The trellis worked as planned. The clever little sparrows, blackbirds, and silvereyes slipped down in the trellis triangles and managed perfectly. The mynahs were foiled for fully a day, and then they worked out how to stretch their necks down through the trellis. My next move was to get some chicken wire and nail it across, and this still allowed the little birds to slip in all around the sides.

Looking for recipes for dinner with Graeme and Joan, and Annie and Mike, I found myself reading Nigella Lawson's *book Feast*. Compulsive reading, the chapter on funerals contained much deeply felt experience and hardly-won wisdom. The first funeral recipe is fish pie, which she says she made on the evening following her mother's funeral. She goes on: 'I don't think anyone wants to cook in the immediate shock of bereavement and in my experience you are anyway likely to need something like a.... Chinese takeaway, but a few days on cooking can be a calming act, and since the mind knows no rest and has no focus, the body may as well be busy...'

I was interested that she also offered lentil soup for funerals, which has always been a standby in this family... if ever Eugenie was ill or 'fluey', she wanted me to make, and now makes her own, lentil soup. And like Nigella, I've always felt that fruitcake is the only appropriate cake for a funeral. The common sense and heartbreaking advice from one who has seen her mother, her sister, and her husband die is never to ask a bereaved person a question. Decisions are impossible, she writes. Just do what you think will be helpful. She described the kindest thing anyone did for her: a friend left bags of shopping with a short note at her side door.

Nigella also discussed that quote of M.F.K. Fisher's, which I knew for truth, when she writes of the *mysterious appetite that often surges in us when our hearts seem about to break and our lives seem too bleakly empty*. She goes on, *'the truth is most bereaved souls crave nourishment more tangible than prayers: they want a steak'*

I remember being puzzled and appalled at my grossness when I was twenty-one, and had just said goodbye for some months to a dashing young cavalry captain I had realised in that instant that I loved. I had felt a deep sense of desolation as he left (only decades later did I discover that this was long forgotten father going-to-war memory pushing away underneath). So I tottered weakly back inside, and carved a hunk of whole meal bread, and plastered it with butter and thick gobs of honey, and stuffed myself. I now know that emotional stress causes a sudden drop in sugar levels, so we crave food to re-balance the system.

All this reading took me back to when I tried to make myself drunk on a couple of glasses of port the only alcohol in the house at the time – when my Cavalier King Charles spaniel had died on the vet's operating table. It wasn't that I was crying with great sobs, it was just an endless flowing, running tap, so that as fast as I mopped, the tears poured down my cheeks again. I thought if I could stupefy myself with alcohol, it would stop the tears. It just made it worse. So much for reading cookery books.

August 28

The mynahs are winning. They still managed to crane their necks through the wire and the trellis. It wouldn't have mattered, except that their dominating and menacing presence, some six or eight of them, drove the little birds away. So I got a series of large stones and put them round the edge of the bird table, under the trellis, leaving small gaps for the little birds. To my amazement, I watched those clever, infuriating mynahs, fly in and under, at jumbo jet angle, and crouch practically on all fours – if they had all fours – and still manage to gobble all the bird food. I finally gave up, and stopped feeding the birds. They don't need it here in the country. It was just my little hobby. On the other hand, Kate has asked me to feed her hens while she's away skiing. I shall enjoy it.

August 29

Eugenie invited me to a concert of Vivaldi and Purcell performed by an Italian group that specialise in Vivaldi. She couldn't give me anything I enjoy more. Sitting next to the mayor I had an interesting talk with him over a remark he'd made in the paper about stray cats having as much right to live in the city as people. Knowing I was talking to a man who used to get on his motorbike to ride to Albany to feed the chickens when they were still there, I brought up the cats.

We discussed our experiences feeding stray cats, and he told me he spends eight $800 a month driving to various places around the city, at the end of late night council meetings, where gangs of strays await him. This, of course, is the man who went to Russia to adopt one orphan, and came back with three, two brothers and their sister.

Re-reading Gitta Sereny's book: Albert Speer: *His Battle With Truth,* I find it hard to believe that he was ignorant of the Final Solution. He could see one manifestation of it all around him in every factory he visited to drive more inhumane efforts out of the slave workers for war production. Airey Neave, who Rebecca West described as having *'that special quality the Romans call pietas'*, estimated that under Speer's aegis, 4,795,000 foreign workers were torn from their homes to work for Hitler. And it's made me curious to know more about the Nuremburg Trials, which Gitta Sereny is always referring to.

One of the most intriguing stories was during the last months of the war. Wilhelm Furtwängler, conductor of the Berlin Philharmonic, and under suspicion from Nazi party chiefs, was told by Speer to stay in Switzerland after a tour there. Speer promised him he would look after the orchestra on its return to Berlin. Later, discovering that Goebbels had ordered the musicians to enroll in the People's Militia to defend Berlin, Speer had their cards secretly removed from the files.

He then told them to schedule a series of last concerts, and said when he told them to play Bruckner's Romantic Symphony, it would mean the end was near, and the musicians should leave Berlin. Hitler's ADC Nicolaus Von Below wrote of that last concert on 12 April. He sat with Speer and Admiral Doenitz, and they listened to Beethoven's Violin Concerto, the Finale from Götterdämmerung and Bruckner's Romantic

Symphony, before walking silently back to their mad master in the Reich Chancellery.

Speer had had the electricity switched on for the occasion, and the hall was packed with Berliners who had been bombed into survival in cellars and ruins, but who still came out for the music. On the way out, Speer was horrified to find the Hitler Youths holding out baskets for concertgoers, containing cyanide capsules. He never discovered who had ordered this final macabre gesture. I think we can guess. Good old Goebbels!

Berlin aside, it fascinates me to learn how often music disrupts cruel wars, and uplifts people in the middle of despair, from the carols both sides sang together in the trenches during World War One, until they were stopped; to Shostakovich conducting his new Symphony No. 7 for the starving people of Leningrad during the terrible siege in World War Two; and the violinist who went to play every day outside the baker's shop in Sarajevo after his friend had been killed there by a sniper. The queues outside the National Gallery for the lunchtime concerts during World War Two were legendary, and I wish I'd heard Beethoven's Symphony No. 9 being played there after the fall of the Berlin Wall.

6

Sep/Oct 2008

September 9

Patrick's seventy-ninth birthday, and the excuse for a slap-up lunch at Pigeon's Perch. We'd done a dummy run the week before, and sussed out a diabolically delicious hot chocolate pudding, somewhere between a soufflé and a mousse... that day we shared it. Today, we both had our own. We were late for our table, because as we drove through a wet, muddy day, we came upon a car driving slowly towards us on the Whangateau bends, with two wet, muddy farm dogs galloping after it. The driver, a rather daffy woman, waved us down. So I opened the window and asked if there was a problem. Yes, indeed. They had been following her for some miles, and she didn't know what to do.

My heart sank, because I could see that this was going to become my problem. Cars were trying to drive past and not slowing down, so I jumped out and tried to inveigle the dogs into the back seat of our car, with Patrick quietly fuming in the front. I got one in, but the other plunged ahead looking even more bewildered, and people driving past were looking at me with the animosity of people who think you don't know how to control your dogs, and are now creating chaos – in fact, yet another stupid townie.

Finally, the other large, muddy, hairy dog joined its mate on the back seat, and the daffy woman drove off with a sigh of relief to her dancing exam!

Now all I had to do was find where our passengers had come from.

They were very friendly and very relieved that someone was looking after them. I stopped at various likely places on the road, but drew a blank, so decided to drive to the vet at Warkworth, a long way out of our way, and hopefully, leave them with him. The dogs had collars and registration numbers, but no phone numbers.

I was worried that these gentle creatures belonged to a farmer who would be like the one I had spoken to in Matakana the previous week ('a loved dog is a spoiled dog, and won't work') and he would be furious with them... my imagination had plenty of country living experience to feed it, and I felt miserable. The vet didn't exactly welcome me with open arms, but he could see the problem when I explained that we were on our way out to lunch.

Though I've sat through a wedding reception with a large, lost, muddy, and starving Springer Spaniel in the back seat, nipping out to give her hunks of ham and chicken, I didn't want to do it again. She had been retrieved from a forest clearing on our way down to Rotorua, with me tiptoeing through the rain and mud in my high-heeled shoes. Another time we had dinner in a restaurant in Kerikeri while a lost retriever puppy chewed up the tartan rug on the car seat, and also the armrests, before we got him to our friendly vet. The armrest still bears the scars.

The last I saw of these two they were gently resisting going into a cage. Back home, after lunch, the phone went, and it was the dogs' owner. No, not a farmer, but a doting owner, who grows roses for market, and whose sister had inexplicably let them out. She was grateful of course.

I'm re-reading yet again Jane Austen's *Mansfield Park*. It's the one I read more regularly than any of the others. It's the one I'd take to a desert island. Though Fanny and Edmund are both so irritatingly virtuous, I enjoy not just the other characters – especially the villains, Henry and Mary Crawford – but the drama of the amateur theatricals, the much ado about nothing in the garden of Mr. Rushworth, and above all, Mansfield

Park itself. A picture of England as Gainsborough would have painted it, described in words by another master. I'm intrigued by the simplicity of eighteenth century country life... Mary Crawford is so bored by days of rain and no one in the village to see, that when she spies boring Fanny sheltering under a tree from the rain, she rushes out to bring her in, and keep her at the vicarage for some amusement (anything for a change!).

And so begins a tentative friendship.

I can remember something of that feeling when I was eighteen, in the days when we didn't have television, I had to have permission from my parents to use the wireless, and we lived miles away from anywhere in a Queen Anne house in the middle of the country. A boy living down the road, the elderly bachelor accountant on the corner (aged thirty-four) all seemed romantic in my isolation. The boy took me to a hunt ball, and the accountant invited us to his pre-ball party, and on closer acquaintance, one seemed callow and ignorant, and the other, elegant, erudite and intimidating. Back in the eighteenth century, the boy would have continued to try to court me, and I would have yearned after the un-attainable older man, and we would all have gone on meeting hopelessly for years.

September 16

Drinks with Mike and Annie. Two of my favourite people – and devoted goat owners – the exploits of Robert, Billy Goat Gruff, Goggles, The Wild One, and The Old Mother, keep us constantly amused. Some weeks ago, a friend who is actually a violinmaker, had accompanied Mike and Annie up here with a pre-fabricated goat house he had made, a carefully de-signed one-off, de-luxe apartment to replace the tum-bledown shed at the bottom of the hill. This magnificent edifice was constructed at the top of the hill, so the goats could do what goats like to do, which is to sit at the top of a hill and survey the landscape below... in this case, the incomparable view of the har-bour, the sea, and the islands beyond.

On returning a couple of weeks ago, Mike and An-nie found to their distress that Robert, Billy Goat Gruff, had been behaving in a very male chauvinist way to The Old Mother, refusing to allow her to enter the shelter, and behaving to Goggles, the rescued wild goat, in a bullying, racist way by also preventing her entry to this superior dwelling. So the two outcasts were sheltering underneath the goat house in wet, muddy, windy conditions... not the luxury that Mike and Annie had envisioned.

Mike spent the weekend building a partition, a side entrance and another ramp, so the two outcasts could use the new back apartment. Dear Mike got up at 2 a.m and made his way down the hundreds of steps into the valley, and up the other side to the goat house, to peer in, in the moonlight and see if all was well. All was indeed well. Everyone present and correct...

Having discussed the tribulations of the goats, we passed on to 'The Wedding', a subject never far from Annie's thoughts these days, though there's still five months to go. She told me she had found a wonderful rose grower in Whangateau, and though she could supply white roses, yellow ones were non-existent since the ferocious storm last year, which had destroyed the yellow rose greenhouse. It turned out, of course, that the rose grower was the owner of the large, muddy dogs.

I've just finished a *new biography of Harold Nicolson* by Norman Rose. I ended it with a feeling of real distaste for both Harold and Vita.

I hadn't realised how skillfully his son Nigel Nicolson had expurgated the diaries I've always enjoyed so much, of all Harold's prejudices against Jews, Coloureds, Japanese, Turks, Persians, Arabs, Slavs, Catholics, and the vulgar – known to them as 'bedints'. Vita came across as selfish, snobbish, unprincipled and promiscuous, a neglectful mother and rather prosaic writer, though a great gardener.

I wonder if I will enjoy re-reading Nicolson's diaries again after this.

The Sound Of Water

The Palestinian situation is enraging. Why does everyone pussyfoot around the Israelis when they're behaving like everyone else who's indulged in ethnic cleansing? No wonder the Arab world doesn't trust the West. I shy away from mentioning it when in the company of Jewish or Israeli friends, just as I avoid mentioning that, I lived at Belsen to Germans... near Hanover, I murmur vaguely.

October 10

I went to the doctor this morning. My damaged hand from the car accident at Hunua thirty-three years ago, when I was flung through the windscreen, has suddenly been playing up. At first, I thought it was a boil coming. As the weeks went by the area in my palm, which has always been too painful to touch, seemed to be swelling, and then something broke through the surface of the skin.

Slowly, after several excruciating weeks, a shard of glass appeared, and it kept catching on things, and then the hand would bleed and the pain get worse. David Davie, a phlegmatic Welshman, was amazed, and proceeded to give me a local anaesthetic in order to carve the glass out. Injecting through all the existing scar tissue was the most painful thing of all. Then it was out; a piece of glass about half an inch long and deep, with jagged edges. No wonder the hand had always been so painful. He told me that old servicemen still have pieces of shrapnel popping out in odd places!

October 12

Coffee with Marjorie at a tea place. It feels as though it's trying to be like one of those comforting English tea places where we used to congregate in a group after doing the shopping. But this one isn't full of life and chat, and feels in fact rather bleak and cheerless, with mean, expensive helpings of scones, sandwiches and tiny slices of cake. Marjorie drew back the curtain on her life and I heard things that saddened me.

Patrick seems to have a new lease of life, and is spending more time in the garden, which means that a number of things I wanted done are now in process. I've given up trying to make a hedge of the garden by the garage and the drive, and have now surrendered to a flower garden stuffed with daisies and foxgloves, asters, catmint, cherry pie, grannies' bonnets and the like, and some roses, including Albertine to smother the trellis arch along with clematis, and a mutabilis rose which I propagated myself.

I've probably over-planted but I want quick results. Now we're beginning on the garden outside, where I've always wanted to develop some borders so that passers-by enjoy a spilling over of flowers and shrubs. Inevitably, there's agapanthus to fill gaps, and daisies, pink cannas and foxgloves, orange arctotis and purple salvia. It should look good by next summer. And the liquid ambers, planted three years ago, are now streaking towards the sky. So much mulching, watering and warmth this year has seen more than two feet of new growth on most branches. The couple we planted last year are still plodding, but they should take off next year. The end of the road will be bright with autumn colour within the next few years.

With Patrick's help I've now got the front lawn re-shaped into a circle instead of a boring rectangle, and by next year I hope it will be a circle of textured ivy, with the added advantage of not needing to be mown.

In autumn, I shall eliminate the flowers around it, and turn it into mounds of green and grey plants, so I get the effect of a green shaded garden like Nicole de Vesian's Provencal garden. Ambitious I know, but worth a try. The pots of clipped box are a great starter. Everything we do is on such a tiny scale here, that it's possible. And though I'd like it to look elegant like Frances's disciplined plantings, I have to fall back on charm, as usual.

Two books on Nuremberg have arrived from Amazon, Airey Neave's and G.M. Gilbert's. Airey Neave's eyewitness account from the day he delivered all the indictments to each accused in their cell, and G.M. Gilbert's account as the prison psychologist. He records the words and thoughts of Hitler's willing accomplices. Looks like some thought-provoking information.

7

Nov/Dec 2008

November 1

I had a long conversation on the phone with Piers last night, covering architecture, including Rome and their holiday there last year, God, philosophy, conspiracy theories, Obama, history... Twice, we were interrupted by Halloween trick or treat knocks on the door, and each time he said, 'I'll hold on, and then you come back.'

It took me back to all the times we had when he was little. I remember tucking him into bed when he was about six, and telling him about Mrs. Bedonebyasyoudid, and Mrs. Doasyouwouldbedoneby, from The Water Babies. He lay with his hands behind his head on the pillow, considering, and then said, 'Well, I think I'm a bit of both, Grannie'.

I've been re-reading Nancy Mitford's biography of Frederick the Great, in the hope of finding a reference to the King of Saxony who started the Dresden china factories in his efforts to reproduce Chinese porcelain. No luck there, but found a charming story about Bach. Mitford writes of Frederick at the Palace of SansSouci playing his flute in the concert, which they held every day after supper at 10 p.m. The King was handed the list of passengers who'd disembarked from the daily coach.

Frederick read it: 'Gentlemen, old Bach has arrived!' It was Johann Sebastian, whom the King had never met. A carriage was sent for the old man and he was told to come at once without changing into his cantor's robe. The King made much of him; the concert was abandoned and the two men went to try out Frederick's new Silbermann pianofortes, Bach extemporising on them to the King's admiration.

Then the King gave Bach a theme, at Bach's request, (it turned out to be a difficult one) and the old man wrote a fugue for the King.

An encounter between a master of war and a master of music. Checking up in a reference book, I find this was in 1747, when Bach went to stay with his son, Carl Philip Emmanuel, who was court harpsichordist at Frederick's court.

November 2

The garden is beginning to bloom, the pots are tumbling with flowers, nasturtiums sprawling, marguerites and shasta daisies flowering. Marjorie's moss rose from Kerikeri is blooming in heavily scented bunches which perfume the steps and the courtyard, blue campanula overflow the pots with Abraham Derby roses which are also flowering, pansies are rampant, and the standard crab apples and the plum tree are foaming with blossom. It makes me feel like a gardener... almost.

The saga of the goats continues... Annie and Mike were very upset when they came up at the weekend to find that Goggles had taken a leaf out of Robert's nasty notebook, and she was denying elderly Old Mother shelter in the back bedroom. Poor Old Mother was left to crouch under the house in the rain, while Robert pee-ed and pooed above her, on the slatted floor. Mike spent the weekend digging out a basement apartment for The Old Mother, and devising a shallow peaked roof, so that The Old Mother was sheltered both from the stormy blast and from anything that Robert happened to release. Phew! Will they now live happily ever after?

November 3

A quick dash into town to see The Phantom of the Opera with Eugenie – at last – I must be the last per-

115

son in the world to see it. To my surprise, I enjoyed it, and then drove home through the clear, starry night.

November 11
During the obligatory evening stroll round the cemetery with Cara, there were many signs of visits to old servicemen's graves after the Armistice Remembrance ceremony there today. The one, which puzzled me, was a vase nestled into a pohutukawa tree where the graves look out to sea. The flowers were beautiful, roses and lilies from a garden, not the stiff sort from a florist. Then I turned round, and realised that the headstone behind me had no grave, and the tree was the nearest place to put some flowers.

It was the grave of Trooper Angus Matheson, of Lord Liverpool's Own. He was twenty-one when he died at Trentham army training base on 29 June 1915. The inscription reads:

Mourn not for him, nor lay your hearts within that quiet grave,
Think you those narrow bounds could hold that spirit pure and brave?
Earth's uniform discarded now, beneath the sod is laid.
He had his marching orders - as a soldier he obeyed.

A poppy had also been tucked into the carving at the head of the stone. But the heart-stopping thing was; who cared enough, eighty-three years later, to pick those scented flowers, bring a glass vase and water, and tuck them into the fork of the tree?

Driving into Matakana earlier today, I avoided driving over the feathery corpse of a little bird with long legs and long claws. I peered through the rear vision mirror, convinced that the speckled brown and cream on the feathers looked like kiwi markings. Driving back later that day, I looked across at the spot, just before the one-way bridge at Whangateau, and though it was considerably more squashed than before, could still pick out these intriguing colours.

Back home, I gathered up a shovel, a pair of gloves and several plastic bags, and hurried back. It seemed a bit small for a kiwi, but maybe it was a young one, I theorised. So the little bundle was stowed carefully in several layers of bags in the deep freeze. It being after-hours now, I left a message on the answer phone of the Department of Conservation.

November 12

They rang today and seemed quite excited, and said they'd come out. A gorgeous young man arrived, just exactly what I'd imagine a Department of Conservation employee to look like – golden haired, very brown, athletic, piercing blue eyes, sort of gentle Crocodile Dundee, and courteous, even with a time-waster like me. It was not a kiwi, but just as interesting he assured me. It was a banded rail, and though they knew the species had made it across from Little Barrier Island to Sandspit, they didn't know it had spread to the mangroves at Whangateau, a long way away in banded rail terms.

He seemed quite delighted, and I... I felt as though I had discovered a new species, or a new star in space, and I had never realised just what joy such a discovery could be.

I looked up Buller's *Book of Birds*, but was as usual sickened by his heartless description of the distress of his captive, 'It could be heard night and day tapping the bars (of its wooden cage) with its slender bill as it wandered up and down its little prison, and it seemed never to relinquish for a single moment the hope of delivery from its unnatural bondage.'

Buller also complained that, 'it was so incessantly active in its movements that I had the utmost difficulty in making a life sketch of it.'

He described letting it loose in a room and it running 'swiftly from one corner to another seeking concealment'... In spite of Darwin's stated belief that creatures have feelings like homo sapiens (a misnomer, if ever there was one), Buller seemed totally oblivious of the mental torment to which he subjected his captives.

November 14

Mary Millen has died. I am sad, I shall miss her, and I don't know how Anthony will live without her. But I'm glad, because she had been in such pain from diabetes, ulcers, heart and thyroid for so long, and never ever complained. Now she is with Robin, her beloved son. I was touched that Anthony wrote that we were among their closest friends. It had never occurred to me, even though I've always loved them.

Staying with them at Ampleforth, in Yorkshire, was an old-fashioned pleasure, reminding me of a way of life taken for granted in my childhood with my stepmother. Regular, proper meals, regular routine, drink before dinner, the pleasure of good beds and freshly laundered linen, spick and span spare bedroom, a feeling of comfort and old-fashioned good taste. The breakfast table, equipped with teapot, toast rack and a posy of flowers, the homemade marmalade, and the smell of frying bacon, brought back so many leisurely breakfasts staying with friends for weekends, or Sunday mornings at home. Few people gather round a breakfast table together any more.

Mary's style was traditionally English, thick carpets, cosy flowery linen sofas, gold-rimmed prints, family portraits of imperious men and women looking down on us in the hall – walking sticks and shooting sticks in the umbrella rack, good antiques, fine silver and pretty china – and of course, cushions, flowers and books.

One shining morning, with cobwebs sparkling in the sun after a light frost, Mary took me to Rievaulx Abbey, a grey ruin sprawling across a green valley. It was surrounded by beech trees in all the autumn shades from pale apricot to dark copper, and a clear stony-bottomed north-country river flowed alongside. Apparently, the monks re-routed it to enlarge their building site. And it was certainly a magnificent one. Even now, in ruins, it was possible to feel the immensity of the soaring ruined arches, and trace the refectory and hospital, the kitchen and the cloisters. And no sound but the running river and the faint cry of sheep up on the hills behind. In this solitude it was easy to imagine the quiet industry of the monks, and bells ringing for the office, chanting in the chapel, and silence in the cloisters. It was one of the earliest Cistercian abbeys in England.

Whenever Mary – a devout Catholic – was short of a man for a dinner party, she would ring up various monks from Ampleforth Abbey, and they couldn't get out of their habits and into their cars fast enough to drive over for a good dinner and some fine wine! On a visit to the Abbey, I felt somewhat the way Henry VIII must have done, as I surveyed a priceless oriental rug which stretched endlessly the whole length of the cloisters. It had been especially woven as a gift to the reigning Abbott.

November 18

The bleakness of the last year feels like *'The Journey of the Magi',* in the words of Dean Lancelot Andrewes' Christmas sermon in 1622:

It was a cold coming they had of it at this time of the year, just the worst time of the year to take a journey, and especially a long journey. The ways deep, the weather sharp, the days short, the sun farthest off, in solstitio brumali, 'the very dead of winter'

It has felt like this for months. Yesterday I went to Jan, who does aura soma, and when I had pointed to the bottles that were beckoning at me, she said, 'I'm worried about you – those are all rescue bottles.'

How astounding that you pick colours in bottles that have symbolism you know nothing about, and they turn out to mirror your inmost feelings.

This morning, feeling fragile, I've made some resolutions about how to survive the journey... and try to have no more 'cold comings'. One of which is to write something each day. I feel so much better when I've let some words trickle out, instead of damning them up, hoping for better days before I enjoy the pleasure of writing again. I have to MAKE the days better, instead of waiting and hoping and becoming more and more hopeless... One of the bottles I chose symbolised being cut off from my spiritual source, which is how I've been feeling, arid and cheerless.

Last week, I started acupuncture to try to shift the total tiredness all the time... maybe it will help... The acupuncturist is enchanting, a fragile little woman, who left her professor husband in China, came here alone, not speaking the language, and after a few years, buying two acres in the country, with a substantial house, where she nurtures a Labrador, two steers (for meat), six goats, which she milks, two hens, for their eggs, and grows her vegetables. Two days a week she plies her acupuncture.

Today, after my second session, I woke early for the first time in years, and put on my dressing gown and went out in the half-light. I dead-headed all the daisies and then, at a quarter to six, wandered up to the corner to watch the sun come up over the sea. It was still too early, but an old farm motorbike came racketing down the road with two youngsters on it. Propping it up against the wall, they pushed through the cemetery gate and strode down the slope in the direction of the harbour. I knew what they had come for. They were going to the grave of the boy who was killed at work three years ago. They were there till half past six, by which time the sun had come up, and was a burning orb above the horizon of the sea, too bright to look at, only the pink reflections over the water safe to gaze upon.

Later, I went to see if they had left a flower or drunk the bottles of beer other mates had left at the headstone, but they had left no trace of their presence. At the nearby grave of another child, someone had also visited, leaving a purple pot with purple campanula at the sad empty grave where there are no trinkets, just the emptiness of grief.

Some mourners seem to gain comfort from making the grave of their beloved a home from home, like the teenager's, with photos, trinkets, shells, china angels, and bits from his car arranged round the head-stone, even his cell phone buried with him. The other child's grave speaks of grief so inconsolable that no comfort could be gained by dressing up the grave. It remains, empty, austere, and every now and then, a tiny token left.

Annabel rang me yesterday and ended up discussing her subjects for next year. When she read out the syllabus for Classics, including Aristophanes, Juvenal, Augustus, I pressed her to take Classics. I would have loved to study those magic names at school. At twelve I read The Complete Works of Shakespeare, in a new edition, which my grandfather gave my parents for Christmas 1950. I laboured through it because I was so curious to discover what this reverberating name was all about. My inaccurate ideas of English history were based on Shakespeare's plays for years, and I think I was the only person who ever opened the pages of that book.

Later, I remember the thrill in class when we came to those hackneyed words 'Veni, vidi, vici,' feeling kinship with every schoolboy for hundreds of years who had also translated them, (Mr Chips has much to answer for) and then, tackling Virgil, I revelled in our amateurish word-by-word translations of those stately lines. Back in London after three years in Malaya, starved of books, having relied on the school library, and dog-eared and ant-eaten Penguins with orange, black and white covers lying around tropical rest houses and hotels, I gazed longingly at tables in Selfridges and Foyles. They were stacked with paperbacks with names like Euripides, Aristotle and Erasmus, Plato and Marcus Aurelius on the covers. I had no money to buy them.

My weekly allowance only covered my lunches and the odd pair of nylon stockings, which laddered almost as soon as they were bought. We tried everything to prolong the life of the wretched things; wearing gloves to put them on, so as not to snag them on a fingernail, and trying to stop the ladders running by dabbing them with blobs of nail varnish. And nothing betrayed the slut or heedless teenager as quickly as crooked seams. Redemption came eventually, but not for years, in the shape of seamless panty hose and nylon mesh. And so the whole company of heaven, ancient historians, philosophers, dramatists and poets remained untasted and unknown to me.

November 30

The loquat tree by the veranda is still laden with bunches of amber-coloured fruit. The two extremely fat wood pigeons who consider our garden to be their territory, and who freeze out any lone interlopers, lumber into the tree like jumbo jets coming in to land, and stuff themselves with the big berries. I watched one in profile the other day, as it swallowed the whole fruit, and it slid bumpily down its gleaming, green and bronze throat, and then into the safety of its smooth, swelling white breast.

Buller says: *'...in spring and early summer it is generally very lean and unfit for the table; but as autumn advances and its favourite berries ripen, it rapidly improves in condition, till it becomes extremely fat.'*

I have news for Buller. He should visit this small corner

of New Zealand. The pigeons feast on the berries of the loquats and the karaka tree in spring and early summer, as well as the kowhai and the puriri fruit. Then, as summer progresses, they move into the squat guava trees, sitting in the top as though they are sitting on a huge nest, and reminding me of a partridge in a pear tree. At no time of the year are our resident pigeons 'lean and unfit for the table'; they remain delectably fat, but forbidden, all the year round.

The last sentence of Buller's text reads:

Its relative abundance may be inferred from the fact that in July and August 1882, Rawiri Kahia and his people snared no less than eight thousand of them in a single strip of miro bush, about two miles in extent by half a mile in width, at Opawa, near Lake Taupo. The birds thus snared are preserved in their own fat and potted as ' huahua kereru'. Food of this kind is esteemed a great delicacy and elaborately carved kumetes are sometimes used for serving it at tribal feasts.

No wonder they needed protection from the Animals Protection and Game Act of 1921. Back in the 1860s in this village, the European settlers would go out and shoot twenty in a morning. They often used the fat instead of butter on their bread – cows were thin on the ground here back then, as was the wheat for bread, which the settlers had to grow.

Read The Guernsey Literary and Potato Pie Society in one gasp tonight. Was really gripped by the beginning, but felt the end tailed off. As we (Cara and I) walked in the cemetery tonight, I saw dolphins leaping below in the harbour. At last I had seen them. There were five or six, leaping, diving and circling. Oh joy. Our neighbours, Joe and Kitty, joined me, but I feared that if I rushed home to get Patrick the dolphins would have disappeared by the time we returned.

And then, unbelievably, a speedboat with a man and two children, shrieking with laughter, roared across the water, right through the middle of the dolphins. Then they turned and came back. Wherever the dolphins moved to, the boat followed and drove into them. I yelled at them, but, as Kitty said, they would never have heard above the sound of the engine. I tried not to agree with Kitty who was asserting that the world was going to hell in a handcart, whatever that means.

December 6

Yesterday was our little Christmas party. I spent most of the week preparing for it in a carefully planned sequence. Doing finger food is much more time-consuming than a meal, and I would simplify it if I did it again. The greatest successes were the tiny pork chipolata sausages, six dozen, which all disappeared, and also the devils on horseback. The salmon rolls were a success, but not the chicken vol-au-vents. The tiny mince pies went down well, and the meringues sprinkled with rose petals looked beautiful. The big stone bowl filled with lemons and holly and ringed with tealights looked Christmassy, and every-one seemed to enjoy the place... Patrick really enjoyed himself too, and so did I. I always enjoy my own parties!

The gardeners, Barry and Rachel, loved the garden, and couldn't believe we'd been here such a short time, while Jackson, the architect, admired the trellis and the canopy on the veranda. Harry, the potter, surprised us by not being interested in Patrick's precious plate from the Japanese Master Hamada's kiln, which he produced for Harry's delectation. Rachel, like Marjorie, noticed things, and was ravished by John Edgar's sculpture, the silky stone called 'Lightstone', with bands of crystal ringed through it. She also loved the story of how I gave Annie Dillard's book Teaching a Stone to Talk to a friend for Christmas, and then I unwrapped her present to me, and it was the Lightstone!

December 7

I'm feeling very contented after the fun last night. We're looking after Lucy while the family are exploring the Bay of Islands, and she is as large, ingenuous and boisterous as ever, too strong for me to enjoy walking her as she drags me all over the road from one good smell to another. We sat on Eugenie's veranda in the sun with her, rather than upset Cara by bringing Lucy into her territory, and spent the whole morning looking at the dark blue sea, framed by flowering pink and red pohutukawas. It was one of those hot, still, perfect days that almost feel hushed with the beauty of it.

I noticed three or four boats motionless in a large circle, and suddenly realised they were watching dolphins. They were back! We sat there for the next two hours watching the display below us, with the dolphins leaping and swimming from one boat to another, performing, it seemed, for the joy of their transfixed spectators.

We tore ourselves away, and went to see Barry and Marjorie's garden.

It also enchanted... the meander through the water gardens and lawns with water lilies and flowers in full bloom. The trees are still bright with spring green, dragonflies swoop over the ponds, and then there's the climb through the dark bush, emerging into sunshine and roses, at the bottom of the three terraces.

Looking up to the villa at the top always makes me envious, and when we've climbed the terraces, and reached the house, I nearly melt with envy again at the position of the house, looking across valleys and hills,

with the majestic, forested mountain Tamahunga behind, and the valley edged with eucalyptus on the other
side. Grapevines crawl down another slope, and the
terraced gardens crammed with roses, lilies, hedges
and topiary, and the fountain in the middle, step splen-
didly down the slope in front of the house. We sat with
Marjorie and Barry on their veranda looking out on yet
another incomparable view in one day. We had real flat
whites and blueberry cake served on dainty art deco
china. A day to be savoured.

December 27

I lost most of December to the dentist. After a routine visit in the first week for a small filling, I fell into a
black pit of pain, which no painkillers could reach. Finally, I went to the doctor in the second week who prescribed some heavy-duty pills, which took several days
to work. Thereafter, I went around like a zombie, until
weaning myself off them on Christmas Eve.

Christmas with everyone was routine family cele-
brations. Since the Christmas when I rebelled and said
I wasn't going to church, (I can't stand the non-
conformist informality and folksy sermons, the modern
banal English of the Bible readings and the thin unen-
thusiastic singing of the hymns, no gusto or joy) the
family have given up too. Instead, we all find a reading
and bring it over to my little sitting room, where we

make our nod to the Divine, and then unwrap the presents.

Philosopher Piers, no longer convinced of the First Cause, found a reading with no mention of it. His reading was:

> *He who knows others is wise;*
> *He who knows himself is enlightened,*
> *He who conquers others is strong;*
> *He who conquers himself is mighty.*
> *He who knows contentment is rich,*
> *He who keeps on his course with energy has will.*
> *He who does not deviate from his proper place will long endure.*
> *He who may die but not perish has longevity.*

A note says: '*The difficulty of knowing does not lie in seeing others, but in seeing oneself. Therefore he who sees himself is enlightened.*'

And secondly: '*He cannot deviate from his place because he becomes one with all things; he cannot perish, because he lives as long as heaven and earth.*'

Later on Christmas morning, Roland arrived with Annabel and Raymond, and brought various electronic toys and games, which kept all the grandchildren occupied like old times when they were little, and spent hours playing with sticky frogs or magnetic lizards I had found. Annie had given me a box of Philharmonic crackers, with a different note whistle in each one, and a conductor's baton and music for Eugenie. We never achieved a tune, but we laughed a lot. And my game with naff presents from a catalogue worked.

Everyone guessed the names I gave them, from Mr Toad for Patrick (an old joke about his vintage cars), the Queen of Sheba for Eugenie, James Bond for my car-mad son, Aly Khan for Julian (race horses), and they even correctly guessed Wittgenstein for Piers. Last year was the Christmas of charades. This one was the Christmas of Scrabble. I first became aware of it at the beginning of the holidays, when Piers knocked softly on the door while we were all asleep, to ask if he could borrow the dictionary! It stayed next door for the holidays, and I became addicted too.

We left out 'thank you' cards and half a dozen beers each for the paper chasers and the bottle collectors.

To our chagrin, the paper chasers stole the other lot's beer too, so I had to rush up to the store to buy some expensive replacements. Maybe the world is going to hell in a...

December 28

The days after Christmas are known as 'The Long Silence' in this house, when we all hunker down with our Christmas books, and there is no sound or movement, except to carve off another piece of Christmas cake.

I'm re-reading Robert Massie's Dreadnought very slowly, trying to take in and remember all the detail. As I slowly worked my way through all the biographical stuff on the various English statesmen of the period, I began to notice a rather surprising pattern – which was not repeated in the biographies of their German counterparts. It began with the account of the great Lord Salisbury's childhood, and how he survived his mother's death before he was ten and the indifference and hostility of his father who thought he was hopeless. Then there was his brilliant and equally successful nephew Arthur Balfour, also prime minister, like his uncle. Balfour's father died when he was seven, and his highly-strung mother Blanche struggled to bring up a large family alone.

Lord Lansdowne, another brilliant statesman, was lucky. His father survived till Lansdowne was twenty-one, but Herbert Asquith, another prime minister of the time, grew up in an impoverished solo parent home after his father died when he was eight, of a twisted intestine after a village cricket match. My favourite statesman of the period, Sir Edward Grey, was also fatherless by the age of eight, while Admiral Jackie Fisher, the great mover and shaker of the navy, was sent back from Ceylon at the age of six, never to see his father again, who died when he was sixteen. Fisher was an adult before seeing his indigent and disinterested mother again'

Winston Churchill's childhood was famously deprived; brought up by his nanny, deprived of her when sent to boarding school at eight, and writing letters begging his parents to come and see him – they didn't. On one occasion his mother, a famous beauty, returned his letter after reading one page. She required him to write to her in French, and told him his French was so appalling she had no intention of reading any further. The emotional deprivation and abuse he suffered is legendary, yet neither he nor any of the others ever made excuses for not living a useful, constructive life. They lived lives full of achievement, unhampered by chips on their shoulders or theories of deprivation and emotional maladjustment.

It was much the same with an earlier hero, the great philanthropist Lord Shaftesbury, who, among many other causes, stopped the employment of children as young as five in the mines. He also opened Ragged Schools for slum children, opposed vivisection, and stopped climbing boys being sent up hot, sooty chimneys from the age of five onwards (small boys, because only small boys could squeeze up the chimneys). Like Churchill, he too was neglected and emotionally deprived by his hostile parents, and the only love he received as a child was also from his nanny, Maria Mills, who died when he was nine. Then there was wonderful William Wilberforce, orphaned at nine when his father died, and a year later sent to live with relatives. These men also endured dreadful years at bullying, inhumane schools.

Yet in spite of all the angst we hear now, about children of single parents being handicapped in the so-called race of life, these people all achieved great things, and apart from Balfour, who never married, all had loving marriages too. Was it because the communities they grew up in were united by values, principles and religion? They also all believed in a 'divine source' to sustain them, and, perhaps just as important, their sole parent usually had no money worries, so they were properly educated and thus equipped to make their way.

Walking in the cemetery at dusk I found several graves embellished with Christmas decorations, a big white stone Celtic cross draped with silver chains and Christmas bells, another with mock holly, and another, a sad headstone commemorating two sons who died in their early twenties, and their father, who died a few years later in his early sixties, sprouting two miniature, faux Christmas trees, decorated in red and gold. Years later, people still loving them and visiting them. Many other graves had little bunches of fresh garden flowers.

The weather continues to be clear and sunny, with bright star-lit nights. It feels as though summer has already lasted forever.

December 31

Looking back, this has been the toughest year for a very long time. Patrick has not been well for most of it. Now that he no longer drives I spend a good chunk of my time taking him to his board meetings, hospital appointments with the heart specialist, to the geriatric clinic, for check-ups, X-rays, scans, to the hearing aid specialists, the doctor, the eye specialist, the pharmacist...

I haven't been good at coping with his deafness, so often I feel our communication seems like non sequiturs, and I get ratty repeating everything two or three times. I've given up our nightly reading aloud, as I have to speak unnaturally loudly for me, and it feels a strain. I want silence and solitude, and can never have enough, and yet, though he is such a hermit, those are not things he wants. And because I have felt so off-balance, and cut off from myself, I haven't had much to do with my friends at all this year

My comfort has been writing this diary. I have often felt, all my life, out of touch with people I could talk to and discuss the things that interest me. When I joined the army at eighteen, instead of going to university as I had always thought I would, I spent my time hiding that basically I was a serious person, and joined in with the rather surface life we lived. I remember the shocked silence in the Officers' Mess when they suggested cancelling the Manchester Guardian, as it then was, as part of a round of cost cutting. A table was laid out in the mess, with all the daily newspapers, including several copies, of course, of the much read Daily Telegraph. 'No one reads it,' said the colonel, of the Manchester Guardian. 'I do,' said the junior officer in the mess. Long, astounded pause. 'Well, we'll let that go,' and the colonel moved on from an embarrassing moment. Was I a commie or something?

It wasn't any better as an army wife, and even now Stella is probably the only person I can talk with about literature, books and ideas, and she is far too busy for me to spend much time with her. With other friends I can talk about gardening, decorating, the spiritual life, cooking, but not that life of the mind that I hunger for. So writing this diary gives me the illusion that I am communicating... however trivial the communication. Even when I belonged to a book club, it was, as Stella once said, the wrong book club... they read novels, and I read everything except novels. Exile is not necessarily a matter of geography. But I've done a lot of reading this year and I feel I understand much more about the world than I did.

Hannah, our cleaning lady is now recovered from the health hiccup she had at Christmas. I suggested she take, besides the doctor's antibiotics, calcium, magnesium and zinc. She tells me she's now feeling calm and energetic, sleeping properly and various other physical symptoms have disappeared. Best of all, the doctor was going to give her iron injections, because she was so anaemic, but in the interval between seeing him, and taking the nutrients I suggested, her blood count is now normal, to the doctor's complete mystification, 'It doesn't make sense,' he said.

8

Jan/Feb 2009

January 16

Rachel rang unexpectedly and invited me to
dinner (Patrick was in New Plymouth with his
sister). I drove across country through a calm
summer evening, and down their long, curving drive
edged with poplars and banks of blue agapanthus and
pink geraniums. The house was settled in a hollow surrounded by specimen trees and looking out to forested
hills and pastures where a few calves were grazing.

As we sat out on the deck under the trees a succes-
sion of birds made their presence felt, beginning with a
couple of loudly chattering kookaburras who sat above
us, and then plunged down into the field next door.
They were followed by wood pigeons and tuis, and
pheasants and pukekos in the fields.

Jackson told us anecdotes about the tiny quail's
families who've returned since their neighbour, Don-

ald's shooting and extermination of most of the quail-eating pukekos.

Mosquitoes drove the said Donald inside – he rushed back home to change from shorts to longs when he took in that we were going to be outside on a warm summer's night. He returned and shortly needed mosquito repellents – he was offered three. He ended up incongruously swathed in a pink mohair shawl, and finally fled indoors, so we followed with candles and penumbra.

Rachel showed me the plaster cast of her grandmother's hand. She was a well-known Budapest pianist who perished in Auschwitz. Whenever Rachel plays the violin, she feels the presence of this grandmother, a Hungarian Jew. The irony of it was that the family had converted to Lutheranism long before, but when it came to the crunch, the Lutherans didn't want them and the Jews didn't want them back. The grandmother died, but her son, Rachel's father, and her daughter went to labour camps being young and fit, and thus survived (Hungarian Jews wasn't rounded up until the later stages of the war.)

The daughter, whose elegant scarves Rachel now wears, went to Paris, the son, Rachel's father, met another survivor, and they married and came to this country, where her father pioneered New Zealand's wine industry. Rachel grew up in Hawke's Bay on her parents' vineyard. Like me, she loves food and cooking, and we spend much time discussing dressings and chutneys, fragrant teas and ways of using lemon peel or a surfeit of plums.

She gave us a bottle of her elderflower champagne for Christmas – delicious.

January 21

The day Obama was inaugurated. Like many others I watched it for the first time in a life where I've seen Roosevelt, Truman, Eisenhower, Kennedy, Johnson, Nixon, Ford, Carter, Reagan, Bush, Clinton and Bush junior come and go, and was never faintly interested in their enthronements. And, like many others, this time I was exhilarated by the extra dimensions of it all, and the hope we cling to that this really will start to change the world...

One story in the paper caught my eye – an old black butler who also had seen many presidents come and go while he buttled in the White House – talked of his fondest memory.

When the Queen came to the White House, after the banquet Prince Philip stayed behind in the Red Room to look at the pictures on his own. The old butler with his assistant found him there, on their way through to serve brandy and liqueurs to the other guests. They stopped and offered a drink to the Duke.

He said, 'Only if you will let me pour one for you too.'
And he poured them a drink and they talked together.

An uncharacteristic picture of a much-maligned
man. So civilised – a painter himself – he wanted to
look at the pictures... red brocade walls, ornate gold
frames enclosing history and mastery... and so sensitive, that he not only invited them to drink with him,
but he himself poured the drinks so that they could not
be blamed for it...

An email from Eugenie today, enclosing this quote
from Emerson:

And yet the compensations of calamity are made
apparent to the understanding also, after long intervals
of time. A fever, a mutilation, a cruel disappointment, a
loss of wealth, a loss of friends, seems at the moment
unpaid loss, and unpayable. But the sure years reveal
the deep remedial force that underlies all facts. The
death of a dear friend, wife, brother, lover, which
seemed nothing but privation, somewhat later assumes
the aspect of a guide or genius; for it commonly oper-
ates revolutions in our way of life, terminates an epoch
of infancy or of youth which was waiting to be closed,
breaks up a wonted occupation, or a household, or a
style of living, and allows the formation of new ones
more friendly to the growth of character. It permits or
constrains the formation of new acquaintances, and the
reception of new influences that prove of the first im-

portance to the next years; and the man or woman who would have remained a sunny flower garden, with no room for its roots and too much sunshine for its head, by the falling off the walls and the neglect of the gardener, is made the banian of the forest, yielding shade and fruit to wide neighbourhoods of men.

I like the metaphor of the flower garden and the forest. What he is discussing is surrender, and non-judgement of all events. Hard to practice, but incredibly consoling and comforting if the effort succeeds. Once I reached a rudimentary understanding of Buddha's injunction to give up attachment to our suffering, and realised that resisting what is happening is what creates the suffering, it made some sense to me.

But it's easier when dealing with my own pain, than observing the pain of others, whether animals, children, grandchildren or others further afield. The serenity prayer, about knowing the difference between the things I can change and those I can't, reminds me that other people's suffering is not necessarily my responsibility... God's business, but not, perhaps, mine. None of which stands in the way of doing something when possible.

I took Kate to Helena's party – another painter, and a beautiful, civilised person. She wears wickedly expensive, but rather kooky, clothes, picked up for a song in Ponsonby or Paris or London. She has big black eyes, a lean, sensitive face and a curtain of dark hair endearingly streaked with silver-grey in front.

Helena was as surprising as ever. She mentioned the time she worked in the Faroe Islands for two years. How come, we asked? Oh, there was an old chap in his eighties and he needed someone to look after him. His religious group advertised and Helena answered the ad, and went up there not speaking a word of Gaelic. She had to earn a living, as well as look after the old chap, so did a tourism job.

Another time, discussing architecture, and from there to the cost of maintaining all the great museums of the world, when I asked how she knew so much about the Victoria and Albert, she airily disclosed she used to sell them Persian antiquities... and then there was the Brideshead discussion, and Jeremy Irons, and her time with him at the drama school where he was famous for being eccentric.

Her Native American stepmother was there that night, bringing with her a charming young gay man all dressed in white, and a pretty girl called Begonia from Peru. When this fascinating Red-Indian lady talked about her spiritual journey at one of our meetings, I was very taken by her account of her childhood. She was brought up by her Red-Indian grandparents, and said there was very little talk in their house. They taught her that silence was sacred, and only worth

144

breaking if you had something worthwhile to say... no idle chat. Idle chat breaks most silence in most homes.

January 22

I went to Rita to get my haircut. We communicated this time, and instead of ending up feeling frustrated and shorn, I came away with a good head of hair, that was nicely shaped. She told me about an owl which must have crashed into the house as it was diving for a moth or night-flying beetle, and broke its wing. The neighbours took it to the vet, who was pessimistic about its chances.

But what is really upsetting her is that its mate is constantly swishing around the house at night, looking for its love.

Buller says nothing about the matrimonial habits of moreporks, and a great deal about the little birds like sparrows and chaffinches, which they add to their diet of rats and mice. We have a couple of moreporks here, who call to each other at night, but it's a long time since I actually saw one.

When we were living at Ellerslie over ten years ago, the garden was ringed with oaks and plane trees. One night I began hearing a great many birds cheeping and, over a period of an hour, it grew louder and louder, until the din could be heard above the sound of the music playing.

Finally I went outside to see what was going on, and, to my astonishment, all the trees were alive with dozens and dozens of blackbirds, all flapping and calling in the same direction. When I worked out what all this racket was directed at, I was heartbroken. A little owl was sitting on a branch of one of the plane trees. There was nothing I could do, but wait till the blackbirds had frozen him out with their noise and hostility. Which they did. I wondered where he found refuge, if everyone reacted to him like this. Obviously our resident blackbirds, on seeing this intruder, had called for help. Blackbirds must have come from miles around Auckland to support their own species against a single morepork.

January 23

It's nearly the end of January, and so far all I've done is bake endless cakes for grandchildren, lunches and parties.

At Helena's the other night the charming young gay man came up to me and said, *'Are you the lady who baked this cake?'* – Lemon cake, French recipe, first try, decorated with ivy; swirls of it round the base, ivy leaves on top. He said he'd eaten three pieces, and asked whether I was married.

A different sort of lemon cake, made with almonds, for lunch at Eugenie's for Ilona and Kenneth, a reunion after thirty years. How they had changed... and I had too, presumably. Ilona was so warm and gentle, Kenneth so utterly urbane and charming... I felt hungry for more of their company, I so enjoy the quality of their intelligence, their wit, their irony, the scope of their conversation, with the backlog of their years in places like Washington, London, Paris, Poland, and so on. It wasn't so much what we talked about, but the quality of their response – their humanity, intelligence and sense of fun being the background to every topic, however trivial.

Next, looking forward to lunch on Sunday with Mike and Annie. Now, back to marinating the meat for supper; lamb in port, lemon, rosemary, olive oil and garlic. Also intend to make a pumpkin hummus to have with it instead of potatoes, and green beans picked from the garden.

I'm re-reading Barbara Tuchman's The *Guns of August,* after a diet of Taylor, Toland, Terraine and others on World War One, Versailles, and the Revolution in Germany.

I had forgotten the German atrocities in Belgium... how could one say that, but I had... not just outbreaks of savagery like the sacking and burning of Louvain, and the destruction of the medieval library with 250,000 ancient manuscripts, as well as everything else, but the actual planned, systematic brutality.

The posters, which were already printed before the invasion, were displayed everywhere, threatening hostages, promising shootings, burnings, and destruction. A promise which each German general, and most German soldiers, kept and multiplied exponentially, and then blamed it on the Belgians because some had resisted occupation, and thus held up General Schlieffen's timetable for the march on France. Hundreds of men, women and children were shot as reprisals for the blocked roads and damaged bridges, which briefly held up the German invasion. Whole villages sacked and burned to the ground, in France as well as Belgium, forerunners to the atrocities of Oradour and Lidice in the next war.

Remembering all this makes one realise that the savagery of World War Two was nothing new to the Germans. They'd already had good practice in the previous war, and then they didn't have the Nazis or SS to blame. Neither, in 1918, did they have to answer to a Nuremburg Tribunal, but got away with it. In World War One they were pretty brutal to their own soldiers too, shooting them if they became too exhausted to stay on the march. I had also forgotten how the Germans had not only grabbed Alsace-Lorraine in the 1870 invasion, but imposed reparations which were supposed to cripple the French for a generation, plus an army of occupation paid for by the French till the reparations had been raised.

I read that some Germans are still complaining about the cruelty of the Versailles reparations – payments to Belgium and France for the devastation they suffered. The reparations were halved back in the twenties, suspended in 1932 because of the Depression, and then Hitler refused to pay any. After the Second World War, Germany's debts were in the billions, so at the London Conference in 1953 most of the debts were written off. The principal on the First World War still had to be paid, but interest payments were deferred while Germany was divided. The Germans who complain forget the merciless terms they imposed on Russia when it surrendered – Russia lost 34 per cent of its population, 32 per cent of her agricultural land, 85 per cent of her sugar beet land, 89 per cent of her coal mines and 54 per cent of her industry. And Ludendorff had actually hoped to keep all this, plus Belgium, when Germany asked for an armistice!

When Germany reunified in 1990, many Germans were shocked at having to start paying their old debt, having supposed that the interest payments had melted away in time. The delayed payments end in 2010, but Germany had already become prosperous and powerful again on Marshall Aid after the war. On the other hand, Britain, one of the victors –crippled by the First

World War and ruined by the second – struggled for years, including rationing until the early fifties, and finally finishing paying off Lease-Lend to America in 2006.

Reading Gitta Sereny's book on Albert Speer, she described how when he was transferred from Nuremberg to Spandau in 1947, he looked down from the windows of his plane and was thrilled to see bridges rebuilt and people hiking, and he felt that Germany was being restored, rebuilt and was on the move again. And I think back to those same grim days of 1947 in England, with rationing more stringent than during the war, even bread and potatoes rationed, and whale meat on sale to eke out tins of corned beef and Spam! The Prime Minister, Clement Attlee, was talking about reducing food to subsistence level, 1700 calories a day per person, dingy and damaged cities were still crumbling and unrepaired after the bombing, railways and industry run-down and needing overhauling. Rose bay willow flowered over craters and derelict bombsites. I still can't bear the sight of this innocent flower.

We were at Belsen then, where my father had been stationed, living in the 'Beast of Belsen's old flat! We sat in the dark when the candles ran out, like everyone else during the nightly power cuts, and ate army rations, delivered once a fortnight in a cardboard box. What are we going to do with cucumbers for a fortnight, I remember my stepmother asking despairingly, when cucumbers were delivered for the next two weeks.

Back to Barbara Tuchman, who I find witty and erudite after the surfeit of men I've been reading. Amazon has just supplied me with a book I've wanted to reread for the last 35 years, Edmond Taylor's Fall of the Dynasties. It was as absorbing as I had remembered, I first read it in 1974, and back then it set me off on all the reading I've done since. But this time I was struck by how he ignored the part which England played in the whole drama, including Sir Edward Grey's role as peacemaker in the last few days before the war broke out.

I explained it away to myself by saying Taylor was writing about the three doomed dynasties. But when I got hold of his autobiography, I found his anti-British bias in it so marked that when he was posted to Mountbatten's staff in India, he did his best to white-ant the British during the war and to work with Indians for Indian Independence. It never seemed to cross Taylor's mind that this was disloyal to the ally with whom they were fighting against the Germans and the Japanese.

Walking round the cemetery with Cara last night, I noticed that the grave for the father and two sons, which had been adorned with miniature Christmas trees at Christmas, now has a big red pottery fish propped up against the headstone... a memorial to their fishing prowess?

January 26

Yesterday, lunch with Annie and Mike and their guests, Jon, a literary agent, and his wife Polly. Sitting round the table in the sunshine looking out at the panorama of turquoise harbour, green hills and dark forest, blue sky and purple islands, we ate, talked and laughed till five o'clock. It was particularly challenging in a way, because Jon had given me a very cold shoulder years ago when I had once contacted him... I wondered why he was so dismissive then, and still don't know, but I enjoyed his company yesterday; he was so quirky and witty. Fishing boats that looked like toy boats occasionally chugged doggedly into the harbour below.

We drank Pimm's No. 1 during the afternoon. Annie was planning to serve it with cucumber sandwiches on the lawn after the wedding ceremony, before dinner in the evening. No one else knew what it tasted like, so Annie produced a bottle and we sat and sipped. The well-remembered taste brought back memories of sitting with other guests in the tropical evening before dinner, by the flame tree in the garden of the Runnymede Hotel in Penang. Since it was always cloudless, the sky was always bright with stars, and the black sea lapped right up against the garden wall.

I was fifteen, and the grown-ups (not my parents, they gave me lemonade) treated me to this delicious adult drink. Dusk came early in the tropics, so it was dark by six thirty, and we watched the waves ripple against the sea wall and little spills of phosphorescence spurt into the air. Sometimes a sampan drifted past, and as the fisherman moved the oars, or shifted his nets, the sparkling phosphorescence glowed where he sat silently in the darkness. We lived in this colonial beauty and splendour at the hotel for over a year. The Pimm's went down a treat with us all today, but Mike pointed out how their mint was sagging in this heat, and they needed it for the drinks for 150 people. I rashly said, 'don't worry, I've got plenty.'

Ilona sent Eugenie the eulogies from Charlotte's funeral. Ilona's was tender, erudite and beautifully written, Kenneth's, honest and loving, witty and vivid. Ilona's quote I haven't read for a long time... she suggested that this was Charlotte's view of life and death. The Venerable Bede spoke thus:

O King, when we compare the present life of man on earth with that time which is unknown to us, it seems like the swift flight of a sparrow through the banqueting –hall where in you sit at supper in winter with your thanes and counsellors. In the midst there is a good fire to warm the hall; outside, the storms of winter rain or snow are raging. The sparrow flies swiftly in through one door of the hall, and out through another. While he is inside, he is safe from winter storms; but after a short space of fair weather, he vanishes out of your sight into the dark winter from which he came. So this life of man appears for a short space, but of what went before or what is to follow, we know nothing.

The simplicity of Bede's phrasing is so appealing – intriguing that some people thought and spoke in such vivid and descriptive ways back then – I can't imagine any 'um's or 'er's or 'sort of's or 'ya know's or other lazy impedimenta cluttering up speech of such simple and yet profound rhythms and images. Bede uses the word 'winter' four times in five sentences. Many people – myself included – would have tried to find a synonym, rather than repeat... but the repetition has a rhythm and beauty of its own.

The homely picture of Anglo-Saxon winter I find rather touching... the light of the glowing embers from the fire, the shadows beyond, and the jumping flames of rush lights and candles... the warmth of many bodies huddled near the fire... the long table with dishes of food, and the feeling of safety from the storm outside; icy winds soughing through the trees, and whistling round the corners of homestead and castle; darkness outside, and any shelter or comfort wrested from the perils and dangers of the night. And beyond the manor farms the untamed country stretched across downs and marshes, valleys with unpolluted rivers, and undisturbed oak forests, still alive with boar and wolves and deer, and even, I've read somewhere, a large bird now extinct, similar to an ostrich.

Bede was a Geordie.

And he wrote in Latin and in 'Englisc'. It was he who invented our system of dating from the birth of Christ, 'anno domini', in the year of our Lord. Before then, time had been reckoned by the accession dates of Roman emperors.

He began using this system in his best-known book called The Ecclesiastical History of the English People.

Charlemagne's tutor had been a student of Bede's, and he took Bede's dating system with him to the seat of civilisation in the western world then – Charlemagne's court – and from there it spread through the Holy Roman Empire and beyond.

And to a foodie like me, to know that Bede enjoyed cooking and had his little personal store of peppercorns which he kept to spice up boring monastery food is very endearing... before he died, he bequeathed them to the other monks, along with his handkerchiefs.

Finished Barbara Tuchman's *The Zimmerman Telegram*, which I had always mixed up with the Zinoviev

Letter. I learn that the *Zimmerman Telegram,* written by the German Foreign Minister, Herr Zimmerman, decoded by the British and handed on to the US, finally provoked President Wilson to reluctantly join in World War One. In the telegram, Zimmerman announced unrestricted submarine warfare and a plan to arm Mexico, so that they could attack America behind its back, and keep the US out of the European war.

The Zinoviev Letter, which is thought to be a forgery, suggested some sort of an alliance with the Bolsheviks and British Communists, just before the election of 1924. It made sure the fledgling Labour government was thrown out of Parliament and allowed the Conservatives to get back in. I won't be muddled again.

February 1

The sun didn't shine today, and it was a relief after the blazing brazen days of the last few weeks. The garden is so dry, but at least it's not dying like Kitty's. I can't imagine letting everything wither and die just for the sake of saving water. We'll have to buy water for our tank if it doesn't rain soon, but I'd rather that than a sad sack garden. I water most days, even when I'm exhausted, rather than let the flowers wilt.

Did great tidying up today, lots of dead heading, and cutting dead wood off the out-of-control white marguerites, the bullies of the garden. The hard pruning I did on the Jean Ducher and mutabilis have meant a glorious flowering now, when most gardens are looking a little weary. At last, this year, the hydrangeas have spread luxuriantly, and the Queen of the Night behind them is now scenting the night air as intended. Pink lavatera and the frilly pink heads of dahlias are intertwining with the roses, and there is a look of profusion and tangled splendour even though the whole garden is so tiny.

After watering, I treated myself to a couple of gardenia blossoms and a spray of the delicately scented crepuscule rose, which is also re-flowering with great enthusiasm. They are now in a glass vase on my bedroom windowsill where I can see them from every angle of the bed. I don't know which is most satisfying, enjoying the flowers, or picking fresh beans, spinach and tomatoes for our supper, just before we eat them. It seems the most enormous luxury to have food so fresh. And so to bed.

February 4

On Tuesday, I suddenly remembered that Kate had an exhibition with other local artists at the Fisherman's Rest. Since I was meeting her with Marjorie and Rachel for coffee on the Wednesday, I thought I'd better go and see her paintings. We booked for supper, and sat in the garden in the unending summer weather, and ate a fresh seafood pizza.

The paintings were not great masters, or even minor ones... Kate's were the only ones that had any style or skill, it seemed to me. But they weren't my thing. So I don't know what to say... perhaps I can get away with mentioning the one I liked best. With most of the works, it's that riddle of how to encourage people with little talent or skill, who think they have both, and who can't see the difference between their work and the work of someone with a gift, who has unrelentingly trained their hand and eye. Looking at the stuff on those? walls reminded me of the terrible poetry that many amateurs write, who don't see or feel the gulf between it and genuine poetry. But then again, maybe that's how my writing seems to my betters, alas.

However, Kate didn't turn up for coffee, just Rachel and me for a while and later Marjorie arrived, not sure if she had the right day. We had a stimulating morning, intimate with Rachel, and then a talk with Marjorie about her showplace garden... talk then developed into a rather cerebral and very satisfying discussion about art, mastery, craftsmanship, technique and fraud. Rachel comes from the terrible, physically exhausting grind of musicianship, I from the discipline of writing, and Marjorie from sensitivity and perceptive observation.

On the strength of my careless promise to Annie, I'm watering the mint twice a day now, hoping it's going to make it luxuriantly to the wedding day. The hydrangeas have faded to shades of antique dusty pink and purple, and muted faded blue. I couldn't resist picking a big bunch, which not only look beautiful in a tall glass vase now, but will soldier on through the winter when they have dried.

February 8

I've been watering and worrying about the mint for the last two weeks and now it's all over. Annie's weekend was a triumph of organization, taste, and love. She'd spent months touring the area finding places to book wedding guests in for the weekend, which being a holiday weekend was always going to be a challenge. She thought of everything, from the flowers, to the Gold Service Portaloos with handbasins and Vivaldi playing, to the collection of little baskets she'd amassed, lined with doilies, tied with ribbon, and filled with rose petals for throwing, parasols for the sun and shawls for the evening chill.

She'd spent months making paper roses to decorate arches and paths, she baked and iced the three-tiered wedding cake, she tested thirteen different types of sausage in her laboratory, to find the best ones with the most sausage meat and the least preservatives, she cooked a dinner party for thirty the night before the wedding, organised the big, white, festooned and flounced marquee, and dinner and dancing for 150, and then invited people like us to join them for brunch the next day, when we feasted on those best sausages, ham, and bubble and squeak which she had made herself the day before the wedding – enough for 130 people.

Their long drive lined with palm trees was festooned with white garlands and flowers, and lit at night with candles sitting in sand in white carrier bags – enchanting.

Their son's friends were well-mannered young people, good-looking young men, and wonderful looking girls, who'd flown in from all parts of the globe; London, Hanoi, Melbourne. I could imagine the thrill of delight, having left London or New York in snow and bitter winter, walking down the shady, palm-lined drive, and then emerging into sunshine on the lawn with the harbour below. Across the turquoise waters of the harbour, steep rock walls emerge topped with trees stretching to the sky. Toy fishing boats rock at anchor. Annie had even calculated that it would be high tide, and thus, perfect!

February 10   Annie arrived with the bride and her sister to return various small things like lace cloths and baskets. The sister was interesting; back from Hanoi, where she teaches English and loves it. How fascinating that Hanoi for them means fun, the lifestyle, and the good money, while for my generation, Hanoi was the Forbidden City of Ho Chi Minh, sinister and beyond reach. The girls had soft, gentle voices. As they said goodbye and climbed the steps talking with Annie, it was like listening to doves cooing.

Yesterday, I took Patrick to the hospital geriatric clinic (he hates the name, but when you're nearly eighty, there's no escaping the label).

While they rustled around to discover that they should have sent him to the clinic at Warkworth, three quarter of an hour's drive nearer home, I fell in love with a print on the waiting room wall – Raeburn's picture The Rev Robert Walker skating on Duddingston Loch.

I'm determined to bribe the hospital authorities to swap it for something similar for their walls.

February 11

Have had a quiet few days reading. Too hot to do anything else. The temperature not much below 30 degrees, humidity 100 per cent, and all the while Australia burning. Patrick is away for the night being interviewed for some TV programme, which we will never watch.

Valerie Davies

I dropped him at his board meeting, and hurried home, using the new shortcut through the tunnels. Stopped at the butcher to get myself a little treat for lunch. With a nice little lamb rack, I arrived home nearly fainting in the unbearable heat, but undeterred at the thought of giving myself a gourmet lunch in blissful solitude. I intended to savour the whole day to myself. In the garden, I found four small broad bean pods, a handful of flat green beans, and some young spinach leaves.

I sliced half a leek very finely, and sautéed the rings in butter and oil, while the lamb rack was roasting in the little oven. I picked some mint to boil with a few small new potatoes, blanched the flat beans, and then with the tiny, green jewels masquerading as broad beans, put them all in the pan with the leeks. I crumbled in some chicken bouillon cube, added a dash of Dijon mustard, a touch of nutmeg, and poured in cream. After it had boiled and the vegetables were cooked, I stirred in torn up spinach and some potatoes sliced in half longways. They absorbed some of the flavoured sauce, and then this delectable mixture was poured onto a plate with the lamb. The only thing missing was a good glass of wine, but I couldn't bring myself to open a whole bottle just for myself, and then condemn my wonky liver to finishing it up, so I made do with a glass of sparkling apple juice.

The Sound Of Water

I watched the news headlines about the Melbourne fires, which began with a New Zealand TV reporter going back to their burnt-out home with a husband and wife from New Zealand. They picked their way through ash and debris, twisted corrugated iron and sooty posts, melted fridge and broken blackened bricks.

'Welcome to our home,' the wife said grimly to the reporter.

'Thank you,' she replied in a vacuous society tone and smile, 'How does it feel?'

At this I switched off. It was getting dangerously close to: 'apart from that, Mrs. Lincoln, how was the play?'

I rang my brother Derek in Devon to wish him happy birthday, and since I'd just finished reading Castles of Steel, by Robert K. Massie, mentioned the footnote I'd found on the dreadnought HMS Vanguard. It sank at anchor in Scapa Flow on the night of 9 July 1917, with nearly all the 800 crew lost, including our great-uncle, our grandmother's brother. I remember when I was seven, listening to my grandmother, Mabel, still bemoaning how the family with four girls, Lizzie, Mabel, Jessie and Violet, had read the telegram, telling them that the precious only son and brother had been drowned. Then, six weeks later, they received a sodden kitbag, full of wet uniforms. They all had hysterics.

There was always an implied criticism of the heartlessness of the navy. But I've often thought; what else could they do? If they had tried to empty 800 kitbags and dry out the contents, everything would have got muddled up. Derek said he'd found a lot of information on it on the internet, and would send it. He also told me that a number of officers survived the explosion – which they think was one of the magazines spontaneously blowing up for some still unexplained reason – because they were dining with officer friends on other ships.

What a horror, sitting having fun with your mates on a long summer evening, and suddenly your ship blows into the sky in dust and fragments, and amid the noise of the explosion, the smoke, the chaos, all your friends, workmates and possessions are dashed to the bottom of the sea. The ship was a dreadnought, and I used to wonder just what the name dreadnought was all about. I learn from Robert Massie that it was the name Elizabeth I chose for a ship launched in 1573, which eventually sailed against the Armada. It meant what it says, 'dread nought'.

We discussed the fires in Victoria. Derek was as well informed as me, for television brings us all to each other. What mystified and bothered him, as a civil defence expert with a master's degree under his belt, and years of experience as a civil defence chief, was that people had been told they could stay in their houses and fight the fire.

I forgot to tell him about what I call the Plymouth dots. I read Joe Bennett's book the other day, in which he followed the steps of H.V. Morton, in his book published in 1928, In Search of England, a fairly once-over-lightly travel book. When Bennett got to Plymouth, where my brother lives, he went in search of the house where the Pilgrim Fathers stayed the night before they set off in the Mayflower for the New World. In 1928, Morton found an old lady living in it. Not finding it in 2007, Bennett went to the information centre, and the helpful lady there showed him a map of Plymouth covered in hundreds of black dots.

The dots were where each German bomb had fallen as they pounded the city during the war. And the historic house received one of the bombs of course, right by the harbour, which the Germans were trying to destroy. When I stayed with my other brother, it was in a leafy Georgian area of the city, some way away from the harbour. Apparently, Georgian Plymouth survived, because it was further out, but picturesque Tudor and Elizabethan Plymouth, clustered around the harbour, was almost completely obliterated. The stunned and destitute citizens of Plymouth fled every night to Dartmoor and camped on the moors, not knowing whether their homes would still be there when they trekked back in the morning.

When I read about the dots I felt as sad as I did when I realised that in the Baedeker raids when they bombed Exeter Cathedral, the German bombers managed to obliterate the Tudor house nearby where Charles II had hidden when he was on the run from Cromwell and the Roundheads. Morton had gone there too on his travels.

When I stayed with him, my brother Robert had taken me to the steps in Plymouth's ancient harbour, where the intrepid Pilgrim Fathers (and Mothers) had stepped aboard the Mayflower to sail across the Atlantic into the unknown – America. A plaque and a rather beautiful memorial mark the spot, and as I stood there I imagined with awe the immensity of that step from land to sea, a step which changed the whole history of the world, as those brave souls set sail on their perilous voyage, and a future that no one could imagine. Their incredible courage made the world we live in today possible. One small step indeed for mankind and maybe the biggest too.

February 13

A story in the Herald today talked about the debris floating around the earth. NASA estimates that there are more than 17,000 objects larger than 10cm, and

Space Security Index that there are 300,000 pieces smaller than 10cm all hurtling around the world.

So that mystical picture of the world taken from outer space can never be taken again, except through a thick film of rubbish. What a drag on the heart.

February 15

The night before last, I looked up just in time to see Cara strolling past the French windows with something large and black in her mouth. I leapt up after her, grabbed her, and shook her until she dropped quite a large fledgling, which I feared was a tui by the shape of its beak and little white feathers. Cara ran away, and I picked up the baby and tried to take him back in the direction Cara had come from, hoping a bereaved parent was lurking somewhere. But the bird pecked me so hard, I dropped him by mistake onto a pile of branches by the fence, and, to my dismay, he tottered off down into the rubbish heap below, where I couldn't see him, or reach him. I fear that was the end of him.

Then, last night, I was reading and in that state of absorption when I don't hear anything, when gradually the sharp crying of a bird began to penetrate. For a while I supposed it was a seagull shrieking, and then realised it was real anguish I was hearing. I jumped up, dashed outside, and there was Cara at the top of the puriri tree, with a tui circling around, in and out of the branches, shrieking at her. And in the plum tree was another frightened fledgling.

The tui was trying to distract Cara from her baby. I threw bits of bark and twigs to frighten Cara down the tree, and grabbed her. I shut her inside Patrick's room, and returned to the distraught tui family. By then, mother was in the tree with her baby, and I left them to it. Silence fell. Patrick rooted out the litter box from under the house, while I locked all the cat doors, and we imprisoned the would-be murderer overnight. We have not heard a sound from a tui since. I looked up Buller, and learn that tuis nest either in the fork of a shrub, or at the top of a tree, which information was not very helpful.

The usual stuff, imprisoned specimens etc.

February 17

Eugenie's birthday yesterday, and I was reclassified as a girl and invited to her girls' lunch. All the old faces from weddings, christenings and other parties, which was good. Dorothy was telling me that her father has only a few months to live. Already a multi-millionaire, he's had his life insurance paid out, and Dorothy asked him what he wanted to do with the rest of his life. He just wants to meditate three times a day, he said. How interesting. I've often thought that if I was imprisoned, or incapacitated in some way, that's what I'd do; meditate all day, and inhabit outer space, instead of being stuck in inner space. Or is it the other way round?

Some discussion came up about Eugenie's birthday being so close to St Valentine's Day, and I revealed that I had walked all around the five mile perimeter of Kew Gardens and then had a hot bath in order to try to manipulate a Valentine's birthday for her. This led to a rather illogical conversation with Alicia, about her Egyptian family in Cairo, and talk of jumping off a table to try to get a boy – more likely to get a miscarriage, I explained to someone not much younger than me!

From there, we talked of Cairo, and I told her how my father and stepmother had met on a blind date at Shepherd's Hotel. The other couple, who knew each other, didn't stick together, but my parents did... and from there to the burning of Shepherd's and of all the other historic European landmarks in Cairo in the riots of 1952. Alicia, who is still a striking, blue-eyed, golden-haired beauty, told me how she remembered being pushed down on the floor in the back of a car, and covered with a rug to hide her and her golden hair as they fled the mayhem.

Jumbo Hoare was the unlikely and unforgettable name of the man who persuaded my father to go with him to Shepherd's. He had previously been wounded at

Tobruk, and the hospital ship taking him to Alexandria was sunk by the Germans near Sollum. He managed to jump off the ship and cling to wreckage before being rescued. And before reaching Egypt, he'd already jumped out of his burning tank at Arras in 1940, where his regiment was holding off the Germans while the BEF escaped from Dunkirk. Jumbo walked ninety miles from Arras with his troop sergeant whom he had rescued from their burning tank, and eventually reached England.

Jumping from doomed conveyances was Jumbo's thing. Sent to North Africa and wounded, after recovering and back in the desert, he was captured and sent to an Italian prisoner-of-war camp. Another country, another jump. While being transported from Italy to Germany in a cattle truck, he and a friend jumped from the moving train at night, and met up with a friendly shepherd, who hid them in a cave and fed them. When Jumbo went down with malaria, the shepherd took him to the local convent, where the nuns nursed him and hid him and his companion. On one occasion, when the Germans were searching the convent, the mother superior, at risk to her life, hid them under her bed. Lying under the bed, Jumbo heard her saying to the Germans at the doorway: 'No man has ever entered my bedroom'...

The mayor, who knew Jumbo and his friend were there, urged the nuns to send them away, as the sisters' lives were in danger. But in spite of all the atrocities which they had watched from the convent windows, the brave nuns refused to betray the men. When he was able to link up with the advancing British Army, Jumbo became a lieutenant colonel and was awarded the MC, and, after the war, he returned to thank the selfless Italians.

But before then, he had been posted back to Egypt for his historic rendezvous at Shepherd's with my stepmother's friend Joan. She was so nervous that she brought along a friend, my future stepmother, Peggy. Both girls were in the Red Cross. Jumbo's escort was my father, who had the good taste to persevere with Peggy. She was not glamorous, but she was tall, black-haired, black-eyed, and striking. She was gay in the old sense of the word, had a quick sense of humour, and unassailable integrity.

My uncle had much the same experiences as Jumbo, as a prisoner of war on the run in Italy, cared for by heroic villagers, who risked their lives to do it. And so many other Allied prisoners tell the same stories. Mussolini may have declared war on Britain, but his people didn't. Their courage, goodness and heroism were the other side of the Italian war effort. The appalling poverty and starvation, which afflicted Italy, after the

Germans had pillaged, bombed, booby-trapped and terrorised the whole country, match the ordeals of the occupied Dutch. And I always hate it when people mock the Italian army for its record in the war – they never wanted to fight, and were abominably equipped.

February 20
I'm having a lot of trouble finding a reading for our Soul Food gathering on Sunday. The virtues Jocelyn has chosen are reliability and gentleness. Gentleness is easy, but reliability is a liability. I've ransacked my books and found nothing.

February 21
Jon and Jocelyn's place was an old-fashioned hippy fantasy. Hidden at the end of a long, winding, rutted drive, was a handmade house with a soaring, curving wooden ceiling with wonderful acoustics. Inside were Jon's pottery, paintings and carvings by friends, and from the windows, views into the orchard on one side, trees laden with quinces and pears, figs and apples, while an olive grove cradled the house from winds in the other direction. A path led down to the empty white sands and long, slow breakers on the beach.

There was something about the hot afternoon. Somehow, it felt like the peak of summer, and from now on we would be sliding down towards autumn. It had a fullness and sadness. Jon is irresistibly friendly with a bright twinkle in his eyes. Jocelyn is dignified, reserved, and always dressed with style and sensitivity, beautiful details, subtle colours.

The drive to it depressed me; rather desolate, flat, poor pastures with clumps of swamp grass dotted over, and what looked like depressed cattle. The drive back was different. The flats seemed to have a remote, melancholy beauty this time, and every so often there was a pear tree or a windswept apple tree in the hedgerow, laden with ripe fruit. Self-seeded perhaps from a settler's core, tossed away as he trudged these empty, dusty roads. Occasionally I passed an old orchard, with misshapen trees from the prevailing wind, and heavy with fruit. It's a good year for everything this year.

The gathering was rather special. The music, a Baha'i a cappella group, was sublime, and then Jocelyn produced Sinead O'Connor's song to her mother. Never having heard this singer, I felt quite overwhelmed by the power and beauty of her unaccompanied voice. It seemed so appropriate in that setting, that all the singing was unaccompanied.

Then an unusually lively discussion. I started it by saying that I found the word reliable made me angry; that I was tired of always being reliable, and knowing that people always relied on me being reliable! This opened up the floodgates, as other people discussed how they felt taken advantage of because they were always reliable! Later, when we walked around the garden, we saw a patch of carefully cultivated stinging nettles, the food for a particularly rare variety of yellow monarch butterfly. Jocelyn said there's only one other person in the North Island trying to stop them from becoming extinct. Her ordinary monarchs are rather short of food, so I promised her some swan plants.

I took yet another lemon cake. This one an Elisabeth Luard special; Spanish, and it keeps forever. It's the easiest cake I've ever made, and I may never make any other. It's just 175 grams of flour (I lazily use Self Raising), 175 grams of sugar and olive oil, three eggs, pinch of salt, and the zest and juice of a lemon. Stir everything together and tip into a greased lined tin, and I add a thick sprinkling of sugar on top to cheer it up, and a teaspoon of vanilla in the mix in memory of my grandmother. It was delicious, and gobbled up with great enthusiasm. The enthusiasm was probably because it was so hot that everyone else had brought a refreshing watermelon, and as each person brought their offering, a small mountain of green watermelons began to rise from the table.

Helena was as surprising as usual. Talking about Alice Bailey's channelled writings from 'the Tibetan', back in the thirties and forties, she told me that Alice Bailey's autobiography has just been published by the

Lucis Trust, which is continuing to publish transcripts left by Alice Bailey, who died years ago. More than that, the person who runs the Trust is Helena's cousin.

I knew that Alice Bailey didn't enjoy the work she did, transcribing the teachings of the Tibetan, which she heard inwardly, and she actually doubted his existence. So he sent her a parcel, telling her in advance that he would do so. Helena told me that when the Tibetan had finished his teachings, and Alice Bailey had stopped transcribing for the first time in about twenty years, she died twelve days later; her task completed.

February 26
Last night was a meeting of our group. Just four of us, with one in Burma exploring her missionary childhood, and the other in the South Island. Later, I was wakened from sleep by severe pain in my upper right arm, and it kept reminding me it was there all night. It felt like being alerted to another area to work on with the acupuncturist this morning. The area on the upper arm is the heart meridian, according to Lyn. My health is definitely improving, the pain in my right knee almost gone.

February 27
Jocelyn came today, with two ice-cream cartons full of hungry caterpillars. We distributed them among the

healthy, bushy swan plants in the cemetery, and then went for a walk on to the little rocky peninsula looking out to sea and across to Little Barrier Island. There we sat and talked, covering very quickly the universe, the past, and the future. After this invigorating session, we came back to the house! She was enchanted by it, and noticed things that no one had done before, like the precious little Prattware jug on the bookcase, the Michelangelo sketch of a man's head by my bedside, and she even noticed the white stoneware Victorian jugs.

Very satisfying to share a private passion. We bought the Prattware jug at a Cordy's auction. I was prepared to go to any price (within reason) but no one else was interested, and we got it for $40. Inside was a scrap of paper; brown with age, with writing in an old-fashioned hand like my grandmother's. On one side it reads: 'This jug was brought out to NZ by my Grandma,' and on the other side, in more recent ink, and another old-fashioned hand: 'Jug 200 years old'. The note stays in the jug. Definitely written with a fountain pen. Do my grandchildren know what a fountain pen is? I wonder.

9

Mar/Apr 2009

March 1

We attended a meeting at Graeme and Joan's house on Saturday with lots of rich local residents who own blocks of the hills and bush running down to the harbour. They are organising a society to protect the bush, establish a plan to eradicate pests (rats and possums), and get a grant to pay for it all! It was grey and cloudy still from the rain of the last few days, rags of mist drifting into hollows in the hills. Thank you God for the timing. Our tank is full again, the grass is green and the spinach is growing.

Last night, I marched over to the cemetery to inspect what I thought would be some fat, happy caterpillars, and a few chrysalises. Not one, or rather, one caterpillar left. The wasps must have eaten the rest. So now, we must have many fat, happy wasps. I don't know how I'm going to tell poor Jocelyn of the fate of her cherished babies.

So today I rang George, the village's resident handyman, volunteer fireman, churchwarden, Residents' Committee official, Cemetery Committee member, gardener, emergency fixer, to list only a few of his functions. I showed him a patch in the bracken where I'd seen a lot of wasps, and sure enough, there was a big hole in the ground. I didn't realise they nested in the ground, as well as on Eugenie's fence! I left him climbing into his white overalls, preparatory to doing battle with them. He says they can't see white, so you don't get stung... he also told me that the flowers in the pohutukawa tree on 11 November were for his mother, whose ashes are scattered there. He had sprayed 'Wet and Forget', the mould remover, on all his family graves in the cemetery, which explains their pristine look, compared with the other blackened, weathered, lichened graves!

He tut-tutted over the broken memorial bench in memory of another family, and said he'd have to replace the rotten plank, and had got the wrought iron seat-back at home where he was riveting the broken bits together. He also checked several gorse sprouts that needed spraying. I think he must be about fifty-five, but it's hard to tell. I count the years, and hope I will not still be here when he's too old to go on being indispensable. He comes from one of the original settler families, which also included the Scots from Nova Scotia, and whose graves people the cemetery. The first settlers arrived in Auckland from England on a ship called Queen of Beauty. Crossing the Atlantic on the long sea voyage, they found themselves being boarded by the notorious Confederate cruiser, Alabama, since this was in the middle of the American Civil War. As an English ship, they were allowed to continue on their way to Auckland. The names of these first settlers are recorded on the earliest records as owning land here.

One of the passengers was a young man called Charles Septimus Clarke, the seventh child of parents who had died when he was three. Now just twenty, he was embarking on this great adventure on his own. With the Wyatt family, he came to this place, and eventually became a man of much influence in the district.

He married Mary Ann Wyatt in 1869 and they lived in a handsome house he built himself from pit-sawn timber felled on his property. The settlers had started from scratch. The cutter Flora McDonald put them ashore on the beach in October 1863, and Mr. Wyatt, who had brought a large tent with him from England for his family, shared it with Charles Clarke until Charles had built himself a temporary dwelling of split slabs. Luckily, it being October, they had the warm summer in front of them.

These settlers worked harder than we can ever imagine today, breaking in land to grow vegetables and even wheat, since flour was hard to come by, building their houses, making their clothes, salting, preserving, drying, bottling, carrying water, chopping firewood, milking, ploughing, fencing, planting orchards and hedges, to name just some of the unceasing chores which had to be done in order to survive. John Wyatt even made a windmill to turn the steel mill, which ground the wheat. When women did the washing they had to fetch and boil the water, scrub the clothes on a washboard, feed them through the mangle, peg them out, starch and blue the whites, dry them and iron and air them, just one of the many back-breaking house-wifery tasks they had to tackle. One lasting aspect of the settlers' achievement is a landscape not so different from the one they had left behind. But while the English landscape had evolved over several millennia, the settlers created theirs in less than half a century.

In spite of hardships and hard lives, they lived to great ages, as their headstones in the cemetery testify. John (The Elder) Wyatt and his wife died at eighty and eighty-one respectively. Charles (Septimus) Clarke died in 1929 at eighty-five, Robert Wyatt, born the year before his family arrived in New Zealand in 1862, lived till 1957, dying at ninety-five. Many of the names on the earliest land registers still figure on local lists today, on hall committees, library rosters, volunteer fire brigade, bowls clubs, cricket teams, road names, place names and on the war memorial.

March 4

Yesterday was one of those days, which catch your breath with the beauty of it. And the interesting thing is that most people are aware of this special quality, something to do with the clarity, the stillness, the shine on the fields, the hills and the leaves. Sunset matched the beauty of the day – not a dramatic one – pink sky which turned to lilac and turquoise, purple islands, navy-blue sea merging to silver on the horizon, and the distant rim of South Omaha on the other horizon, tinged with pink and blue, the hills purple and palest green. It feels like autumn and as I type, the cicadas are rasping away, a solid wall of sound.

I went to Omaha beach to walk through the dunes – sea and beach on one side, larks and builders' hammers on the other. The steel, glass and concrete palaces here are some sort of gross monument to money, and maybe to the straight lines of computer design, but not to style. It seems incredible that there could be so many variations on vulgarity and crass display. And no doubt if I met the owners they would seem perfectly normal and ordinary. The waves were rolling in and breaking with a crash on the long, curving, empty expanse of sand. From the sound, it felt as though a big swell was building up.

I saw a few goldfinches, and one frightened rabbit, which froze among the bushy dune plants. The sun was shining through his translucent pink ears, and his eyes were rigid with fright, so I didn't stop, but hurried past, hoping he gained a little confidence from not being molested. I could see the huge burrows they've dug from the mounds of white sand. I wondered how the burrows held up in this fine powdery sand.

On the way home I stopped for a good cup of coffee in a new coffee place I've discovered, and then did the sort of shopping I enjoy. First port of call, a new bakery where they do genuine artisan bread, and got myself a sour dough stick, and some early hot cross buns. Next stop, the organic vegetable stall, and here I came away with pears to make a pear and almond frangipane tart, a bunch of tomatoes on the vine, and fresh organic courgettes. The last vegetable stall yielded new potatoes, fresh figs, and red peppers, which I shall stew in balsamic vinegar and put in the deep freeze to use at an appropriate moment. Very satisfying.

In the night, the sea blew up, and the bay down below is now a cauldron of foaming white water and green breakers thundering onto the rocks. The huge swells make it feel as though the pot has been filled to overflowing. And one wonders where all this extra water has come from, though apparently it's the same water! The sound of the water crowds in behind everything and never ceases.

On the table as I write, is one perfect Abraham Derby bud in a slim glass bottle, the scent is delicious. And in my mind is the doleful voice of Marlene Dietrich sing-songing: Another Spring, Another Love. Cara, the black witchy cat, is sitting on the table by the computer screen.

I've been reading slowly, at bedtime, Frances Partridge's diaries again. This time I was struck by what a lovely life they led in A Pacifist's War... relays of friends to stay, growing their own fruit and vegetables, feeding the chickens, killing the pigs, making ham and brawn, enjoying the grapes they grew, eating the game and smoked salmon which friends brought, searching for quails eggs up on the downs, writing articles for the Spectator, listening to and making music, staying with other friends, visits to London, sightseeing the bombing... the only grumbles being when Frances had to do the housework and the cooking in the intervals between their 'help' being called up for war work, and finding another willing domestic slave.

When Saxon Sydney-Turner arrived for ten days, they had grouse in his honour and a bottle of Château

Neuf 1923, plus homegrown globe artichokes, figs and plums. Holidaying themselves at Raymond Mortimer's, Partridge described a delicious supper of asparagus, wine, and chocolates, and wrote of lunch at the Ivy in London, when the menu was smoked salmon, cold grouse, chocolate mousse and Nuits-Saint-Georges. This was all a far cry from the hard, cold misery of rationing in the rest of England with two ounces of meat, butter and cheese per person per week, to mention only three items.

They had a good war. Apart from cheering up their friends by having them to stay, I couldn't see that they did anything for their country... other pacifists found opportunities for service... not that I can see how anyone could be a pacifist in that war, knowing that Hitler was trying to enslave the whole world. Even back in the early thirties, Vera Brittain and her ilk were informing people of Partridge's ilk about concentration camps, anti-Semitism and the like.

Three weeks after Mike Partridge's sudden death she was in France, travelling and socialising to try to deaden the pain. She went on travelling and socialising for years trying to deaden the pain, and I wonder if she had stayed still and grieved, allowing herself to feel her feelings instead of trying to escape from them, whether she would have been able to move on from that burden of misery. She wrote of missing her little black cat, but came back a few months after Mike's death, and sold Ham Spray and we never hear of the cat again. Presumably it was expendable, like the poor old epileptic pauper ladies they watched for fun at an asylum where a friend worked.

The old ladies, 'incurables', were given shocks to see how they reacted, in a series of experiments put on for the Partridge's amusement. The old ladies thought they were having treatment for their epilepsy, not realising they were just entertainment for the idle rich... 'Shall we trigger them?' the Partridge's friend would say. It seems amazing that a lifelong and committed socialist should have felt so unconsciously superior, so callous, and so unimaginative. On the other hand, the loves and lives of all her intriguing friends make for fascinating reading. I must get the rest of the series.

March 5

A grey, billowy day with squaly showers, and the sea as relentlessly rampant as yesterday.

The noise of the water and the wind in the trees is a permanent backdrop to everything else.

The water tank is filling. I had an acupuncture session with lots of acupressure. So painful as she hits the spot that you have to be a masochist to persist, but I do, because I feel this is my best chance to improve my health.

Valerie Davies

I was thinking about Barack Obama last night, and Prime Minister John Key. They are both symbols of hope to unprejudiced people (I was appalled at Graeme's on Saturday when a little old lady told me how worried she was about Obama's Muslim connections, and 'that Muslim preacher of his.') Apart from their youth, the thing they have in common is that they were both brought up in responsible, caring, solo parent homes. I've always believed from my experience with boys brought up by their widowed mothers after the war, that they are more understanding, compassionate and easier to talk to than macho men.

John Key confirmed it for me, when he and Helen Clark were asked on TV about their definition of being rich. Helen wittered on about her little house in Mt Albert. John Key, millionaire, and product of a single mother and a state house, said he felt that being rich was having enough money to pay for the car when it was at the garage, and enough money to buy new shoes and other needs. I knew exactly what he meant. I know, and he knows from our single parent experience, what it's like, worrying about where the money's going to come from for absolute essentials.

Today, I was reading the *Weekly Telegraph*, and the story of David Cameron and his six-year-old son who has just died. Another rich man and his wife, with a child so badly disabled that they never knew if he understood them, and who spent hours at a time screaming in pain. He had a combination of cerebral Palsy and epilepsy and needed twenty-six injections a day, and had to be fed through tubes in his stomach.

I read that David Cameron had tried to take his share of the twenty-four-hour care giving, so that many political meetings were held at his house while he held the baby or prepared his injections. This meant that that child's influence was felt in circles well out-side the family. The child looked beautiful and cher-ished. When he died suddenly, many people were greatly affected by it.

Patrick asked if I thought people should be kept alive in such circumstances. I had no answer, but I could see the great purpose of that soul's life. But a few pages further on in *the Telegraph,* was the obituary of Christopher Nolan, the novelist with cerebral palsy who could neither talk, walk or use his hands, and spent his life confined to a wheelchair. His heroic mother held his head in her hands for hours, while he used a rod or 'unicorn stick' to tap out each letter on a typewriter. At twenty-one, he won the Whitbread Prize for his autobiographical novel Under the Eye of the Clock.

His mother read his acceptance speech, which in-cluded the words: '*Imagine, if you will, what I would have missed if the doctors had not revived me. Can it be right for man to turn on his handicapped brother and silence him before he can ever draw breath?'*

He died at forty-three.

Reading all this made me conscious of the hidden mysteries of the universe, when in Francis Thompson's words:

> *... ever and anon a trumpet sounds*
> *From the hid battlements of Eternity:*
> *Those shaken mists a space unsettle, then*
> *Round the half-glimpsed turrets slowly wash again.*

March 7

I rang Hilde last night.

Contact is increasingly hard work. I spoke to her for half an hour.

In other days, the ground we covered would have probably taken ten minutes.

The combination of her deafness, her loss of vocabulary in English, and loss of memory, make it a slow and painful process.

She had fallen and broken her arm, to which I gave the full attention it deserved, but as we meandered down other labyrinthine byways, punctuated with long, groping silences.

I had to grapple with impatience.

Example: *'Sat place people go by ze road...'*

Me, *'Er, to a shop?'*

'No. No. No. You know. Sat sing zat people walk on when sey haven't got a car...'.

Me, *'Pavement?'*

'Jah, jah'.

Hilde: *'Sat place where you get money from*

Me, *'Bank?'*

'Sat country next door to us'

'Australia?'

'Jah, jah'.

The storm has faded away. The sea had calmed by the time the storm actually reached us, which was interesting, and most of yesterday was rain and wind, but not the towering seas. Now the sea is a pale turquoise with purple patches, and has a contemplative air. Crickets cricking noisily, lots of water lying around in big puddles in the grass, bringing the grey heron out on the low-lying patch near the road at Whangateau, and the pair of devoted paradise ducks preening and snacking.

On my way round doctors, hearing specialists, and geriatric clinic with Patrick yesterday, I popped into the vet's for Cara's biscuits. And there was a man carrying a baby grey heron. I opened the cage for him, and watched sadly as the skinny little thing with scaly yellow legs longer than its body kept falling over, crumpling into the blanket beak-first, as he was too young to have any strength in his legs yet. The storm must have blown him out of his nest. The vet gave him a glucose injection, but I fear for his future.

Pumpkin soup for supper, followed by courgette and salmon slice with freshly picked tomatoes, and then fresh figs. I found some golden cape gooseberries the other day, and we had them poached in a little juice to eat with fresh vanilla gelato made by the chap who sells strawberries and went to Italy to learn to make Italian ice cream. It was well worth the trip.

I had a giggle when Lily rang to say she'd been trying to get me when we were at the doctor's, to get the recipe for my pink pudding. She ended up ringing Eugenie on her cell phone. Eugenie was at the airport. The idea of those two girls on their phones discussing Mummy's pink pudding, while planes landed and the world roared all round them, tickled me. For good measure, I gave Lily the recipe of the newfound lemon cake. As a lemon cake aficionado, she was delighted. Eugenie tells me this morning that she's made it again, and swears by it.

And Roland rang, full of the usual plans for the weekend's father-son bonding, meaning cart-racing with Raymond. I asked him what he was giving Annabel for her seventeenth birthday... when I was seventeen a pair of nylons would have been well received, and a good handbag would have sent me into seventh heaven. I find the contrast between the austerity of my war-time childhood and the almost universal affluence of western childhood constantly amazing.

While I was waiting for Patrick at the geriatric clinic, I went into Bookworms, the second hand bookshop. The intriguing woman who owns it reads palms, and when we talked, she looked at mine, and amongst other things said, 'Are you writing a book?'

I'm reading *The Decline* and *Fall of the British Aristocracy,* by David Cannadine. I'd always wondered why the countryside of Cobbett, in which the British farmer and his workers lived in such prosperity and plenty, became the hard up, desperate place described by Thomas Hardy, Laurie Lee, Ronald Fletcher and others.

What I gathered from this book, was that besides the Industrial Revolution, the decline of the big landowners, who were squeezed by ratings, death duties, taxes, land and property taxes and so on, meant that they no longer ploughed profits back into the land, because they didn't have enough. This was followed by raising rents, lower wages etc. and then the invention of refrigerated ships, which meant cheap meat, and cheap wheat could be imported from the colonies with no controls. This caused English agriculture to be further depressed. Free trade certainly didn't work for the English countryside.

So much for the blessings of the British Empire and cheap imports. I felt regretful that progress like free trade, one man, one vote, monetary policies, and so many other factors have not just demolished the aristocracy, (who may have deserved it,) but also destroyed the English countryside and ancient agricultural way of life. And these things, which in one way improved the lot of everyone, also accelerated the exodus from the country to the squalor of spreading industrial cities.

And then there was World War One, in which junior officers died at a faster rate than other groups. They were heirs to estates, small squires, and country gentry, so that land, farms and ancient communities dating from Saxon times were sold in the years following World War One, dismembered, and disappeared. Laurie Lee described this process in the changing face of Slad, his country village. This is not the thesis of the book, but that's how it strikes me at the moment, and only halfway through. Cannadine also pointed out what I'd never thought of; that until the destruction of the landed classes, they were great collectors of art. Now they are great sellers of art!

I felt sad reading this book, at so many standards of conduct in public life having disappeared because of people, who for generations had felt it their duty to govern (though many of them refused high office,) now being sidelined. Sidelined by people who had ambitions to rule, some for good reasons, like long overdue change, some for simple ambition and the desire for power. And having just had a solid diet of biographies of people like Grey, Balfour, Salisbury, Lansdowne, Shaftesbury, Churchill, and so on, we just don't seem to produce many brilliant and ethical people like that in public life now... which sounds hideously old-fashioned and reactionary...

As usual, I have another book on the go as well. I'm re-reading Cecil Beaton's collected diaries and was intrigued at this paragraph which dovetailed with the aristocrats book:

Two tall officers of venerable age... speak to one another with an offhand perfection of manners. There is a bond or link or understanding that goes much deeper than mere politesse. None of these people are looking for slights, for grudges, neither are they surprised or impressed. They live on terms with each other, and do not need the framework of formality that is part of the social exchange in other echelons. These people do not need to meet each other at given times at lunch or dinner in answer to an invitation. They come across each other casually in the course of duty or pleasure – in their study, corridor, palace or club. They go about their jobs with ease, knowing their like are not jockey-

ing for position or trying a little knifing in the backs. This is the reason for the prevailing mood of generosity. One of the officers of venerable age says casually to the other, "I'll look after it now, and when the Queen leaves, you can come back and fetch it". *It is the jewelled Crown of State.*

Roland has spent this weekend like every weekend; cart- racing with Raymond, from six in the morning to six at night, both days. They stagger home deadbeat every Sunday.

March 8

I learn from my calendar that tonight is a gibbous moon. I've never known what a gibbous moon is. I now know that it is a three-quarters moon. I went to see the film *Australia* this afternoon, thinking it would be a good thing to know more about Australia, and I was curious to see Nicole Kidman. I only lasted for twenty minutes of a three-hour production. By then, we had watched a chap droving cattle across a river in searing heat, wearing an unlikely thick, English tweed suit with thick checked winter shirt and tie, being dragged off his horse and snapped up by a crocodile, tweed suit and all. The tiny eight-year old aboriginal girl (It's a boy – Nullah, actor Brandon Walters.) hiding so as not be stolen, then seized his huge black stallion, and apparently was able to vault into the saddle, because the next thing she was galloping through the outback.

We then switched to a stately home in England in 1940, where Nicole Kidman as Lady Ashley, wearing sexy jodhpurs as tight as Princess Anne's, and quite unlike the baggy jobs we wore in my forties childhood, was having an improbable business conference in the stables, saying she was going to Darwin.

Back to Australia fair, and a sleazy bar where the stock agent sent to meet Lady Ashley took on punching all the other sweaty, unshaven drunks in defence of the 'Abo's'. Then to Government House, where a caricature of an English Governor, wearing a topi and monocle, which might have been realistic in 1880, but not in 1940, made a fool of himself in an affected voice, lisping to another caricature of an English twerp.

Down on the docks tough Aussies were sneering at the English Sheila, and one managed to pinch her bottom.

When I saw her swanking improbably and imperiously along the dockside followed by a line of Aboriginal porters, each with a matching blue and cream trunk on their heads, looking like a caravan of African porters off in search of David Livingstone, I gave up. Two and a half more hours of old prejudices, clichés, caricatures, and dead animals lying in the dusty desert. No, thank you!

Valerie Davies

March 9

In town, this morning to go to the chemist, inevitably I also looked in at the bookshop (and came out with a book). The woman serving was on the telephone and so deeply involved in her conversation that I didn't like to interrupt, so went on browsing until I thought enough is enough. She apologised, and I demurred, but said:

'Would you mind me asking who you were talking to? It sounded like a very deep encounter group or an in-depth spiritual counselling session.'

She looked straight at me and said in a level tone, which spoke volumes:

'Yes. It was all that. It was about coaching a seven-year-olds' netball team! The adults are far worse than the children. I don't know why I do it.'

I had a good cup of coffee at my newfound coffee shop on the way home. The two women who make it, both blonde, pretty and kind, one young, one middle-aged, gives pleasure just to look at them.

It was one of those sunny autumn days with a southwesterly wind, so it was chilly.

But there's always a soft romantic haze in the air when the southerly blows. The blue haze made Mount Tamahunga look even more mysterious.

March 10

Patrick has been in Auckland at a board meeting, and going on to stay with Eugenie to see some Japanese play at the Festival. I've spent most of the day fielding calls from radio stations all over Australia, and funnelling them on to Patrick at his board meeting. Since he wrote his column this week telling the truth about the Mr. Asia drug ring, and fulminating against the glamorisation of chief crim Terry Clark on TV, the whole media have gone mad. He's all over The Dominion in Wellington, and radio stations from Perth, Canberra, Adelaide, Brisbane and Melbourne, National Radio and Radio Live, have been interviewing him. Flavour of the week. Peacock today, feather duster tomorrow, in Winston Peters' memorable words.

I went to bed early with a book, after my last acupuncture session for a few weeks. Lyn is going back to China for a holiday to see her family.

I asked her what presents she was taking with her. 'Aah,' she smiled, 'New Zealand honey. It is so good, cannot get honey like that in China.' (I was surprised; I didn't think the Chinese ate honey, or toast and marmalade for that matter!)

She went on, 'Then I take macadamia nuts, so-o good. And I dry figs and bottle them for my son. He love figs, when he come here before. So-o good that it is the season for my tree to have fruit.'

Valerie Davies

I found it rather touching that her presents were so sweetly simple. She was a teenager during the Cultural Revolution, and snatched from her secondary school to go and work on a farm in a remote area of China. She described working thigh-deep in icy water in the paddy fields in freezing winter weather, and thinking she was going to die from misery and cold during her period. She felt homesick and terrified, and didn't earn enough money to feed herself. Her scholarly parents were also slaving somewhere else on a remote collective, she didn't know where.

Reading a book on the White House. I was fascinated to read Nixon's Freudian penultimate sentence in his farewell speech: '... others may hate you – but those who hate you don't win unless you hate them, and then you destroy yourself.' And by coincidence, another book I was reading called *Too Soon Old, Too Late Smart,* by Gordon Livingston, also quoted what must surely have been an apocryphal Freudian slip by Nixon in a speech to Congress during Watergate. He said, 'It is time to get rid of our discredited president... I mean present welfare system.'

In the White House book, one of my favourite anecdotes was about one of my favourite people, Sam Grant. Every time his son Jesse had a puppy, it died, and the boy was, of course, heartbroken. Finally, he was given a Newfoundland. Sam Grant called in the

White House steward. He asked no questions, made no accusations. He said, 'Jesse has a new dog. You may have noticed that his former pets have been peculiarly unfortunate. When this dog dies, every employee in the White House will be at once discharged.' The dog, called Faith, lived to a ripe old age!

It reminded me of when Grant was a newly made colonel right at the beginning of the Civil War. He had to take his regiment from Camp Yates to Quincy. The first day the regiment only managed five miles. The next day no one was ready at 6 a.m., and they didn't get on the road with all their gear and rations until late morning. The third day, with many of the men still asleep at marching time, Grant started without them. Half-dressed, breakfast-less recruits raced frantically to catch up with Grant and the rest of the regiment. The next day, with Grant not having said a word, everyone was ready. A man of few words, but a master psychologist. He refused to watch bull-fighting put on in his honour in Mexico when he was president, refused to go hunting or shooting, and, a superb horseman, punished his men if he saw them ill-treating their horses.

The authors of the White House book did their usual moan about the British burning Washington and the President's house in 1814, and brave Dolly Madison saving Washington's historic portrait. But they

199

omit to say that the British were retaliating after the Americans' unprovoked attack on Canada, where many people had fled from the War of Independence some years before. The Americans had been burning Canadian towns and villages, leaving people homeless in the arctic winter. They burnt York, the capital, twice (a few years later it reverted to its Indian name, Toronto). Madison and Jefferson had attacked Canada, thinking it would be a soft target and would fall into their hands while the British were busy fighting Napoleon in Europe.

After the British had burnt the President's house, the scorched walls were whitewashed over, thus giving it the distinctive nickname 'The White House'.

However, many British soldiers, fresh from Wellington's careful invasion of Southern France, where they paid for all their food, and protected property – unlike the French army which simply pillaged – were horrified by the destruction in Washington.

March 13 Friday
Yes, it was a black Friday.

When I reached Rita for my hair appointment, I could see how strained she was looking. With a sick husband and her cherished dog having just died, I wasn't surprised. But the hairdressing turned into a counselling session, because she was also distraught about her son-in-law. At one point I said, could we do my hair at the same time as we talk?

She ended up in tears as we pin-pointed the real crunch, which was nothing to do with her son-in-law, but her relationship with her father... and when I got home I ended up in tears too. She'd completely forgotten, or ignored, what I said about wanting a bob like the last time, and I'm back to square one again with short feathery bits all over my head, instead of a nice, chunky, well behaved bob. I was torn between frustration and despair. Bad hair days for another six weeks.

I'm also depressed by two items in the newspaper yesterday. One was about a chimpanzee in a Swedish zoo who had stockpiled a heap of rocks, and had then thrown them at the gawping visitors. Smug, blinkered experts were marvelling at his intelligence, and ability to plan. I was in despair that he obviously hated being in prison so much, and how we have taught this poor creature to hate.

The other item, which plunged me even further into the pit, was the story of a Syrian woman of seventy-five, married to a Saudi. She'd been arrested for taking bread from two men only distantly related to her. They are in prison for the offence but she is about to have forty lashes, four years prison and then be deported back to Syria. If she survives, she'll be nearly eighty then. Why do fundamental Muslim men hate women so much? It's as bad as the hatred of the Inquisition for women and their witch-hunts, which killed so many women. I can only think of two things which have built up this culture of hostility to women. One is the way boy children are conditioned from the age of about seven to see women as 'other'. The other is the prohibition on having pictures of the human body in art, so that all art is wonderfully intricate, but left brained calligraphy and geometrical patterns and design.

The creative, compassionate right brain is never acknowledged or developed, and the masculine, logical mind, basing life on justice, which seems to mean punishment and revenge, rather than love, dominates the whole Muslim culture.

I also thought to myself that Mohammed would probably have commended the men for caring about the old woman and feeding her. I must get a copy of the Koran, and read it.

And talking of reading, I found it pretty depressing to read in the Telegraph that the top five authors that most people read are J.K. Rowling, John Grisham, Sophie Kinsella, Jilly Cooper and the Mills and Boon collective. I haven't read any of them. No wonder I'm out of step with the world. No, I must be positive, and tell myself that I march to a different drum. Well, I certainly do that.

I see also, on reading the paper, that scientists believe that baby turtles hitch a lift on those Pacific currents I read about, riding the East Australian Current, then skipping past the tip of Cape Reinga and catching the Humboldt Current to the coast of Peru and Chile. Then they return to Australia using the Southern Equatorial Current. Fascinating.

March 14

It poured with soft, warm rain all day, and the sea has been rough and noisy for the last few days. The moon has been obscured by cloud, but last night the full moon was so bright it lit up the garden. Moreporks very near, calling to each other in the night.

I went to the market to deliver my extra candle-snuffer to a friend, since she had fallen in love with the one on my coffee table. She wasn't there, so I handed it over to her husband. It was too wet to drift around shopping while holding handbag, umbrella and shopping bag. But since I was there, I naturally gravitated across the road to the antique market, umbrella and all, and only spent two minutes there. My eye fell on the only thing that wasn't junk: a little mirror, an elegant colonial copy of an Empire style mirror, carved gilt frame, inside which was a beautifully mottled walnut frame, and inside that another carved gilt frame. It was a paltry $25 and I didn't even need to think about it. It had my name on it.

Flushed with this triumph, Patrick and I drove over to the Warehouse, where he wanted to get weed spray. I found three large snow-in-summer, which I've been looking for at all the garden centres, with no success. They were reduced too. Then to Provedores, where I bought the makings of our lunch to eat when we got home. It was superb. Delicious hunks of freshly cooked ham in fresh artisan-made ciabatta roll and Danish butter, followed by a wickedly rich, moist carrot cake and coffee. Not very healthy, but so enjoyable for so little effort!

On Sunday afternoon, TV3 came and interviewed Patrick over the Hillary-Mallory-Archer controversy... a storm in a teacup over Jeffrey Archer's latest book, and a beat-up by the Sunday newspapers about whether Hillary was first to the top, or Mallory. It wasn't the usual disruptive performance, they didn't turn the house upside down as usual, and they actually used quite a bit of it on the news, which is unusual!

March 17

My brother Robert's birthday. He must be sixty-seven. I remember the day he was born. I was four, and my sister and I were staying with our grandmother at Bexleyheath on the fringes of London. She had a flat at the top of a large Edwardian house set in rambling gardens, where I was fascinated by the dog cemetery with its little headstones.

But I was frightened by the large, dark laurel bushes along some of the paths in the shrubbery, and anxious that a German soldier might be hiding behind them, and would jump out on me when it was getting dark.

And I was very fearful of bombs falling... I had seen plenty of ruins and bomb craters by then.

The day Robert was born, my grandmother had taught me to sing the skipping rhyme:

'Wallflowers, wallflowers, growing up so tall,
We're all the old ones, and we shall surely die,
Excepting you, and you, and you...'

As I jumped over the skipping rope.

In the early evening, in the spring sunshine, I was down in the courtyard by the stables, still learning to skip and singing this old jingle to myself, when the window at the top of the house was flung open, and my grandmother called down:

'You've got a little brother. He's called Robert John.'

I went on skipping and singing to myself and thinking about my new baby brother called Robert John.

I didn't see him till some weeks later, as he and my mother stayed in hospital in Dorchester for another month. When we went back to my mother, it was not to the farm cottage in Wool, but to a little red brick Edwardian villa in a hamlet outside Weymouth. As we walked in the front gate, my grandmother told me that the flowers in the front garden were forget-me-nots, and the shrub was called mock orange blossom. The new baby was forever linked in my mind with forget-me-nots and orange blossom.

One more baby was one too many for my young mother. I became responsible for the baby, and used to feed him and look after him when she was out, which was often. The first time I discovered she was out, my sister and I went calling for her round the streets of this new place we lived in. On a late summer night in June, the neighbours rescued us, and were waiting for my mother when she returned some hours later. She listened meekly to their lecture, and after they had gone, she spanked our bottoms hard, and said: 'Never do that again.'

We never did, but another night when she was out, we began dancing round our beds in our white cotton nighties, playing at being fairies. Unbeknown to us, she had returned, and was watching us silently from the door. She spanked us again. This was the mother who, back in the country cottage, had sung us to sleep in her

rich contralto voice with songs like Where the Bee
Sucks, There Suck I; Cherry Ripe; and One Fine Day,
from Madame Butterfly.

She disappeared just over a year later, and fifty
years later I learned that she had fled to Sydney, where
she made her living singing... in nightclubs, presumably. The year she left, when I was six, I didn't know
that the Allies were invading the continent. That the
American soldiers bound for the horror of Omaha
beach left from Weymouth Bay. All I knew, was that
one day the golden sands were no longer covered in
khaki trucks and tanks and other vehicles, and all the
barbed wire had gone.

I had thought until then that all beaches were covered in trucks and barbed wire and that all seas had
rows of iron spikes to stop the Germans coming. But I
didn't know what their disappearance meant, so when
one terrible night hundreds of bombers had roared
over for long hours, I didn't know that they were ours,
and were bound for Germany. I thought they were Hitler's planes, loaded with bombs for us. I lay there in the
dark, petrified, feeling totally alone since my mother
was out, not daring to get the others into the air raid
shelter, since the sirens hadn't rung.

Yesterday morning I rang a friend, since I hadn't
heard from her, and thought maybe she hadn't received
a gift I'd sent her. But no, she and her husband had had

a hard weekend with family. He poured it all out before I spoke to her, and when she came on the line, I got it all again. When I put down the phone, with no mention of my little gift, having spent the whole time being available to their misery, just like I was with the hairdresser on Friday, I thought: this is a pattern. Do I want people who lean on me in my life, or do I want friends? It was a no-brainer. At that moment, the phone went, and it was Beryl, could she come and see me in the afternoon. I was delighted – a friend.

She came, and we talked about everything – except books – she said she wasn't educated. But neither am I, in that sense. It's only reading and living that educates. Beryl was born in Germany just after the war. Her father was in the German navy, and left his ship at Athens when peace was declared. He made his way back home through devastated Europe, discovering what had happened in Germany and elsewhere, while he was sheltered from it all on his ship throughout the war.

He decided he didn't want to live in Germany ever again. His best school friend had come back from England where he'd been a POW and had had a happy relationship with the farmer he was billeted with. He was planning to go back and continue working with his friendly farmer. Beryl's father went too. They went to live in Northamptonshire, the very heart of England geographically and, perhaps, symbolically. So Beryl grew up an Englishwoman. We've got to know each other in our spiritual group.

March 19

Phone call from Jane, she was passing through Warkworth on her way back from the dentist. So I jumped in the car, and we had an hour and half nattering over coffee, and then meandering round Bookworms. After which, she drove home to Paihia.

I took home from Bookworms a book on Islam and the Arabs. Rather heartbreaking, because it was written fifty years ago, and the writer is continually explaining how the Sharia law is being liberalised in each country he deals with. And now, here we are full circle, with the noose of Sharia, which means 'the road to the watering place' – the right road to follow to reach the goal set by the Koran – being tightened in nearly every Muslim country. So women are back to being hidden, covered, uneducated, raped, helpless and totally exploited, blamed and victimised, while justice means stoning and beheading and chopping off limbs...

I remember hearing a talk on Islam by a western believer, and how reasonable and logical he made it sound, explaining that Islam gave the balance that Christianity lacked. Christianity preached love, but Islam redressed the failings of this creed, by preaching justice.

Valerie Davies

My new book quoted the creed found on Muslim tombstones, which ends with the words: 'Islam is what He sent, religion is what He decreed, truth is what He said, justice is what He ordered'. Depends how you interpret justice...

On the other hand, the opening sura of the Koran, which Muslims start their prayers with at the five prescribed times during the day, I find beautiful, even though I don't believe in a God who blesses or curses anyone. It goes:

In the name of God, the Merciful, the Compassionate
Praise belongs to God, the Lord of all Being,
The All-merciful, the All-compassionate,
The master of the day of Doom.
Thee only we serve; to Thee alone we pray for succour
Guide us in the straight path,
The path of those whom Thou hast blessed,
Not of those against whom Thou art wrathful,
Nor of those who are astray.

A Christian could pray the first few lines without misgivings. But the last lines, which ring with judgement for sinners and no forgiveness or compassion, are a long way from the ideals, though not the practice, of

Christianity! I have a theory that in fundamentalist beliefs of all creeds, people's ideas of God are based on their own unconscious infantile interactions with their parents. Since so many people have had, what seemed to a tiny child, an all-powerful, sometimes irrational and judging father, that's how God has been personified. And certainly that's how he's been personified by all the male-dominated religions of the world – as an angry, punishing, judging, irrational grandfather!

Such a belief is a good way to keep people in subjection by religions with leaders specialising in power! No wonder that a rational, mature person wouldn't want a bar of such an Old Testament god. But as people become more autonomous, and aware, and they let go childhood conditioning, they begin to move into deeper and more compassionate understandings of a Creative Energy – hence the gulf between fundamentalism and other branches of all religions. The American Indians' benevolent Great Spirit seems closer to the truth of a loving creator than all the angry gods.

March 20

At Frances's marvellous house, Marianne joined us, not just for lunch, but also for an event, satisfying to the eyes, the mouth, the heart, and the soul. The Japanese word shibui expresses some of the beauty and elegance of the occasion, but not the enjoyment between the three of us. There's always a sparkle when we three meet... we sat at a table dressed in starched linen, old silver and crystal, pretty china and flowers – the colours: green and white, and touches of pink, ruby, and plum from the flowers, the pink champagne, and the ruby flowers in the china. The food, delicate and perfectly presented, from the individual cheese tartlets and fragrant salad, to the miniature lemon cream tarts...

From there, having discovered that it was five o'clock, I hurried over to Lily's house to look after the grandchildren. Both were back from school, one off to a party looking, I can only say, like a fashionable teenager (enough said), and Raymond, exhausted, lying on the sofa doing his homework. We played a few games of rummy-o, and then, thankfully to bed. I was tired, having done Newmarket shopping and spent the Christmas book tokens before going to the lunch party.

Next morning, having given Saffy, the cat, as much cuddling as was possible in the time available, I left her looking wonderfully grumpy, with her smoky blue fur and chunky body, flat, truculent little face and big, unblinking amber eyes. At Roland's house I met his sweet new love, Susie.

Roland went to a garage with me, and put air in my tyres, for which I was truly grateful. He was taking the assorted bodies out to the cart track for the rest of the day. Then I raced back home, glad to get away from city traffic, back to the peace of this precious place. I read the book Roland lent me, Paulo Coelho's The Fifth Mountain in one gulp... didn't find it as profound as The Alchemist. Went back to read the biblical account of Elijah. Lots of blood, death and revenge in true Old Testament tradition.

March 23

I was having a quiet day, when Eugenie rang in the afternoon, and mentioned that Julian was thinking of selling their half of this property because they use it so little. This saddened us of course, but we could see the logic.

Then Piers rang, and said he wanted to come and stay the night now he can drive himself. He arrived and we talked endlessly of history of art and Neoplatonism, the driving force apparently, behind Michelangelo's work. I learnt a lot. I made a fish pie, which he ate with gusto, and all the vegetables – peas, brussels sprouts and spinach! Then gelato from Charlie's and a hot chocolate sauce, made with cream, brown sugar, butter, and lots of melted Toblerone and dark chocolate.

Though it was getting dark afterwards, he asked if I was still going to do my walk with Cara, so we had a stroll and chat in the dusk, meandering round the mown grass and tombstones. He said how much he loved this place, the smell of the fresh air, the peace, the remoteness... he said he was going to come more often now that he could drive. He seemed so strong and calm and mature.

As if there wasn't enough reverberating around my life, later Patrick precipitated a discussion which, I felt, was crunch point, and I said things I never intended would ever be said, though they were the truth. Went to bed feeling sick, and feeling guilty, that though I had spoken the truth, I had failed love.

March 24

Patrick and I were extremely polite, gentle and shell-shocked today. He showed me how to do his Kendo sword drill, which I had arranged before this happened. By evening I realised that this was not the end of the world, and in fact, I felt better than I had for a long time, and we seemed to be getting on better than before.

I went to send an email to Derek and Gill in Plymouth to inquire about Margaret's fall, when my computer rang! I realised this was them, and rang back on the phone, but Gill insisted on talking to me through Skype. This was a revelation and we chatted for an hour and a half... gardens, weather, cats, family, politics, books and houses.

March 26

Three quotes from an article I was editing for Eugenie:

Singer Beverly Sills: *'Arts are the signature of civilisation'.*

Actress Stella Adler: *'Life beats down and crushes the soul, and art reminds you that you have one'.*

Jim Morrison, who died young: 'O great creator of being, grant us one more hour to perform our art and perfect our lives'.

Last night, as I listened to Monteverdi's Vespers before switching off the light, I became sure about that perpetual nagging question: 'Which three composers would you take to a desert island?'

Bach, Handel, the never changing greats, and now I've definitely plumped for Monteverdi... something about his unique way with trumpets as well as voices, makes me feel I wouldn't want to live without him. What a relief! Now I know what to pack for the island.

This morning I didn't want to leave here, the day was so beautiful. But Auckland was just as heartstopping, shining air and glittering sea with the perfect cone of Rangitoto floating across the harbour, and huge sails on tiny yachts flying over the water. Took Patrick to his board meeting, and after a few errands, I arrived at Cynthia's house with a posy of pale mauve-pink roses and hydrangeas, plus some rolls and hot cross buns. We had lunch and a long natter. It was comforting to be with someone I didn't have to hide anything from. We both combed through the various tangles in our lives, knowing we were safe to do so. Then a late pick-up from the board for Patrick, and home.

Waiting was an email on Patrick's computer from David Robinson, who I haven't seen or heard from since Hong Kong days – as he says, nearly forty years ago.

When he retired from Hong Kong, and settled in Cape Cod, he began holidaying in this country nearly twenty years ago, and even had a house in Kerikeri for five years, when we were there.

He had found one of my books in a second-hand bookshop in Akaroa, and tracked me down through Patrick. I've replied, and am hoping he'll ring. It gave me such a buzz to read: 'I have never forgotten you, the children, and those wonderful fish stews at weekends at your flat.'

I also spoke with Ilona in Wellington, as Eugenie has booked me to go and see the Monet exhibition in May. Will stay the night with Ilona and Kenneth, which will be the icing on the cake. Had a brief word with Piers, and he sounded good. Went to bed smiling, knowing he was okay.

March 26

Worked hard all day after ringing Marianne for a chat about last Friday's lunch, Caroline, who's coming to lunch next week, then Joan, the hairdresser for another urgent appointment, and Cynthia, to say thank you, and invite her with Caroline. Recreated Cynthia's delicious lunch yesterday; courgette, cumin and feta fritters, with salad, tomato and avocado salsa, and sour cream and beetroot relish on the fritters. So good, I'll be making it again. I hadn't known what to do with beetroot relish when someone gave me a jar. I can't get enough of it now.

When I went to sleep after listening to Monteverdi's Vespers again, I had a great sense of peace and well-being. From feeling rather isolated a couple of weeks ago, I've been in touch with, or seen, nearly all my friends and loved ones in the last ten days.

My bedtime reading for the last few weeks has been the James Lees-Milne diaries, though I don't have the complete set. He gets much more specific about his numerous homosexual affairs the older he gets, and blows the gaffe on a lot of people. When one also discovers that Lees-Milne had an affair with one friend, while unbeknown to him, his wife Alvilde was having an affair with Vita Sackville-West at the same time, the mind boggles. No wonder the lower classes (who knew all the aristocracy's secrets, since they waited on them hand and foot) thought the upper classes were promiscuous. They were!

Lees-Milne, having converted to Catholicism in the mid-thirties, returned to the Anglican Church after the Latin mass was barbarously abolished in the Catholic Church. In spite of his sexual peccadilloes, Lees-Milne was very devout, reading the gospels right through over Easter, attending church regularly, and celebrating the anniversary of his dead mother's hundredth birthday with a private holy communion.

What a strange contrast the two diarists I've been reading are. Frances Partridge, hedonistic, anti-God, moral and faithful, compared with James Lees-Milne, acerbic, God-fearing, amoral and utterly unfaithful! Some of the same literary people figure in both sets of diaries. Partridge is more factual, Lees-Milne gossipy.

His diaries are full of fascinating details, like Kenneth Clark at his second wedding. When the best man held out the ring to the officiating priest, K. Clark said: 'Beautiful, isn't it, it's Coptic'. At which the cleric replied: 'Oh, if you're interested in that sort of thing, what do you think of my chasuble'... while all the while the bride waited with outstretched finger.

When the fox-hunting Duke of Beaufort died suddenly in the night, he had seen two foxes the day before when returning from hunting. One was sitting on his father's grave, the other on his grandfather's grave. He pointed with his whip and said: 'That's where I want to be buried.' The same day, his current mistress, the Duchess of Westminster, heard two owls hooting during the day – a local portent of death. That night, the hounds bayed all night, and couldn't be quieted. Their baying is known as 'singing'.

It was another windless day, the sea cobalt blue, the sky pale, clear and cloudless and I felt I'd missed out on it, because I was inside working so hard. Each moment seems so precious on these shining days. And every night the sky is studded with stars, so bright they seem to be in perpetual movement, and the Milky Way billows with tiny sparks that make it look like a cloud of light in the cloudless sky. The moreporks are very near these nights, calling to each other from the trees around the house.

March 27

Busy day again, working on Eugenie's stuff, articles for a magazine, rewriting and checking a newsletter. These are the shining autumn days. Each one seems more glittering than the previous one. The bracken has turned rusty-gold in two days, and the liquid ambers are beginning their change of life from green to red and purple. Suddenly, the guava tree is covered in red fruit. A couple of days ago the green berries were hardly noticeable amongst the foliage.

Now they are bright red. And the garden is full of flowers again, the purple salvia descended from a cutting from Howick nine years ago, roses and dahlias, impatiens and daisies, and the little blue South African flower whose name I always forget, and my favourite white Japanese anemones. The plum tree is also in flower... why, only the plum tree and God knows.

Over at Eugenie's I found Deepak Chopra's book *Why is God Laughing?,* and laughed my way through it this afternoon. Later, when I was lying down, I went into that gap, the blank space, the dark place where there is nothing, except that sudden tumble into bliss. I think the bliss comes as I come out of the space. First the void, then the bliss. The deafening sound of the bulldozer working across the road didn't make any difference, it was there and not there, and nothing existed. It used to be a dark, desolate space, but these days it's simply what I think the mystics call a cloud of unknowing.

On the return, there is the love, which seemed also to be absolute beauty, absolute joy, absolute peace. It makes sense of words like ineffable. It only lasts for a moment.

And afterwards I know that all's right with the world, and with me. Everything seems perfect, even the problems, which don't seem like problems, but simply part of what is.

The Sound Of Water

Do the moments get longer, or maybe the gaps between the moments get shorter... who knows? But the memory of them sits there in the back of the mind, a rampart of peace and comfort to lean against... or in those words of Boethius, 'a quiet resting place for faithful souls...' and even for souls like me.

March 29

I've reluctantly returned inside, almost dazed with the splendour of the sunset tonight. Another calm, milky day, and then, as the sun went down, the sea turned pink, and the sky lilac, and the islands floating on the horizon, pale purple. At one point, as I looked at the horizon, at the place where the pink sea and the pink sky met, I could almost feel the edge of the world, and the rosy sea running over the brink in an unending pink waterfall.

Then the colours deepened and the water became indigo and deep pink, a wine dark sea, and the sky turned turquoise. When it darkened into dusk, the colours spread to the other side of the firmament, and a celestial curtain of glowing red hung like a backdrop behind the silent village, the church spire and the distant hills, the trees, all outlined in black against the skyline.

Went to Rita to salvage my hair this morning. She tried. On the way, I stopped for a cup of coffee, and there was Belinda, a friend from twenty years ago, when we did courses together. Her hobby is reading Tarot cards at markets, and so she did mine. Without even putting the question into words, she answered it about my work. She felt the house situation would work out satisfactorily.

I did the sort of shopping I enjoy. The market provided me with flat green beans, avocado pears and cucumbers. At a stall on the road to Joan, I bought beetroot and orange relish, two jars of lemon curd for the various entertainments next week, a dozen newly laid eggs and honeycomb.

Back home, Annabel had arrived with her boyfriend, camera and car. Very grown-up, gentle and adorable. She was taking photos for a homework photographic assignment.

A witty little reply from David in reply to my email, and taking me up on the offer of lunch on Tuesday.

March 30
Breakfast on the veranda on another peerless day. The sea silver and still below, the sky clear and blue above. My favourite Connon's wholemeal bread toasted, Danish unsalted butter and the fresh honeycomb. Good coffee in the pot. Later, more coffee with Mike and Annie. After lunch, though I begrudged missing a single hour of the glorious weather, I drove to

Matakana to see the film Dean Spanley. I laughed all the way through and cried at the end.

March 31

David came today. No, I would not have recognised him after forty years, and I'm sure he wouldn't have recognised me either. On the other hand, the things about him that were so endearing forty years ago in Hong Kong are still there: kindness and honesty, the gusto and sense of fun. He remembered fondly what he described as my wonderful weekend parties with masses of food and the famous fish and rice dish. 'You say now you had no money,' he reminisced, 'but you always gave us these wonderful meals.' My memories were only of two or three of these occasions, but I rather fancied the glamorous picture he had of a hostess holding open home at weekends, so I didn't discourage him.

I felt sad at the way his life has turned out. The sudden death of the woman he loved for fourteen years from encephalitis, caused by mosquito bites when they were on holiday in Thailand celebrating his retirement; his sense of having no home, shuttling between America and New Zealand, and neither country prepared to let him in for good... and the sadness I detected from his childhood.

We worked out that we met when he was helping to organise Larry Adler's visit to the Mandarin Hotel, and

I went to hear Larry play magically on his harmonica, before interviewing him for the South China Morning Post. Larry and his then wife took me up in a big way, until the whole thing was soured by Larry's wife leaving lesbian love notes under my pillow and me forever fleeing from her, and wondering if Larry knew what was going on. He left Hong Kong after a month to go on to the Adelaide Festival, and his wife remained in Hong Kong for some months after; a thorn in my side, as I never knew what she would be up to next. She was known to be unstable, and had pills flown out to her once a week, so that she couldn't take too many, and I was terrified of upsetting her.

The next year, I received a telegram from Larry saying he was arriving at 9am Kai Tak Airport the following morning. I went to the office, resolutely determined to have nothing to do with him, but the phone rang mid-morning, and there he was at the end of it, wanting me to meet him for lunch.

Not even my dental appointment would deter him, so I ended up with a numb face at the Foreign Correspondents Club with Larry. (Once I had thought the FCC was utterly romantic, the place where Han Su Yin had met her lover in Love is a Many-Splendored Thing.

But no more. Just lots of scruffy journalists sitting around, frequently drinking too much!).

As we went up in the lift, Larry effortlessly raised his voice to a pitch which meant the others would hear him, without him seeming to shout. He then proceeded to entertain me with expert little jokes and clever little aphorisms, which riveted his captive audience, and caused a little flurry of adulation from them, but not from me. At lunch, I glumly sucked an omelette, tasteless from my numb jaw. I didn't know whether he and his wife had reunited, and didn't like to ask. Halfway through the meal, he asked if I was still seeing my boyfriend from the previous year, and when I said yes, he said: 'He's not the man for you.'

My muffled reply was rather tepid, and he went on: 'In fact, I think you and I would suit each other rather well.' I didn't know what to make of this remark, and changed the subject. A few minutes later he said: 'Ya know, that's the first time I ever propositioned a woman and she ignored me.'

Somehow, I extricated myself from this embarrassing lunch, and followed, with some derision, Larry's subsequent career as a socialite in London.

David had done the derision too, and we both laughed over it and had recognised in the gossip columns in the Express and others of that ilk, all the exaggerations and boasts he had told us, including playing tennis with the Duke of Edinburgh, and having an affair with Greta Garbo.

The Duke was true, I told David, having discovered the link with Baron, the photographer, who was a mate of Larry's and also of the Duke. David had not caught up with the fact that among Larry's lists of supposed conquests, Greta Garbo had now been deleted, to be upgraded with Ingrid Bergman, for a later generation of filmgoers. David, on the other hand was able to tell me, courtesy of the gossip columns, that Larry had moved from the famous Dolphin Square apartments with their tennis courts, to the much more distinguished and exclusive Albany Chambers, the historic Regency bachelor flats in Piccadilly. No tennis courts at the Albany. Funny to think Larry could have passed the time of day with my ex-husband during his Dolphin Square sojourn.

April 2

There must have been a storm out in the ocean; the sea has been thunderous and white-capped for the last two days. Today, in the bright sunshine again, the foam is sharp white and the sea deep aquamarine. After slaving over a good lunch for Caroline, Michael and Cynthia, it was not a success. Cynthia rang to say she had a new granddaughter, and would not be coming. Michael seemed tired and unforthcoming, and when I came to serve him he said that he never ate lunch... and it was downhill all the way after that... I felt he was not very well, and had lost his old joie de vivre and mellowness.

Caroline was impressed with the garden, and I got her to show me how to prune the old moss rose which Marjorie had grown for me in Kerikeri. Like Barry, another talented gardener, she was very taken with my grouping of blue pots and blue flowers on the faded two-toned blue bench by the blue wrought-iron chairs, as we look out of the French windows.

When they left, I had a quick snooze, and then drove off to Auckland to see My Fair Lady. I wasn't particularly looking forward to it, but Eugenie had arranged for me to go with Lily and Annabel. It turned out to be a treat, beautifully staged, sung and costumed. I drove straight back along swift, empty roads, once out of Auckland and its road works and detours. A half-moon lit up the sky and my heart. Cara was waiting for me on the bed, which she never does, and stayed there all night, snuggled up into the crook of my arm.

A rather touching picture of the Queen with her arm round Michelle Obama, and Michelle Obama's beautiful arm round the Queen's tiny shoulder.

Rereading, for the umpteenth time, poet Kate Llewellyn's *Burning*, a diary of a year in the Blue Mountains. I am always stabbed with envy, committing one of the seven deadly sins every time I read it. Her metaphors, her vision, her poetic prose make my pedestrian writing seem even more prosaic! Alas, I would love to be a poet, and I would also like to have straight hair.

April 6

I've finished reading Parson Woodforde's diaries, written between 1758 and 1802, which I had only looked at cursorily before.

Virginia Woolf's comment about him doing nothing but eat had put me off.

I now read them from cover to cover, wonderfully relaxing bedtime reading... coursing hares, eating gargantuan meals (but only in company), walking along country paths to dine and play cards with the friendly squire and his lady. Herculean trips by coach to Bath and Somerset, grumbles about his niece Nancy who lived with him:

'Nancy pert tonight'.

Endless games of quadrille, a few books mentioned, a few concerts in Norwich, the illnesses and pregnancies of his maids, and 'uppityness' of his ever-changing 'boys', who ran messages (no phones then), helped in the stables and the kitchen, and cheeked his footman, his cooks and his maids.

A typical menu for six, which included the Squire, Parson Woodforde and his niece, read:

Couple of boiled Chicken and Pigs face, very good Peas Soup, a boiled Rump of Beef very fine, a prodigious fine, large and very fat Cock-Turkey rosted, Maccaroni, Batter Custard Pudding with Jelly, Apple Fritters, Tarts and Raspberry Puffs. Desert, baked Apples, nice Nonpareils, brandy Cherries and Filberts. Wines, Port and Sherries, Malt Liquors, Strong Beer, bottled Porter etc. After Coffee and Tea we got to Cards, limited Loo...

Much neighbourliness, sending of barrels of apples, a fine hare, a brace of partridges, a treasured cucumber... and much formality among all the calling, and coming and going, and enquiring on the safe arrival or departure or good health of everyone.

Nancy, Woodforde's niece, is frequently referred to in the diary as Miss Woodforde – usually when he's in a good mood with her. When she's been cheeky, she's Nancy.

She was about twelve years younger than him, and came to keep him company, and, I assume, to housekeep, though he never mentions this, but she is included on the list of people he pays once a year. Nancy gets ten guineas a year, twice as much as the maids. But some years, Woodforde pays her three months late because she has not been satisfactory! One year, he comments on how she grumbles about the isolation and lack of company... poor Nancy, stuck in the wilds of

Norfolk with a middle-aged bachelor cousin, who used her salary to exert his power over her.

In spite of the rigours of travel, they were surprisingly mobile, taking the arduous trip back to Somerset which took some days, quite regularly, in order to catch up with family. Those Christmas card pictures of stagecoaches struggling through snowdrifts and freezing winter landscapes were true to life in Woodforde's time. Even his chamber pot froze, it was so cold inside the house, and even colder up in his bedroom. Gifts of money to buy bread and coal for the poor feature regularly, as do the Overseers of the Poor, collecting for the poor in the village. The other regular occurrence was the delivery late at night by the village blacksmith, of a barrel of smuggled brandy.

A black man blowing a French Horn came to the kitchen door to see if they would like to see a female dwarf, who came into the kitchen and sang them two songs. He told Parson Woodforde he had previously lived with the Earl of Albemarle. Woodforde gave him a shilling.

Now he was making his living thus. Which would not be interesting, except for the arresting footnote discussing the great decision in 1772 of the Chief Justice, Lord Mansfield. In his judgement on a slave called 'Somerset', Lord Mansfield decreed that every slave, by the mere fact of landing on English soil, became free.

This was four years before the founding of the United States, which continued with slavery for nearly another century.

I couldn't help contrasting this little cameo with the trials of Hattie McDaniel. She was the African-American woman who played Mammy in Gone with the Wind. She was asked not to attend the opening of the film in Atlanta, and when at the Oscars, attending to receive the award of Best Supporting Actress, she had to sit alone in a segregated area. As late as 1939, she was the daughter of former slaves.

April 7

A package arrived from Mike, with a copy of Yeats's poem, An Irish Airman Foresees his Death, which he had recited to us when we had coffee with them the other Monday. Plus another poem by Yeats, Partition, about India, and some off-beat Economist obituaries, which Mike regularly supplies us with.

I'm always uneasy about Yeats, he seemed such a poseur in so many ways... with his monocle and cloak, and Golden Dawn magic affiliations, and staying in castles and stately homes, fulminating against the English, and then enjoying the pleasures and rewards of being Establishment. When it comes to him writing poems about the war, I can only remember that he didn't participate in either war, but left Wilfred Owen out of the Oxford Book of English Poetry because he suspected him of pacifist sympathies.

Yeats wrote to fellow poet Dorothy Wellesley:

When I excluded Wilfred Owen whom I consider unworthy of the poets corner of a country newspaper, I did not know I was excluding a revered sandwich-board Man of the revolution & that some body (sic) has put his worst & most famous poem in a glass-case in the British Museum – however if I had known it I would have excluded him just the same. He is all blood, dirt & sucked sugar stick.

Lieutenant Owen was killed on 4 November 1918, a week before the Armistice.

He was leading his men of the Manchester Regiment forward to cross a heavily defended canal.

The last anyone remembered, he was with his men, encouraging them with, *'Well done'* to one, and, *'You're doing very well, my boy'* to another. Shortly after Owen was killed the attack was called off, and his body was taken back to be buried at Ors.

It was one of the few unsuccessful attacks by the British on that day when they were heading towards victory.

His parents back in Shrewsbury breathed a sigh of relief when the bells rang a week later for the Armistice. They were still ringing when the telegram from London arrived at midday. Perhaps it was Owen's bitter poem:

'The old Lie: Dulce et decorum est
Pro patria mori'

('The old Lie: How sweet and fitting it is to die for one's country') which prejudiced Irish nationalist Yeats. His poem on Partition was a disaffected Irishman's take on the dismantling of the British Empire, biting, mocking and somewhat inaccurate. Owen's poetry was about facing the destruction of civilisation in what my grandmother called 'The Great War'.

I've given up the Kendo exercises. They hurt my arms and shoulders, and I realised that I would start developing massive muscled shoulders like a samurai (or Patrick).

April 10 Good Friday
We have now lived here for three years, which is a dicey time for us. We always seemed to have moved after three years! I marked Good Friday as I always do, with the playing of Bach's St Matthew Passion ('The Great Work', as Anna Magdalena, his wife called it) right through. No matter how intently I listen, it always finishes before I realise we are getting to the end. I always feel a sense of incompleteness, which is not

assuaged by replaying the last chorus. It was the same when I sang it in the choir; it always ended before I was ready.

A cold day and the fire lit. It's like having another person in the house; a warm, comforting presence. I need it. No family this weekend. I lobbed a hand grenade into the emails and I have heard nothing since... I cried all day Wednesday and Thursday, and am still fragile.

I Ching for me is 'Thunderclap'. Appropriate. Acupuncture was just what I needed on Thursday. Lyn did some stress relief, and then worked on my leg meridians. A weak gallbladder, she said, affects confidence and decision making... the spleen, self-doubt... people who spend a lot of time thinking... it affects their digestion... yes, that's all me.

But as usual I need energy. Oh, to have the energy I had before being felled with chronic fatigue syndrome. This is the Holy Grail that drives me on to try every, and any, form of alternative medicine. It got me on my feet again. I've now started taking extra zinc and St John's Wort.

Anything to feel better than I have for so many years, and not be knocked back by doctors saying things like, 'If you had some purpose in your life you'd feel better', or another: 'You can't expect to feel at forty, like you felt at thirty,' or 'Do you have emotional problems?' People like me are driven to self-diagnose and self-medicate.

April 12

Easter Monday Roland came on Saturday with Susie, his new girlfriend, on their way up north ... Murray, a face from the long distant past, appeared on Sunday. He was a member of Patrick's three-man team working on the Mr. Asia drug ring investigation back in 1979–1980. He was a brave man who risked himself, especially when he went to Singapore and secretly got into the office of Martin Johnson, alias Mr Asia, one of the murderous drug bosses.

He now has a property in Australia with a six-bedroom Georgian mansion, tennis court and swimming pool, a beautiful young Brazilian wife and two small children, as well as his three from a previous marriage. An interesting, intelligent, calm and well-rounded person.

I offered him coffee, but he asked for tea. When he said his wife was Brazilian and they imported their coffee from Brazil.

I understood why he asked for tea! I made him lapsang souchong, and he joined that very small group of people close to my heart who appreciate it – the electrician at Laingholm being one of them! Murray immediately commented on the smoky flavour.

Valerie Davies

The village school had its fete today, and as Dinah, who serves at the village shop opposite the school, stood outside watching, a pleasant looking Maori woman walked past as I was getting into the car. 'Come on, Dinah,' she quipped, 'aren't you coming up with me to buy some raffle tickets?' 'I'm working,' said Dinah, to which the other replied, 'You always were lucky!'

April 13

Thunderclap continues. Things deteriorate. I am in despair and am hopelessly persona non grata.... I knew the consequences for me would not be good. I don't know where we go from here.

Try to carry on with life.

Took Patrick into town to do several errands. I realised how far I had fallen, when I went to the jeweller to collect my pearl and black cross necklace, and it was still unrepaired after six weeks. I could see he was under pressure, so I said I did understand how busy he was, and would just rely on him to let me know when he had fixed it. He said to me: 'you're being so nice about this, some people are so rude to me,' and I felt grateful to him for telling me I was nice! Feel sick all the time.

I'm reading a book on Alice Bailey's work by some chap called Sir John Sinclair. Can't find out what his credentials are, but I don't think he's a professional writer... too many 'but enough of that...'s.

I was interested to read the proof that Djwhal Khul, the Tibetan Master who transmitted the dense and profound material telepathically from Tibet to Alice Bailey, who then transcribed it in New York, was very much alive.

The account of D.K. arriving at the border of Tibet and India, when he knew in some way that a friend of Alice Bailey's was there, and giving him a parcel of incense for Alice Bailey, was rather moving... 'a lama seated on a donkey... attended by four lamas and all the natives... surrounding them and bowing... a very great and holy man.... who had never been known to come down across the frontier or visit an Occidental...'

Apparently, Alice Bailey, or A.A.B. as she was known, was accused by her pacifist friends of doctoring D.K.'s material to suit pro-British attitudes at the outbreak of the Second World War. Apparently, D.K. also referred to all the allies holding out in 'that small fortress of the Forces of Light which is the British Isles.' Answering critics who said that God being love He must love all equally, A.A.B. later wrote:

Because God is love, He had no alternative or the Hierarchy either, working under the Christ, to do anything but stand firmly on the side of those who were seeking to free humanity from slavery, evil, aggression and corruption.

The words of the Christ have never been more true, 'He that is not with me is against me'.

My thoughts, precisely!

I wish I knew where I had read that story of Chips Channon standing with Emerald Cunard, looking at everyone in tails and tiaras at some post-war function, and saying:

'This is what we've been fighting for!'

And quick as a flash, Emerald Cunard came back with, 'Oh, are they all Poles?' It must have been in Nancy Mitford's letters, or similar.

Still quivering inside with the effects of Thunder-clap. Everything passes, I know, but I don't know what is going to come to pass... the weather is so beautiful, the sea like glass, the sky cloudless and a clarity and calmness in the air.

The contrast with my anguish feels like a cruel joke. A tempest would be easier to bear.

April 14

Another exquisite day of Indian summer.

In the garden, red and magenta leaves of the liquid ambers are scattered across the grass in the autumnal untidiness that I love, and so many flowers are still blooming and producing a second flowering.

The guavas are sweet and ripe now, and the wood pigeons know it, and have returned, as well as the little silvereyes.

I still feel shell-shocked from Thunderclap, but am refraining from beating myself up, from inner recriminations, from silent, angry conversations with myself, and trying not to give in to the absolute misery. So I wait. Wait for it to pass, and to see where we go from here. And I feel deep sadness... probably grief. I had a phone call from Ilona about my Wellington trip, which I was planning to abandon, since I feel too miserable to contemplate it. However, Ilona has plans to take me out to dinner, and go to a play, so I felt it would be churlish and discourteous to cry off.

April 18

On Thursday, I had my acupuncture with Lyn, and felt so unexpectedly good after it, instead of being like a zombie, that I collected the new framed picture of Raeburn's skating dominie, and did various other errands.

The Reverend Walker was framed in silver and black, silver grey mount and inner rim of black framing the painting. He looks even more elegant in this setting. I've hung him in the bathroom; the only place left for a big picture, and banished all the gold-framed botanical prints to my bedroom. I've added pewter candlesticks and soap dish to the mix, with the black Spanish soap and black hand towels. I'm now looking for grey towels instead of Patrick's brown ones.

Couldn't be bothered to cook in the evening, so for the first time in a long time, we went out to dinner. The atmosphere has changed at our local since the pigtailed, necklaced chap has gone.

The friendly waitress who makes marvellous coffee waited on us, and the pumpkin and mussel soup, flavoured with lemon grass, was world class, texture, taste and presentation a pleasure (I sound like those TV celebrity chefs) and we had our usual fishy pizza with a decent glass of pinot gris and the perfect coffee. The place was filled with happy families and gorgeous-looking blonde children. It could only have been an Anglo-Saxon society. And so to bed. A warm starry night.

The next day, I needed to get away from festering on my worries, and went off to the village. I took three pairs of trousers to Tracey to be shortened. She was her usual friendly self. Then I returned to the local for more of that perfect coffee. I know as soon as my spoon dents the cream on top whether it's going to be a good cup or not; the creamy topping is always a giveaway. If it collapses or disappears quickly, then the coffee will have no richness or body, but will taste thin and unsatisfying.

Sustained by the perfect coffee, I drove off to Goat Island, and stood and watched the shags in their giant nests with sticks and twigs protruding in every direction, up in the pohutukawa trees on the edge of the cliff. There's a whole colony of them all in one tree, like an avian apartment block, but no one ever seems to notice all these big nests cheek by jowl, with big birds perched on top of them. Everyone is always intent on the sea and the view and getting their wetsuits on and off.

There was a group putting away very professional-looking camera equipment. I spoke to one of them. They were a Canadian TV film crew, filming oceans of the world. They had come here first, since the Marine Reserve here was the first in the world, he said. I pointed out the dozen or more nests in the tree, but he wasn't interested in what was in the air, only what was under the sea.

Captain Cook and his sailors enjoyed eating shags... after a diet of inspissated juice of wort, weevilly ships biscuit, and the rest, we would probably enjoy them too, but the sailors even preferred them to duck. Their first feast of shags took place at Mercury Bay, and then later at anchor at Queen Charlotte Sound, where Cook described them as good roasted or stewed. Since he banned the regulation unhealthy salted beef and pork, and threw out butter and cheese when it went rancid, he knew what he was talking about.

I can only read Georgette Heyer at the moment, and light novels like *The Jane Austen Book Club*, which make me laugh. Georgette Heyer makes me laugh too, and I've read The Masqueraders right through two nights running.

It's one of her early ones, so there's a bit too much tiresome Regency slang, but for the rest, the dialogue is very funny. The heroine is unlike the later stock heroines who were always beautiful, obsessed with clothes, waltzing and Regency bucks.

This morning, I did a round trip to town for bags of compost for the garden, amino acid taurine for my stressed liver, and back to market, where I bought Comice pears and avocado pears. Then, what I had come for, a session with Belinda. Before she even got the cards out, she had tuned in and felt the last week.

I stopped at Bill's village store.

As I walked across the road, there was a roly-poly old lady, sitting on the bench outside the shop, eating a doughnut and swinging her short little legs to and fro, like a happy child.

When I was inside, she came in, and calling Bill 'Silly Billy', took him to task for leaving his van for too long on the pavement outside the shop. She gave him a real going-over.

Bill must have heard me giggle to myself, and after she'd gone, he came over and said: 'D' you know her story?' She is, as I thought, somewhat disadvantaged, but lives a full and satisfying life in the sheltered village community. She is the most sought-after player for teams in the bowls club, in spite of the idiosyncrasies of her manner. She has her own house and wanders round the place chatting to everyone.

'She does odd jobs around the place, picking up rubbish, looking after her little property, and she's part of the church community, and helps on cake stalls, and whatever.'

Yes, I thought, village life is a sheltered community.

April 20

Yesterday took on its own momentum. Woke up tired, and got up late. I was just about to get some breakfast, and the computer rang! It was Derek and Gill. We had a long chat, an hour and a half, so then I was running late for the whole day. Cooked lunch and at the same time baked a lemon cake for Patrick's daughter and husband. We had a gentle, pleasant afternoon with them.

Later we did lots of mulling over the various aspects of the situation we feel we are in over this house. We had thought we'd die before the others left here; they had originally planned to retire here. We wonder if we will be able to stay here ourselves. We have begun looking tentatively for places where we could afford to buy. There aren't many, and they are all remote! I did 'I Ching' on the situation. It seemed apt and comforting, telling me that all is well, that though I sense vague and distant imports of future difficulties, worrying is pointless. I have to remain true to the present well-being, and not allow indistinct fears of an improbable future to affect me.

At five o'clock, we went down to Mike and Annie, with a basket of ripe red guavas. They had a dish of ripe yellow guavas waiting for us. So we did a swap. We had a chat and a glass of wine, and as we were leaving, they invited us to share their roast lamb. We had a happy evening with them, laughter and the comfort of being with kind friends. We said nothing about our house worries; too many other people involved.

Annie talked about her work. As we listened, I realised she uses not just her thorough scientific training, but immense creativity and profound common, or rather uncommon, sense in her investigations.

She described huge, plastic bags of whey. But the problem was that the bags were covered in mould, and she had to test them to see if the inside was contaminated. She described putting enormous swabs on the contaminated parts, and then more huge swabs on the uncontaminated parts, and then having cleaned the bacteria off, comparing the newly-cleaned parts with the clean parts already tested.

Then there was the bacteria which grow in the burnt soil of Chinese paddy fields after farmers have cleared the rice harvest. The bacteria get into other substances, and there's no way of sterilising it, because it actually grows in heat. She was asked to test for it in bandages and other sterilised materials, but was not allowed to import the bacteria from China to do the experiments. So she created her own from her own bonfires! Other intriguing stories were her visits to Switzerland to check mould on a painting, and checking out another millionaire's home, when a carpet rotted under a solid coffee table, caused by some substance in the wood.

I asked her if there are guidelines for these things, but in fact each of her investigations tends to be the first of its kind, so she is continually improvising and creating experimental processes. No one else does her sort of work in this country. At the same time she is a talented home-maker – gardening, sewing, painting furniture, and cooking wonderful food. I must ask her for her mellifluous recipe for lemon custard. She keeps Patrick permanently supplied with her homemade marmalade.

April 26

A hard week... feeling chronic fatigue, dragging myself around with my liver playing up as well, and feeling nauseous and unspeakable. At some cost to my fragile self, made chocolate mousses for an indefinite number of grandchildren. In one of Partridge's diaries, she quotes Princess Mathilde Bonaparte as saying, 'griefs seem heavier as one gets older'... yes.

On Wednesday Lily, Annabel and Raymond came for lunch with the excitable Bichon Frisé puppy. I only just coped. Cooked fish pie and produced the chocolate mousse. Mistake; no one hungry, late breakfast, snacking on the journey... we have been eating fish pie and chocolate mousse ever since.

On Thursday, we did a tentative house-hunting expedition to the wilds of Northland and the Kaipara Harbour. I've had the name Pahi lurking at the back of my consciousness for months, so there we went, via Paparoa, which turned out to be a pleasant village with, among other things, a reasonable restaurant, The Sahara.

Pahi took our breath away. A peninsula protruding into the huge Kaipara, with water views from most angles... truly the last, loneliest, loveliest... huge skies, grey shining sheets of water, low hills, and the feeling of a remote and forgotten country. Lunch at The Sahara, and then back home. I was drained and exhausted, and tottered into bed.

Up in good time however, for the sweep in the morning. A jaunty little Englishman from Southampton, who had been an engineer for Shell, covering the Home Counties as far as Cornwall and up to Birmingham. Somewhat over-qualified for sweeping chimneys. During our chat over the de rigueur cup of tea, he said something memorable: 'You are only as happy as your saddest child', apropos of his wife...

Made a chocolate almond cake since Annie doesn't eat wheat. Disaster. After it cooled and I'd piled on chocolate icing lavishly, I thought I'd cut a piece for a quality check. The inside was completely uncooked. After a little panic, I scooped all the raw chocolate cake out, leaving a circle of iced, cooked chocolate cake, added an egg and more almonds to the raw mixture which also had the sugar and butter from the icing, and put it all back in the oven.

It turned out delicious. I shall try to replicate the amounts of the ingredients in the second version, as I preferred both the taste and texture. In bed and asleep by 7pm, as I have been all this week.

Up the next morning for Anzac Day, and Mike and Annie came for a cup of coffee after the village Anzac service.

Because of the rain it was in the hall, and we didn't go. Apparently, we missed something rather special. They tried both versions of the cake! After they left, I went to bed. Slept for fourteen hours. I am still not good.

April 28

Patrick rang Julian while I was at acupuncture, and we find there is no problem about the house, the garage, and us staying here, when they sell next door. All our agonising was for nothing, and if I had listened to 'I Ching', I would have spared myself much unnecessary angst. It actually took a few hours for the reality to sink through the layers of despair and exhaustion and to begin to feel how wonderful it was.

Since then, I've been in a constant state of thankfulness and thanksgiving. Every tree, every leaf, every bird, every cloud, every ripple on the water, every blooming daisy gives me another little prod of joy... we will always be able to enjoy and savour them in this blessed place. Shafts of delight and relief continually ripple through me.

April 30

I dropped Patrick at his board meeting and drove straight to my favourite department store to spend Roland's Christmas gift voucher. I quickly felt bored and smothered. I used to enjoy the friendly old-fashioned comfort and elegant merchandise. But now, after the inevitable makeover and elimination of various departments like 'Manchester', and the shrinking of departments like handbags and rugs... there's not much left for the likes of me, just acres of makeup counters and smart, skimpy young clothes in tiny sizes which don't have any relevance to people my age and size. I used to spend hours in the china department, but even there, there wasn't one thing I lusted after.

Eventually I struck lucky with a rather chic purple draped knitted jacket, very nice, and an expensive and extravagant black Caroline Sills long coat/cardigan ... had a dreary lunch and left half of it, and fled to the Atrium where I'd parked. Relaxed with a very efficient manicure while I used up more time and more money, and finally went back to the car to go and fetch Patrick. Found to my chagrin, that to park three hours in town costs $30. I don't think I will spend time, money and energy going to town for a while... it used to be a treat, alas. Is this another sign of growing old, and being out of step...?

10

May/Jun 2009

May 6

I've been looking after the grandsons. I left on Friday, and returned yesterday – Tuesday – on my knees with exhaustion. Walking Lucy, running to and fro, and up and down stairs in that big house, up at the crack of dawn to get the boys off to school, and still up at the crack of doom the other end of the day to get them to bed and off the computer, leaves me bleary with tiredness.

It was not helped by arriving on Friday to walk Lucy, and finding she was not there, but Piers was. He had had another mighty nosebleed, and knew nothing of Lucy. His nose bled intermittently for the rest of the day, worryingly, and a phone call from the pound gave us news of Lucy. Late in the afternoon, they rang to say they had run out of time, and would we come and get her, and pay the fee. So off we went into the unknown in the Friday night rush hour traffic, and were reduced to thumbing through the map, parked on yellow lines in the middle of thundering traffic before we found the pound.

Too tired to cook supper, I suggested Kentucky Fried Chicken to a chorus of 'Hurrahs', and drove out once again. At Parnell KFC, they were closed for renovations, so by the time we'd crossed town again to Royal Oak KFC, and had then been rerouted around roadworks, I'd been driving for hours. Piers and Charlie were loving, courteous, and thoughtful. One night I went to bed before Piers, and he came up and said he'd shut my bedroom door so that the smell of his cooking wouldn't filter in.

Unable to concentrate on anything for the last few weeks, I've either blobbed out with Georgette Heyer, or read in desultory fashion another book of James Lees-Milnes' diaries, Caves of Ice, courtesy of Abe books, a new email source we've found. Just before I left for Auckland, three more Frances Partridge diaries arrived, also courtesy of Abe, so I now have the complete set. I read the first two Partridge's over the weekend looking after the boys, as well as Malcolm Gladwell's intriguing book The Outliers, and as I backed out of the drive to go and eat a quiet lunch at La Cigale, I said to myself, I would like to experience an interesting synchronicity today.

At La Cigale I ordered a fresh salad with salmon and puy lentils, and while I waited, I pulled out half a dozen of their old World of Interiors to browse through. They were all dated 1989, so pretty old. In the second one I flicked through, I found a page of gorgeous rooms with lovely fabrics. So I went back to the beginning of the story, and it was about Janetta Parlade's new home in Spain, Frances Partridge's most beloved friend. Reading the text, the person writing it obviously knew Janetta well. So once again, I turned back to the beginning, and the writer was Frances Partridge. So I had had a triumphant synchronicity! Since Frances Partridge was born in 1900, this made her eighty-nine when she wrote the story, and she still had over a decade more to live.

I never fail to be amazed at the constant travelling, visiting, dining, parties, concert-going, exhibition attending, that Frances Partridge did. One night alone in her flat, and she'd be in a panic that her life was empty. A few phone calls from friends would make her feel better. Before I was married, I used to be very pleased with myself when I had country weekends with friends organised six weeks in advance... but now, having reached Partridge's age in the diaries, I would collapse with such constant socialising.

Interestingly, she quotes Sir Walter Scott's journal, which I'd like to read. He writes, 'If the question was eternal company without the power of retiring within yourself, or solitary confinement for life, I should say, "Turnkey, lock the cell. There she and I are at one.

Reading of her London in the late sixties and early seventies, I discover much that I never knew was happening while I was struggling with the vicissitudes of life in Hong Kong and then here. I had no idea, for example, of the hippy invasion of London, of the grubby, bearded, long-skirted, pot-smoking hordes who infested Piccadilly, Chelsea and elsewhere, or of the constant strikes and power cuts, which reduced life to such a misery during the reign of Heath and his cohorts.

And year after year, I delight in her descriptions of winter; the powdering of snows, the pale streaked skies of the north, the snowdrops and the primroses. Never – I notice, sounds – like the glorious cacophony of church bells ringing, or rooks cawing and clacking, circling and soaring around their rookeries before they settle down for the night, or the soft incessant cooing of wood pigeons in summer, which are all things I miss most in this new world. I miss the scent of lilac too.

However, I am amazed at how virulent Partridge is about things like meditation and mysticism, neither of which she seems to have the faintest idea about, taking in only the most trivial and superficially phony aspects of both. A bit like thinking, that all the tourist flags and space souvenirs at Cape Canaveral were what space exploration and the Hubble telescope was all about. She's also very critical of the rich friends she stays with, but many people who have to work for their living would have thought that she was also rich and parasitical.

At the beginning of 'Caves of Ice,' Janes Lees-Milne writes: *'An explanation is now called for. Why do I resume this diary, which three months ago I brought to an end? There is no explanation. I merely missed it like an old friend.'*

Which is much how I feel. Writing this is like communicating with a friend... mulling over thoughts, experiences, troubles and joys. I miss it too when I don't write. And when I stopped writing for some years, I actually felt miserable. I realise now, that I was always waiting for a new computer after my old one collapsed. When it arrived, I was so intimidated by it that I never used it, though I constantly promised myself I was going to. And when Eugenie gave me this laptop, it still took me weeks before I was brave enough to tackle it, and I still struggle with hitting wrong keys and sentences mystifyingly becoming italic or turning red.

Also, I enjoy writing my own stuff. I spend so much of my time proofreading, checking and making suggestions about other people's work, for which, of course they get the credit, that it's balm to write this for myself. I wrote reams in my diaries when I was young, but they were more the outpourings of hopeless love, misunderstandings and despairs. A doctor friend in Hong Kong once asked to read them. I gave him one, and presumably baulked at finding no Freudian insights, he commented on how 'innocent' they were. My memory would be how self-obsessed they were?. But they were still my comfort even then. I had an extra small diary in my handbag, which I kept religiously in colours. The bad days were coloured blue. The good days were red. I coloured them in as soon as I arrived in the office each morning.

There weren't many red days in one year. I was recovering from a month in hospital with hepatitis, jaundice and glandular fever, followed by separating from my husband, and feeling knee-capped by his sudden departure from Hong Kong at a telephone call's notice at the airport, with no arrangements about money. Then the divorce, a job that paid me less than I could live on, so I had to find all sorts of extra odd jobs to make ends meet, an unhappy love affair on the rebound, a terrible bout of dysentery which reduced me to a skeleton in five days, my teeth packed up and I racked up unpayable dentist's bills. Two house moves, the bank's threat of bankruptcy because of the debts my husband had left behind, the incessant worry of trying to find a good amah to look after the children –

even boils under my armpits – to mention just some of the plagues which darkened the days of 1969 and coloured them blue.

Strangely, the mere act of colouring in each day, the little daily ritual, seemed to give a little stability in a frightening world. One more day lived through! I even had William the Silent's grim maxim written in it and read it constantly on the blue days: *'There is no need of hope in order to attempt, or of success in order to persevere...'* a sort of seventeenth century version of: *'just do it'.* Also inscribed on the front page, Clement of Alexandria: *'We may not be taken up and transported to our journey's end, but must travel thither on foot, traversing the whole distance of the narrow way'.* The whole distance of the narrow way seemed interminable and inescapable forty years ago, and the journey's end an infinity away – no longer!

May 7

I drove into town to collect the clothes I'd left behind at Eugenie's and to take Cynthia to lunch for her birthday. Called in to Eugenie's, dropped in the proofs I'd corrected overnight, received an ecstatic welcome from Lucy the dog, gave Piers the TV remote I'd forgotten to bring before, and forgot my clothes again.

I had a good natter with Cynthia, over a tasteless salad and good coffee at the garden centre. We can both talk about our families with complete detachment, neither judging our own children or each other's. We both agree that sons are easier, and that one would never talk to friends who only had sons, because they couldn't understand the stormy tensions and interplay in the intense mother-daughter relationship.

I bought a fragrant blue hyacinth in a pot, and came straight home. Cynthia, who is seventy like me, was wearing an outfit of tights and clinging sweater which revealed her youthful figure. I hoped, in retrospect, that either my (fairly) unlined skin or my still thick hair might be the meagre assets left to keep me afloat in these days of reduced vanity and completely faded beauty.

Wellington looms with various aspects still unresolved. At this stage I'm dreading it. I'm also anxious at the thought of leaving Cara again. She moped when I was looking after the boys, and slept on the bed, snuggling up to me for the first few nights I was home.

May 8

Cold, grey and rainy. It feels like the first day of winter. So I celebrated with a blazing fire, and porridge with cream and brown sugar for breakfast. Our lunch with Brian and Marianne at their bach at Kawau Island on Sunday looks less and less likely. If the weather continues to be stormy there won't be a ferry.

The Sound Of Water

I picked what looked like the last two roses of summer, pink and gold-tipped Abraham Darby blooms, their scent the scent of an archetypal rose. They are in a long glass vase on the bookshelf in my bedroom, their leaves particularly pretty, reflected in the white Georgian style mirror above the bookcase. Luckily, there will be some roses of winter, since I have planted, as always, mutabilis and Jean Ducher to bloom all the year round. Winter feels delicious: piling dry logs on the fire, making pancakes for supper, wearing warm woolly clothes, and pulling the curtains as dusk falls. Thank you, god of small things!

May 10

A wild and stormy day! No lunch at Kawau, but great relief over Wellington. Ilona contacted Eugenie and me, and had apparently never received my email with my ETA. They are going to meet me, and take me to the Monet exhibition and then to a private viewing at an interesting gallery, followed by dinner and theatre in the evening. A Frances Partridge sort of day! Then, just as I was feeling good and relieved about Wellington, all the snafoos seeming to be unravelled, Eugenie tells me Ilona will expect me to be using my mobile phone, and also to text. I can't do either. I hope I can get a crash course with Roland tomorrow night, but oh dear, how daunting I find the technological age.

Having racked my brains for something to take worthy of all this treating and spoiling, I've baked one of my fruitcake specials, have a bottle of Heron's Nest quince ratafia and a box of Bendicks peppermint chocolates. Then, trying to work out a safe way to get the cake in one piece to Wellington, and not sure whether the draconian security checks would allow me to carry a round metal object like a cake tin, I ended up ringing Air NZ, and it seems OK. But I have no confidence in the system. I suspect that the security checkers enjoy their brief moments of power too much not to be unreasonable, and probably make up their own rules as they go along.

I was nearly decapitated by a low-flying tui swooping out of the guava tree as I walked down the path. There are two large fat ones, and our garden is their territory, they rustle around for honey in the loquat tree blossoms, suck honey out of the red flowers on the bottlebrush tree outside the window with their long tongues, and also seem to eat the ripe guavas.

16 May

After all the destroying panics and huge mountains to climb, Wellington was a doddle and a delight. Stayed with Roland the night before in order to catch the early plane and was up at the crack the next day, leaving Patrick to take a taxi to his board meeting. Roland had given me some intense coaching on the mobile, and I think I can now text. However, sailed onto the plane, with 'park and ride' under my belt, the computerised ticketing accomplished, and no need to use the mobile. I learned too, that Kenneth doesn't use a mobile at all, and Ilona had not expected me to text her! Phew!

Ilona was waiting as I came out and whisked me off to the exhibition. Queued for nearly an hour, but it was worth it. I see paintings differently to when I was young. Very satisfying. With a little time before Ilona picked me up, I sat in the sun by the harbour, and savoured Wellington. People were roller-skating and jogging, walking and propelling pushchairs as they skated, skateboarding and talking, laughing and talking, and listening to their earphones. Everyone was enjoying themselves using the waterside as their playground.

Ilona took me up to Jim's and Charlotte's house at the top of the hill in Brooklyn, with views across the harbour to distant snow-topped mountains. She and Kenneth have not only restored the house to the clarity and beauty of Ernst Plischke's – the renowned Austrian architect – original design, but also enhanced it with their own contemporary alterations. So the acres of plum-red Thai silk curtains in the sitting area, tangerine silk in the dining area, and cloud grey silk curtains stretching down the full height of the stairs and along the gallery passage looking into a courtyard, have been duplicated. But the old hair-cord floor-covering with dark red tribal rugs has been replaced with light floorboards, and a gay yellow and turquoise, salmon and cream Bosnian rug of Jim's, which brings the house into the present.

Books, pictures, artifacts, sculptures and treasures everywhere, some Jim's and Charlotte's, others, Ilona and Kenneth's, and bright sunlight streaming in make it such a happy house filled with creativity and enjoyment. In the gallery downstairs, leading to the bedrooms and studies, were more wonderful pictures, Frances Hodgkins, and her father, Toss Woollaston, and others.

After a leisurely lunch, and a walk around the garden, which is being rescued from years of neglect in Charlotte's old age, and Ilona's absence, there was just time to freshen up and take off for the evening. First, the exhibition, then the theatre; dinner downstairs, and upstairs to the play, The Year of the Rat. Tiny, intimate theatre, which I loved, hearing every word of the witty script.

What synchronicity: it was about Orwell, Cyril Connolly and Sonia Brownlow, who all figure in Partridge's diaries. Later, back to the top of the hill, sitting in front of the log fire with a cup of cocoa and a piece of my cake for Ilona, wine and cake for Kenneth, and just cocoa for me. Kenneth dubbed it a 'platonic cake', in that it was the essence of the perfect fruitcake!

The next morning, I enjoyed a long and satisfying talk with Kenneth walking by the harbour, once more in brilliant sunshine, about books, more books, and writers. We agreed on the unlovability of Virginia Woolf, Kenneth saying how incredible that feminists should have chosen her as one of their heroes, me saying that she could enjoy a room of her own because of her relays of servants – cooks, housekeepers, gardeners, chars, etc, and how unkind she was to and about them, and many others.

Then museums, (Kenneth is a trustee of one) and the fact that formerly aristocrats collected pictures and works of art because they loved them and enjoyed showing them, whereas now, museums collect from impoverished aristos, and museums don't love their works of art; they acquire them for prestige.

We strolled past a beautifully incised verse of Eileen Duggan's on a groyne at the water's edge, then had coffee at the airport, and Kenneth left me at my gate.

I had been thoroughly spoiled and stimulated for every moment of the trip. Back to Auckland, and drove through hail and cloudbursts to pick up Patrick from Eugenie's.

Valerie Davies

And so home, and as I write this with the fire blazing, the rain pouring down, and the scent of hyacinths, I rather regret that we didn't move to Wellington when Patrick was offered a job there. I love its atmosphere of refinement, and enjoyment of the arts... the way the life of the city is concentrated in the centre, and not diffused like Auckland. And the people look interesting and intelligent, even their clothes and style were so interesting. I feel homesick for Wellington, its atmosphere and intellectual life. It was so stimulating being with Ilona and Kenneth, civilised and intelligent, humane and urbane, and to be in their city.

Today, I have spent hours on Google reading reviews from the 'Times Literary Supplement,' the 'London Review of Books' and all the rest, on various biographies of Sonia Orwell.

I learned from the play, that Orwell called it Nineteen Eighty-Four, because that was the year of the Rat, the rat being Stalin.

Yesterday, Patrick had his Japanophile friend John to lunch. I was utterly exhausted when he left, and slept for several hours. That night, as I lay in bed, I didn't want to read. Instead I was happy to lie there, feeling the edges of that precious bliss hovering in my consciousness, and so went peacefully to sleep. Was awakened by the pain of what felt like a tight iron band around my chest, squeezing me tight. It lasted for about twenty minutes. Suppose I will have to get checked by the doctor. I am reluctant.

May 18

Feeling very peculiar at the moment. Had a headache all night, and felt nauseous and headachy this morning. Dragged myself around Warkworth shopping, but felt too wretched to have a coffee. Dr Davie is either booked up this week, or I am taking Patrick into his board meeting, so I can't make an appointment till next week. Even the pharmacist, when I consulted him about my rotten digestion and nausea, suggested going to the doctor, so it looks as though I can't avoid it. I hate the idea of getting into a drug ring, and experiencing the sort of side effects that Patrick does. If I do, I won't take them.

The real world continues... a day of bright sunshine, vivid colour and deep shadows... tuis, I counted five, singing and clicking from the kauri and the puriri tree, which is in full bloom speckled with cyclamen pink blossoms from which the tuis suck the honey. Two fat pigeons landed heavily on the telephone wire as we sat and had lunch in the sun, and then edged sideways in perfect unison, like trapeze artists, till they reached the telegraph pole out on the road. A flock of tiny silver-eyes, bright green, flickered in and out of the plum tree and into the birdbath, taking turns.

Zeb, a neighbour's black and white longhaired pointer came to see us, accompanied by deaf and nearly blind little Digger. They enjoyed their socialising, ate a tiny snack I gave them, took a drink from the dogs' water bowl I keep filled at the top of the steps by the roadside, and then meandered off, tails waving like fern fronds. I couldn't watch the film last night on the horror of pig farming and walked outside in the starlight till it was over... no more bacon. I shall bully Patrick to ask why the SPCA doesn't prosecute such outrageous cruelty to animals, whether it's an 'industry' or not. Industry indeed. Animal torture more like.

May 24

Have no energy to write this, but since I was lying on the bed this afternoon, and heard myself saying, 'I feel as if I'm having a nervous breakdown,' I've been forcing myself to do all the things I normally would. So I leapt off the bed, pegged out the washing, folded the clean clothes, went for a walk in the clear, bright sunshine, and now this. Last Monday night, I felt so ill, I rang a help line to check out my symptoms, and they told me to ring 111 and get to the nearest hospital.

The wonderful Volunteer Fire Brigade arrived first. They clomped into the house in what sounded like hobnailed boots, looking like flower pot men in huge hats and yellow waterproof and fireproof trousers, held up by braces, and much too large, so that they seemed to live inside them. A round and kind man who was a charter fisherman attended assiduously to me, while an exquisite and fragile-looking schoolgirl wrestled with an oxygen machine, which didn't work; they decided was a faulty spare. Another moustachioed firefighter baled up Patrick for a quick chat at the other end of the room, trying to pinpoint the year, he'd worked in sales at Patrick's firm when he was/worked there!

The night in hospital was an education – the best and most expert technological care, constant tests, checks, blood tests, blood pressure, ECGs etc, and not an ounce of connection or humanity. After ten hours, no one had even offered me a cup of tea. Thank heavens Eugenie had left me a bottle of water. I said 'good morning,' to the Polynesian cleaning lady who looked a bit surprised and smiled a gold-toothed acknowledgement. Emergency ward, I could understand, though I couldn't understand why no one could give a little boy, huddled on a chair trying to sleep beside his mother, a pillow and a blanket, or even a drink of water.

Transferred to the acute ward, the nurse going off duty at 7 a.m. gave me a cup of life-saving tea, and that was the last contact I had with anyone except the breakfast ladies at 10.30, until the doctors came and gave me the all-clear at 11a.m.; heart okay, but stressed and depressed, with too high cholesterol.

Valerie Davies

The noisy and dramatic cockney male nurse running the ward, who looked and behaved like Jamie Oliver on speed, studiously ignored me the whole time, which was why the doctors missed me on their rounds at 8 a.m. The whole ward was his captive audience. He continued to ignore me after the doctors had seen me, until I flagged down a willing body, who turned out to be head of the department. She helped me peel off the various appendages still sticking to me, so I could dress and go, and make my bed available for another patient. Seeing her doing such a menial task, galvanised Jamie Oliver into a half–hearted lunge in our direction, pretending he hadn't noticed me before.

However, talking to this head nurse gave me some interesting facts to relay to Patrick, as a Health Board member. She told me she had beds for fifty-six people, and she had had eighty-three admissions the day before – with all the complications such figures create.

I was thrilled to find Eugenie, Roland and Piers waiting for me when the ambulance arrived the night before, and Eugenie came back first thing in the morning, and took me back to her home when I was ready to leave.

Roland came in the afternoon and drove me back home to Patrick and a waiting fire, kettle on, and a warm bed. Since then, I've struggled with total exhaustion, and spent much time sleeping.

The Sound Of Water

Kate took me to Helena's for a telling of another life journey on Thursday, and we picked up Marjorie on the way. We had our usual fun in the car there and back, and agreed that this bit made the rest (which is sometimes patchy) worthwhile. We even found we all agreed about the decline of department stores, which made me feel I wasn't as old and out of date as one of my children had hinted. Jackson and Sarah were as loving as ever. Exhausted the next day, but baked a chocolate almond cake for Saturday, when Belinda was coming for lunch.

I'm reading Major General Belchem's autobiographical book *All in the Day's March*. In Belchem's family, out of five brothers who fought in the First World War, only one survived: his father. Of four brothers who fought in the Second World War, he was the only one to survive. Two generations more than decimated. Not one out of ten, but eight out of nine gone. So out of nine young men in just one family, only one survived in the second generation, and he had no son to carry on the name.

Young officers had one of the highest casualty rates in the First World War – they led from the front and were also easily identified by little things; their Sam Browne's, their riding boots and breeches, their revolvers instead of rifles. So they were picked off straight away. This was how my step-grandfather, in the first row of the Northumberland Fusiliers, the first regiment to advance after the bombardment, stepping out at dawn on the first day of the Somme, was wounded and nearly died. This was how the so-called flower of that generation was destroyed, estates broken up with no one to inherit, communities diminished, and an ancient way of life destroyed.

Yesterday, Saturday, Belinda came. We had pumpkin soup on the antique blue and white soup plates, cauliflower cheese sprinkled with toasted almonds, and chocolate cake. We both enjoyed it, Belinda noticed everything: the antique soup plates, the green and white china collection, the dining room chandelier... very satisfying, and she loved the house, and the energy of the whole place.

We walked round the cemetery and out to the headland. It was glorious in the sharp wind and bright sun, and we covered the usual range of subjects: books, courses, clothes, jewellery, diet etc. and discovered we'd been on several large courses together before we knew each other.

Today my colour is terrible again, my energy levels are rock bottom, and I feel near to tears the whole time. I drew a Tarot card to see if I could get a clue to what is happening to me. 'The Hanged Man'... giving up the pattern of the past, to move into a new phase. The giving-up is so painful... which is what I've been feeling. I feel my relationship with the family, including the grandchildren, is dissolving into something much less involved and dear. I know I must step back and not allow myself to be so involved and vulnerable. They are all growing up and away. And this time of transition is hard.

As I read *'The Hanged Man'*, I felt a sort of settling inside. What I am feeling is part of the common experience, others have been this way before. It's my process, but it's part of the human experience too. I took another card, a sort of 'so where do I go from here'... 'Two of Swords' ... march to the beat of your own drum, listen to your inner voice, you have to try another way to resolve the impasse, separate from emotional participation... yes, all that...

So what IS depression? For me it seems to be the need to sleep all the time, no appetite, misery, nausea, apathy... and things like toothache, chest pains, no desire to do anything, unable to concentrate, tears at the slightest thing... I've been taking St John's Wort and zinc, but not for long enough to make a difference, it seems.

Now I understand too, how when you're depressed, it's so hard to motivate yourself to do things that help you, even though you know you must do various things in order to move on. I can see now how schizophrenics get caught in a downward spiral, and stop taking their medication... with consequences we sometimes read about in the crime pages.

May 26

I've found that part of the downward spiral is feeling sick, and so not eating, and then feeling much worse: fragile, shaky, tearful etc. So I eat my comfort food, cornflakes, and they stop me sinking so deep into that state of total fragility.

We've had a good storm, the sea pounding onto the rocks, foam flying, wind roaring, thunderous noise filling the background of sleeping and waking. The birds seem to love the rain, and the blackbird and thrush are continually singing. The plum tree, which lost all its leaves, then came into blossom, is now covered in leaves again. I don't know how long it can keep up this hectic schedule before collapsing into an exhausted fini. I try not to think of the animals freezing in the fields in this icy wind and rain... my annual winter torment. Cara sleeps on the bed every night these days, cuddled up against my back. I love it.

To cheer myself up last night, and to get some endorphins swishing through my system, I Googled Christian the Lion again. I watched that great soul greeting his two former London owners, bringing his wild lioness wife, who sniffed them gently too, and all strolling back to Christian's home in the rocks. There, the lion king, his wife and his cubs lay in the dust in the sun and communed with the two men.

As I watched Christian nuzzling and licking his cubs, so unlike the normal behaviour of male lions, who have a reputation for destroying their offspring, I wondered if this gift of loving was what he had learned in London, and whether he would pass it onto his progeny, and set up a chain of new child-rearing habits in later generations of lions. It was so moving, watching his joyful recognition of his old friends, his exuberant leaps, putting his front legs round their necks, hugging them and licking their faces.

The pig debate continues, thank goodness. We've all known the horrors of it for so long, and yet somehow, it never registered with the public. Let's hope that this time, we really do grasp the nettle and outlaw cruel farming. And I find I can't even eat free-range pork now, having learned that the pigs go through the huge fear-infested abattoirs with all the other terrified animals.

Today I cooked a luxurious lunch... fresh terakihi, gently fried in butter with a few acid free tomatoes, then brandy added, along with cream and fennel. Delicious, eaten with chopped carrots, golden kumara mashed with butter and nutmeg, and silver beet from the garden. A cup of coffee and a piece of fudge completed this delicious repast. Perhaps I should eat well more often. While I felt sick this morning, I do not now!

This message has just arrived on the email from Eugenie. It could not be more apt:

When God takes something from your grasp, He's not punishing you, but merely opening your hands to receive something better... the will of God will never take you where the grace of God will not protect you...

Trouble is, I can imagine a Jew on the way to Auschwitz saying, *'yeah right.'*

On the other hand, a Jew on the way to Auschwitz would also have known Psalm 121:

I will lift up mine eyes unto the hills, from whence cometh my help.

My help cometh from the Lord, which made heaven and earth.

He will not suffer thy foot to be moved: he that keepeth thee will not slumber.

Behold, he that keepeth Israel shall neither slumber nor sleep.

The Lord is thy keeper: The Lord is thy shade upon thy right hand.

The sun shall not smite thee by day, nor the moon by night.

The Lord shall preserve thee from all evil: he shall preserve thy soul.

The Lord shall preserve thy going out and thy coming in from this time forth, and even for evermore.

All of which is saying roughly what Eugenie's email is saying too.

So belief is not logical.

But I want to believe. And I do believe the words of Psalm 139:

O Lord, thou hast searched me and known me.

Thou knowest my downsitting and my uprising, thou understandest my thought afar off.

Thou compassest my path and my lying down, and art acquainted with all my ways.

For there is not a word in my tongue, but lo, O Lord, thou knowest it altogether...

Whither shall I go from thy spirit? Or whither shall I flee

from thy presence? If I ascend up into heaven, thou art there: if I make my bed in hell, behold thou art there.

If I take the wings of the morning, and dwell in the uttermost parts of the sea:

Even there shall thy hand lead me, and thy right hand shall hold me.

And if I did not believe, I think the magnificence and the poetry of these words would seduce me into a longing for belief.

May 28

I've wondered if I'm indulging in one of the seven deadly sins, accidie, but searching the Desert Fathers, Gnostics, and others, I find to my relief that the sloth, and torpor of accidie, is not so much depression, as idleness and being tempted by idleness into turning away from God. Accidie, or sloth, was thus considered a sin, causing people to neglect their spiritual and other duties.

The cure was regular physical hard work, discipline and penances.

Depression seemed to be defined as melancholy, and the old remedy for this condition was to eat well, rest and be kind to oneself, with no guilt and no stress. Exactly what I need. What interesting ancient wisdom and insight into the human condition.

Later took Patrick to his board meeting, and after a birthday coffee with Roland on his forty-fourth birthday, went to see Cindy, who Belinda had put me in touch with, it was like a miracle.

I realised that my depression was caused by suppressing the feelings from my difficult childhood, of fear and anger, grief and despair and so on. I'm now getting in touch with all that misery, and by facing it, and examining how it's influenced all my thinking, relationships and responses, I can start to change those old patterns of thought and behaviour.

I've always reached such a plateau with each counsellor I go to see, but Cindy works in a way I've never encountered before, and we went straight to the root of a problem that's dogged me for years. Cindy has a PhD in biochemistry, and used to teach at a university until deciding to do this sort of healing full-time. She is wonderfully ordinary, and therefore authentic and very convincing. I go to Dr Davie tomorrow to renew my thyroid prescription. I do not think I will be sharing this information with him!

Took myself off for a good cup of coffee at Matakana, where my two lovely friends, Jill and Julie, spoil me. I sat in the sunshine, and Mel delivered the coffee and talked about the tiger that killed the keeper at Whangarei, and her indignation at the shooting of the poor creature. We covered a number of other contentious issues as well, and ended up talking about trees.

The most beautiful view of the water, which skirts the road into Matakana, is at Whangateau, on a series of tight hairpin bends, where you can't stop to look. Each time I drive past, I try to snatch the beauty, slowing down to gaze as long as possible, while on the run, and hoping no car comes speeding up behind me. No matter what the weather, it's always beautiful.

Today, a sheet of still, shining blue water stretched across the perfect semi-circle of the bay, the tide so high that the bright white sandbank where sea birds congregate was shrunk to a thin ridge. All the yachts at anchor just inside the harbour entrance were floating over their reflections. At low tide, the pastel colours of pale blue water, pale gold sand, coffee-coloured sand banks, lines of white surf beyond the bar, yachts leaning on their side, and huge sky, are always a symphony of seaside colours, reminding me of primitive pictures of the Norfolk coast, with tiny toy boats in the distance. As I crawl past in the car, not daring to stop, I can never get enough of this tantalising view.

May 31 Queen's Birthday Weekend

It's been cold and rainy, a good winter weekend.

I cooked pikelets for afternoon tea yesterday, eaten with unsalted butter and strawberry jam, a winter treat.

Today, I achieved an ambition I have long secretly nourished! Baked a crème caramel, which I've never felt I was clever enough to do. It was delicious, preceded by lamb racks, roasted parsnips tossed in flour to crisp them up, roasted sage leaves, carrots stewed in butter and brown sugar, and brussels sprouts.

The caramel custard was eaten with ripe persimmons in Patrick's case, and in mine, with bananas cooked in rum, brown sugar and butter. Waistlines no object... but supper may be frugal... a lettuce leaf at the most.

I'm nearing the end of the first two volumes of the *Lyttelton/Hart-Davis* letters, full of allusions, books and jokes. Like *Oscar Wilde* on being served a very chunky watercress sandwich... 'Tell the cook... that these are the very worst sandwiches in the world, and when I ask for a watercress sandwich, I do not mean a loaf with a field in the middle of it ...' and little bon mots like 'No cause was ever finally lost until the Bishop of X made it his own...'

My little dark night of the soul has come to a triumphant end, with the recovery of what I had forgotten yet again... that the inner life and reality is the truth... that outward things are the creation of man and his imperfect free will. Mother Julian's, 'All is well, and all is well, and all manner of things are well,' is not mindless optimism, but the understanding of other levels of reality, and the mystical knowledge of the Divine Source, the One Love, Intelligence and Power. In the I AM Discourses I found the sentence: 'The human or outer defects or discrepancies have nothing to do with the Omnipresent Perfection of God, for anything imperfect is the creation of the outer concept of mankind.' That sentence may not speak to others, but it took me back into the sunlight and out of the shadows.

June 4

We had good friends to dinner at the weekend, and it was a total flop. Not sure why. Every topic of conversation fell flat... long pauses between conversations, every subject I introduced or tossed in for some fun or badinage failed, sending myself up didn't work, and many times I felt such a sense of boredom as I persevered, that I lost heart and petered out. Things were taken up or argued in a pernickety way, and I can only think that the extreme tiredness of one person in particular, and maybe us as well, just killed the usual fun and bonhomie. Patrick and I both felt the same way, we discovered afterwards, and felt sad. Hope the friendship recovers, but I fear dreadful pressures on them are mounting with the recession, and the stresses are going to tell in various destructive ways. I hope not.

Today, the cloudless sky and bright sunshine continues. The nights are crystal clear and silver with moon, and very cold. The colours of the trees, the gold-leafed poplars, the bare red and gold branches of the willows, the silver of the birches, means the countryside is bright with colour.

Sitting in the garden, I watched a tui drinking in the bird bath, a huge pigeon swaying on veritable bent twigs in the guava tree, plundering the berries, and tiny, lime green silvereyes flicking in and out of the bottlebrush tree sipping the honey in the red flowers.

If I had a favourite bird, silvereyes or wax-eyes would be near the top of the list.

Buller called them silvereyes, which is one up in his favour for once.

They are supposed to have arrived in New Zealand in June 1856. Buller wrote:

...in the early part of June of that year, I first heard of its occurrence at Waikanae, a native settlement on the west coast, about forty miles from Wellington. The native mailman brought in word that a new bird had been seen, and that it was a visitor from another land. A week later he brought intelligence that large flocks had appeared, and that the 'tau-hou' (stranger) swarmed in the brushwood near the coast; reporting further that they seemed weary after their journey, and that the natives had caught many of them alive

Buller tells us that they were then seen in numbers in Wellington, and greatly welcomed as they ate the aphis known as American Blight, which was ruining the settlers' apple trees.

The little silvereye has flourished here ever since its epic thousand-mile journey across the Tasman.

Why did they come, flocks of them, not just a few blown by the wind? What a great heart in a tiny frame, and what impelled each one to embark on this huge migration across an ocean? Flocks of them sometimes clung exhausted to the masts of ships in mid-ocean. How did they know that land, New Zealand, was awaiting them at the other side of the trackless sea? And how sad, that at the end of the endless journey, tiny wings beating against the winds, they were so exhausted, that many were caught by hand by Maoris and ended their lives precipitately in the Promised Land. Whenever I see the tiny green creatures flitting in and out of the bird bath, sipping the honey in the bottle-brush tree, and nibbling the apples I put out in winter, I remember their great journey and noble hearts.

Marjorie has sent me that beautiful rhythmic poem by E.E. Cummings. She had sent it to our local doctor whose son was killed in a car crash a few weeks ago, with those wonderful repetitive phrases: 'i carry your heart with me (i carry your heart),' to its ravishing last thought, 'this is the wonder that's keeping the stars apart... i carry your heart.'

I hope it comforts those grieving parents the way poetry sustained me when my father died when I was in Hong Kong. I had lent a friend my copy of The Towers of Trebizond, by Rose Macaulay. As soon as day broke after the phone call in the night, I rang her, and asked if she could return it to me as soon as possible. The poem in it was like a lifeline back to sanity. Every time I felt overwhelmed with grief, I read it again, and it brought me back to a place where I could still stand being alive. It was *John Davies of Hereford's* dirge for his friend *Mr. Thomas Morley:*

Death has deprived me of my dearest friend.
My dearest friend is dead and laid in grave.
In grave he rests until the world shall end.
The world shall end, as end all things must have:
All things must have an end that Nature wrought...
Death has deprived me of my dearest friend...

Both poems build up such an insistent and some-how, satisfying rhythm with a limited vocabulary. The repetition of the same few words becomes a comforting rhythmic beat... the comfort of rhythm is why mothers rock their babies, and desperate babies and people rock themselves to and fro.

Children love to move and chant rhythmically, and the chanting and rhythm of maths times-tables at school, first thing every morning when I was a child, was, I'm sure, an activity which calmed us all, and 'en-trained' us, which is what chanting did for monks.

It meant that everyone moved onto the same ener-getic wavelength, and cooperated. When monks stopped chanting, their communities began to disintegrate.

June 6

I went to Warkworth to get my hair trimmed. Even before I got home and looked in the mirror, I had sunk back into deep depression and despair (my hair was dreary enough to produce a depression when I finally did look in the mirror). As I walked down the steps to the house, I was almost overwhelmed with despair, and could see no reason to go on living, except that there was no excuse for not dragging drearily on.

I tried to blot it out with books and sleep, and early bed, but woke at midnight with that deep corroding load lying like a dead weight on my heart. It felt so unbearable, that I was almost panicky with it. Even to live the next moment seemed unbearable, quite apart from the next day and the next week. I tried to reason with it, and decided that it was such a free-flowing existential thing, that maybe I had carried it since before birth... maybe it was my poor mother's despair... I actually felt a bit better and lighter, and more able to cope when I reached this point.

I knew I had no hope of getting back to sleep, and looked around for something to help me move on. I picked up Deepak Chopra's book on 'synchrodestiny', and found what I needed. Reading his sanity shifted me from little local ego and its limiting fears, into the fresh air and clear realms of the higher self, from local to non-local, in Deepak Chopra speak, from the separation of the ego, to the sense of connection with all that is, and the sense of goodness and peace which comes with that knowledge.

This morning, Patrick and I went to see the film Beethoven at Matakana. Very moving... not the real sadness of his story, but the exquisite music, and the astonishing beauty of the musicians talking about it. Some of them combined such physical, intellectual and spiritual beauty that tears just sprang into my eyes. The architecture, the photography and the scenery were all ravishing. I hadn't realised that the London Philharmonia had commissioned Beethoven's Symphony No. 9... I felt patriotically proud that they had been so enlightened! We are planning at the moment to go back and see it again next week.

Beethoven wrestled with the desire to end his life several times, and wrote that: *'only the knowledge that no man has the right voluntarily to quit this life while he can still do a good deed,'* prevented him, as well as his belief that the gift he knew he possessed had to be expressed.

How could I have left him off my list of desert island musts? Monteverdi will have to go, so it'll be Bach, Handel and Beethoven. Their collected works should see me through the rest of my life on that persistent island.

June 7

I've reluctantly finished the sixth volume of the *Lyttelton/Hart-Davis* letters, and the only way I can handle having finished all six volumes is to turn round and start at the beginning again... some delicious bon mots... In 1958 when Eisenhower seemed moribund, and was running the free world from the golf course, the White House became known in the US as the 'Tomb of the Well-known Soldier', while Churchill at the same time, quipped after some disaster, 'It wouldn't have happened when Eisenhower was alive!'

Good jokes, like Churchill (known as Winston in these books) when tactfully informed by a backbencher in the House that his fly buttons were undone, replied, *'No matter, the dead bird does not leave the nest,' or Lyttelton's witty reference to a sonnet, which we were taught at school was the essence of bathos, writing 'Here there is always work of some kind in the garden – not much with the spade with which Lyttelton (Not Wilkinson) hath tilled his land, but with axe and saw.'*

Many of the books and people they referred to I didn't know, but I fully appreciated *Lyttelton's* abhorrence of *D.H. Lawrence*, and *F.R. Leavis*. When *Rupert Hart-Davis* unveiled his town wife, as well as his country wife, I found *Lyttelton's* vicarious enjoyment of the London wife, and the coy compliments he sent her, rather distasteful. Particularly when *Rupert Hart-Davis* had jaundice, and since his country wife, whose delicious name was Comfort (the mother of his three children), was out all day teaching, she invited Ruth, the London wife, to stay and look after him, and take him away for health-giving, rapturous weekends. *Lyttelton*, after commenting how civilised all this was, then sent his love to Ruth the town wife, but not to Comfort, who he had known for much longer, and who was the one being so civilised.

I finally came round reluctantly to Ruth, when she wrote notes to *Lyttelton*, and sounded genuinely charming. Rupert Hart-Davis sounded a lovely chap, and when, after eighteen years, he and Ruth were finally able to marry, it seemed the saddest thing that she died of a heart attack three years later. His descriptions of Swaledale, where he fled regularly from London, pressed my nostalgia buttons. Swaledale: my favourite place on earth. His descriptions took me straight there, and the years that he wrote of, were the years that I too knew Swaledale.

Good gossip... *Diana Cooper* was *Hart–Davis's* aunt, famous trumpet player *Humphrey Lyttelton* was *George's* son, while *Lord Cobham,* cricketing Gov-General of New Zealand, was his nephew. *Joyce Gren-*

fell was *Hart-Davis's* cousin, *Humphrey Lyttelton* learned to play the trumpet from a book while at Eton, *George Lyttelton's* wife was related to numerous figures at the court of the young Queen Elizabeth, while his daughter was the Queen's PR. Comfort's cousin was *Adlai Stevenson.* And so on. *T.S. Eliot* and Evelyn *Waugh, Sitwells* and *Sassoons, Somerset Maugham, Malcolm Sargent,* known as *Flash Harry;* names and faces crowd the letters with anecdote and incident. Back I go, to start reading them all again.

Obama has been to the Middle East and made a great speech, quoting the Koran. Let's hope this is the beginning of the turning point, if there is such a thing.

June 8

It's been pouring with rain for days. I enjoy the weather until I see the sodden animals standing glumly in the fields. Worst of all are the newly shorn sheep tensed and bent like hairpins against the freezing south wind and cold, with no shelter. How cruel or greedy can you get to shear a sheep in the middle of winter?

I spent a happy few hours on Google. Looked up *Rupert Hart-Davis,* and was amused to see a young pundit in the mould of *F.R. Leavis* who *Hart-Davis* and *George Lyttelton* hated so much, writing *Hart-Davis's obituary.*

He wrote him off as a snobbish old fuddy-duddy. Which he was, but he was much more than that, and a kind and decent, loving person. It was his kind heart, which prompted him to offer to write to George Lyttelton when George was complaining at a dinner party that no one ever wrote to him anymore.

I also explored the genealogies (one of my hobbies) of various royal houses, and was much struck when scrolling through the Danes to see how they treated a divorced Danish princess. She was part Chinese, Czech and English, an unlikely choice for a royal bride, and married Danish prince No. 2. When the marriage inevitably broke up, she was given her own rank as a Princess of Denmark, and a title of her own. She was no longer HRH, but became Serene Highness, though she wasn't even the mother of the heir to the throne, as *Diana* was.

And she was not stripped of her rank and titles, or humiliated the way Diana was by the Windsors. She was treated with dignity and honour, and remains a person of consequence in Denmark.

It seemed so typical of the decency and humanity of modern Denmark... as when the Jews were forced to wear a yellow armband by the Nazis, *King Frederick* and all the Danes wore them too, while at the same time they spirited the Jews out of the Nazi grasp, ferrying them across to Sweden.

June 13

A week of Kultur! Wednesday was the usual board meeting stint, and after delivering Patrick, I nerved myself to go and see Hilde who has shrunk to half her size, and is so bent, she doesn't even come up to my shoulder. Her English is beginning to go, she doesn't hear unless I shout, and then she often doesn't understand. Her memory is so bad she says things like, *'you know, that place where I had the big house and garden,'* for Epsom, where she lived for over thirty years.

Or, *'you know, that illness everyone gets when they get old...'*

'Alzheimer's?'

'No, no, you know, that one that hurts'...

'Arthritis?'

'No, no, no! Much more painful than that. You know, everyone gets it when they get old' ... (getting impatient now) Parkinson's, shingles, multiple sclerosis, Hodgkin's disease run through my mind. Finally I make a lucky, if inaccurate, stab at it: cancer...

'Yar, yar. Well, Dora's daughter...' and so on.

Thursday night we went with Marjorie to the grand premiere of the Spinning Sun Company's latest creation, Left and Right. This is the village's very own modern dance company with Arts Council grants, and our tiny community takes it very seriously. All the seats were booked for all four nights and it was a wonderful atmosphere of informality, enjoyment and participation, with most people knowing each other in the audience, even we Johnny-come-latelies knowing a surprising number of people. It felt the same at the market this morning, I knew so many people to greet.

This morning, back to Beethoven again, just as good, just as moving, the people just as exquisite, their souls shining out from the screen, pianists like *Hélène Grimaud,* conductors like *Gianandrea Noseda*, pianist, Ronald *Brautigam, cellist, David Waterman. Hélène Grimaud,* I've discovered, is the French pianist I'd read about some years ago, who has a deep connection with wolves, and has now opened a sanctuary for wolves in Switzerland. She is descended from *Sephardic Jews* from Corsica and *Berber Jews,* whose name was Grimaldi. They changed their name to *Grimaud* before *Hélène* was born. Sometimes one wonders where western culture would be without the Jews.

There was a magnificent German bass, who sang *Don Pizarro* in *Fidelio.* He talked of the genius of Beethoven, comparing it with the dumbing down and trashing of all art today, the trivial Facebook level of communication, versus the profundity of *Beethoven's* interpretation of the human condition, the hope, the suffering, the greatness. He was so vehement and really upset about the 'trashing' and the 'dumbing down', and I so agreed with him. I knew how he felt, and it was pain and grief for lost beauty and understanding, for our lost culture and heritage. Visions of *Tracey Emin's* unmade bed at the Tate Gallery, and *Damien Hirst's* diamond-covered skull rose before my reluctant eyes, along with the image of our unused television with a cloth over it. Patrick wrote of it as: 'the cloth of rejection.'

Rachel and Jackson came with us. Rachel is playing at St Matthew's, in Haydn's Great Mass, tomorrow morning, so we are up and off to Auckland first thing in the morning.

Annie rang yesterday to thank us for telling them about the Beethoven film, which they had now seen, and they were fresh from the Michael Hill Violin Competition.

June 15

Up early for the drive to Auckland. Patrick decided not to come, which makes it easier, not having to deliver him at the church door, find parking and all the other manoeuvres.

The music was sublime.

Haydn's Great Organ Mass in E-flat major, the choir Musica Sacra, and the Orchestra, including Rachel on the violin. The choir's little carved green and gold organ had been especially made for *Prince Charles's* wedding in St Paul's Cathedral, just to accompany *Kiri Te Kanawa* singing *Handels's* Let the Bright Seraphim.

The Mass was joyful, filled with exaltation.

Wonderful hymns too, including the appropriately chosen tune of Austria.

The same could not be said of the ritual of the Sung Eucharist, or Communion, which had been bowdlerised and ignorantly chopped up, rewritten and freehanded. The Benedictus was followed by a prayer in Maori, so I don't know what we prayed then... the Gospel, in some modern version, may have been about the wheat and the tares, but I couldn't really recognise it.

The Lord's Prayer was rolled up into a rambling and scrambled collection of modern clichés, and political correctness... praying masochistically to: 'Pain-bearer', and then inaccurately to: 'Love-maker' (it makes me wince just to write these words)... we then prayed ungrammatically to:

Father and Mother of us all,
loving God in whom is heaven:
the hallowing of your name echo
through the universe!

The way of your justice be followed by the peoples of the   world (why not 'Thy kingdom come'?)

Your heavenly will be done by all created beings!

293

(The exclamation marks were in their text, not mine. And what was wrong with 'Thy will be done'? And are there any uncreated beings?)

Then, more ungrammatical banal nonsense:

Your commonwealth of peace and freedom sustain our hope and come on earth. (what's wrong with 'On earth as it is in heaven'?)

With the bread we need for today, feed us.
In the hurts we absorb from one another, forgive us.
In times of temptation and test strengthen us

And so on ...

Yet the point of what was known as The Lord's Prayer, words that were traditionally believed to have been used by him, was that they were simple, direct, and everyone could remember and use them.

The use of those words for two thousand years had imbued them with the sacredness, power and patina, that anything well-used and well-loved always acquires.

Even though the accurate translation from Aramaic is longer, the brevity of the traditional version worked for generations of believers.

I remember a gentle country boy from Norfolk, talking on a BBC/TV documentary, about how, when catapulted into France with the BEF in 1940, he shot his first man. He described a German soldier running across a field in front of him, and he knew he had to shoot. He began praying the Lord's Prayer in his agony as he pulled the trigger. Would he, could he, have remembered that wordy arrhythmic collection of clichés that passes for prayer now, to sustain him in such an extremity?

Then there was the pilot, shot down and rescued from the sea, dying on the deck of a Japanese ship... he asked for someone to pray with him, and the only English-speaking Japanese, an officer, knelt down by him and recited the Lord's Prayer with him as he died...

I felt that splendid German bass's same anger and grief over the trashing and the dumbing down, the loss of our culture and our heritage. However, at the end, the vicar began the wonderful words of the Charge, and I perked up. They always used to send me out feeling strong and happy, and full of good cheer.

Dust and ashes!

After the first line, he free-handed a bit, and then tailed off into the words of the Irish blessing about the rain falling soft upon our fields, the wind at our backs and so on. Fine in its place, but it doesn't compare with the power and beauty of:

Go forth into the world in peace;
Be of good courage;

Hold fast that which is good;
Render to no man evil for evil;
Strengthen the fainthearted;
Support the weak;
Help the afflicted;
Honour all men;
Love and serve the Lord, rejoicing
In the power of the Holy Spirit.
And the blessing of God Almighty, the Father, the
Son and the Holy Ghost, be upon you, and remain with
you forever.

With no respect for the wisdom of ages, for the value of tried-and-true ritual and custom, for the memory of beautiful words that creep into the fabric of the mind, heart and memory's grooves of habit, so that years later, the old words and responses revive and come back to comfort, these arrogant liturgical reformers have destroyed something ancient and precious.

And it hasn't even worked!

By dismantling the old liturgy, its language and poetry, they haven't attracted hordes of new Anglicans into the churches...

The faithful remnants just hang on, obediently going through the new unsatisfying motions. Others, like me, leave.

Worse still, to me, a whole generation have minds empty of the glorious prayers, words and phrases, which lifted the spirit and gave peace or comfort when needed...

Lord, now lettest thou thy servant depart in peace according to thy word... Come unto me, all ye that labour and are heavy laden, and I will give you rest... Thy word is a lantern to my feet; and a light unto my paths...where your treasure is, there will your heart be also... to everything there is a season, and a time to every purpose under the heaven...

The Authorised Version of the Bible had a vocabulary of about 8,000 words of *Anglo-Saxon* and *Latin* derivation compared with Shakespeare's 60,000 or so, but the scholars and translators kept the rhythms and idioms of the original Hebrew, and that is what is always missing from the clumsy modern translations. Many of the phrases too, were straight from the Hebrew, according to Benson Bobrick's book *The Making of the English Bible... 'the apple of his eye...a stranger in a strange land...a man after his own heart... a labour of love... the root of all evil.'*

The old translators also used the rhythms of Hebrew, as in a *'man of strength'*, instead of a *'strong man'*, or *'the holy of holies'*, instead of the *'holiest place'.* It's rather moving to think that the eloquence which formed the minds and thoughts of English-speaking peoples were based on the actual speech patterns of Jesus. But not anymore.

And I think it's one of the reasons that the use of English has deteriorated. When people grew up hearing the Bible, the simple, elegant language of *Wycliffe, Tyndale* and *Coverdale,* polished by the skill and scholarship of the authorised scholars, praying in the beautifully chosen words of Cranmer, using and reciting the Lord's prayer regularly, the balance and rhythm of simple resonant prose and poetry subconsciously influenced and educated them in a way that children no longer experience.

When ten-year-old *Piers* was at St Kentigern Prep School, and exposed for a few years to these very influences, he met me by chance one day, coming back from school, laden down with books, and desperate for a lift. He took another way home, and there was Grannie. As he climbed into my car his first words were: 'God moves in mysterious ways'...

Elfrida Vipont, who as a Quaker worships in silence, described Cranmer's work as 'the re-shaping of the Liturgy in language so beautiful that it has become part of our national heritage,' and the Authorized Version of the Bible 'which has powerfully influenced the lives of the English speaking peoples.' And a handful of philistines in the Anglican Church have felt free to dismantle the culture of the English-speaking peoples. I feel the most incredible grief at this careless and ignorant destruction – actually, vandalism... it feels worse than the burning of the Great Library of Alexandria.

Annabel rang for a chat. I told her about the homeless people in the doorways who I stopped to talk to after the concert, and what warm, friendly people they were, and how it was misfortune and having no one who cared enough to help which had brought them to this pass. She told me she had a friend who went to help in a soup kitchen every fortnight, and how he had taken his girlfriend and his mother too. I asked Annabel if she would go, and she said yes.

She then told me a little vignette of school and teenage life, which wrings the heart for several reasons.

It was about a girl who had no real friends 'she was a bit nerdy, always swotting, and she was always criticising, so no one liked her.' She told them all it was her birthday, and she would be having a party at a shopping mall. Annabel cried off, since she had a rehearsal of the inter-school concert.

One of Annabel's friends went out to St Luke's to meet her mother who worked there, and the birthday girl rushed up, and said, *'Oh, thank you for coming, you're the only one.'* So Annabel's friend said, *'Look I've just got to get some money from my mother, and I'll be back.'* She rushed to her mother, and rang Annabel and another friend, and they dropped everything and drove out as fast as they could. So the poor girl had a party, and was grateful that at least three of them had turned up.

Annabel, on the other hand, has really got her life working ... great exam results, nice boyfriend, good car, good job, and all's right with her world. Talking to her, I learned about party buses. A bus, a driver, some seats, and they dance in the aisle. They all pile aboard, shut the doors, and the driver drives them all over Auckland (I'm not sure why, maybe to various pubs), and they get home in the small hours. Her mother says it's wonderful, because you know they will be completely safe, you know where they are – in a manner of speaking – and there aren't any gate-crashers or stoushes!

I thought back to the little girl with no front teeth who would come and stay the weekend with Grannie. She would arrive, unpack her bag, hang up her clothes, spread her white embroidered nightie on the bed, place her 'pigs' (the pink piggie-faced fluffy slippers I'd given her years before) by the bed, arrange all her jewels, and toiletries, toys and dollies, and within five minutes would have transformed the spare room into a little girl's boudoir. I miss those days. This was the little girl too, who I promised I would 'move' all her dozens of dollies when they moved house, so they could sit on the back seat in my car and have 'fresh air'. Even today, tucked away at the back of her cupboard they are all propped up in various positions so that they can still breathe!

June 17

Yesterday, after leaving notes around the house for months, with the word 'passport' on them, I finally drummed up the emotional strength to look for it in the place I hoped it was, but feared it wasn't. And if it wasn't there, where was it? But it was! Now I regret that I hadn't grasped the nettle earlier. For the last year I've been suppressing low-level anxiety about it, even having nightmares of arriving at the airport and finding I had no passport, and I could have cleared it all up in a moment if I had had any strength of character, and had stopped procrastinating!

It was out of date, as I had suspected, so I rang the British High Commission, and did all the hopeless ringing of endless extensions with just an answer-phone message, and the endless instructions to ring this extension and that extension, none of which had any relevance to me. Finally, I rang a number that wasn't on offer, and struck a human being. Now I have spent hours filling in the arcane form she sent, after having the most hideous passport photo taken this afternoon. My only hope is that I am unrecognisable!

I'm struggling through a book on the Desert War, which Roland lent me, *Setting the Desert on Fire*, by *James Barr*. The intricate Arab politics and devious British diplomatic manoeuvrings are bewildering and rather boring. However, I have discovered that *Lawrence's* celebrated tale about being sodomised by the Turkish Bey was apparently not true. He told no one at the time, and only revealed it eighteen months later in his book, The Seven Pillars...

Lawrence's account is mystifying. As the book asks, how did he know what the stripes on his back – which he described in such detail as each lash fell – looked like? How come they then put him in an insecure hut, where by astonishing good luck, he also found some old clothes, and was able to escape? How come he looked fit and relaxed on his return to Aqaba, as film footage of him in Jerusalem two days later showed? And the by-now dead Bey's outraged relatives produced evidence to show that the Bey was an inveterate womaniser, rather than a sodomiser!

But I do find what the book has to say about Palestine very interesting, including Balfour's words: '*It being clearly understood that nothing shall be done which may prejudice the civil and religious rights of existing non-Jewish communities in Palestine, or the rights and political status enjoyed by Jews in any other country.'*

But it didn't work out like that and the Palestinians lost out, and so did the Jews in other countries who ended up being expelled as scapegoats for the Zionists.

According to *Sheik Abdullah*, the Arabs were *'annoyed and insulted by the Zionist immigration, but not alarmed by it.'* In the 1920s, Jewish immigration was small, but in the 1930s, the Depression and Hitler's rise to power caused a huge jump in the figures. Speaking in 1947, Sheik Abdullah told an audience, that in 1932 only 9,500 Jews came, but this didn't bother them as they never thought their Arab majority would be in danger. But the next year 1933, when Hitler came to power, immigration jumped to 30,000, in 1934 it was 42,000, and in 1935, it was 61,000.

And, of course, it has never stopped, the Arabs have been kicked out, and the Israelis are still stealing more land and still squeezing out the remaining Arabs in the West Bank.

Their policies in refusing to allow Arabs to travel from the West Bank and be with their families beggars belief; even, I read today, denying an orphaned eight-year-old girl whose parents had been killed in the fighting, the right to join other members of her family in Gaza.

The west nags on about human rights abuses in Russia, China, Myanmar, and Zimbabwe, but we leave the Israelis to systematically annihilate the Palestinians, squeezing them into ghettos with not enough water and a lack of everything, which was what the Nazis did to them. The Israelis even seem to have got away with building what they euphemistically call a 'wall'. It's actually a barrier stretching several hundred kilometres, averaging seventy metres in width, constructed out of concrete, barbed wire, electric fencing and ditches with tank patrol lanes, and no-go zones, which disrupts and interferes with the movements and livelihoods of all Palestinians.

I did enjoy the vignette of Allenby and his troops entering Jerusalem after the Turks had retreated. A cable from London had told him to walk in and not ride, since when the Kaiser had pranced in on horseback by the same gate, comments went round the world that a better man than he had walked in. Allenby cabled back to set his government's heart at rest, and tell its anxious members that he and all his soldiers had all entered on foot.

June 19

My seventy-first birthday, cards and calls from everyone. We enjoyed a sumptuous lunch at Ascension Winery – duck breast on sweet and tangy red cabbage, and a salad of rocket, pear, walnuts and Gorgonzola, plus a glass of ordinary Pinot Gris. Patrick had a steak inevitably, and a huge helping of kumara chips. We shared a delicious hot chocolate pudding, and I savoured a glass of dessert wine too.

Then we had a wander round the Red Barn. I came out with a treasure for $5: a deep willow-patterned cup – it looks very fine with a lighted beeswax candle sitting in it at the moment. My requested birthday presents were *Albion's Seed,* by David Hackett Fischer, a feast, 1,000 pages long, full of facts, maps, family trees and history, meat and drink to me, and an antique book, *The Myths of Greece and Rome* by *H.A. Guerber.*

Last night, Derek and Gill rang via Skype from Plymouth, and we talked about everything from botany to books for over an hour. Derek sloped off to make coffee and came back to tantalise me by waving rich tea biscuits (unobtainable here) in front of the screen, and recommended books to read, while Gill rushed out to the garden to bring in, and waggle in front of the screen, her penstemons, Mrs. Simkins and other treasures she'd bought the day before. The rescued cat, Monty, was also dangled in front of the screen (reluctantly). Good fun.

Valerie Davies

A freezing night, and so contentedly to warm bed, with a cup of hot chocolate spiked with a dash of Kahlua and my great new doorstop of a book.

11

Jul/Aug 2009

July 13

I've spent the last three weeks looking after the grandsons, walking sweet, boisterous Lucy, answering Eugenie's emails, and occasionally drumming up the energy to see a friend. I visited Ginny in her stark penthouse, Stella in her gracious art deco home, lunching on the new terrace on one of the few sunny days, and then Marianne in her huge ground floor flat, crammed with her covetable paintings, and grey, painted French furniture... everyone else was away, or working.

I cooked a roast dinner for Roland and all the grandchildren; watched him watching Annabel prattling on about the arrangements for the pre-ball and after-ball parties, and was touched by the tender expression and loving half-smile on his face as he listened to his darling daughter being deliciously featherheaded and very practical at the same time ... watched Kristin Scott Thomas in *I've loved You so Long*, and bought lotsa' books – ten in all – all with birthday book tokens

Apropos of all the moon landing anniversary articles, I was very taken, when I mentioned to Roland that I had taken him and Eugenie as four and five-year-olds to view the moon rocks in the Ocean Terminal in Kowloon, that he remembered. He remembered the endless queue and then when we finally got there, the sense of disappointment at how small they were, and wondering if they really did come from the moon. I too remember thinking how disappointingly small they were, and without any presence.

Apart from a rather one-dimensional first novel about East Prussia when the Russians invaded, which I read because I wanted to piece together the refugee situation that I'd been conscious of at Belsen as a child, I only read Antony Beevor's '*D-day*.' I found it less interesting than his other books, which had covered so much ground that no one else, had done. Here, he was walking in the footsteps of so many others, including Max Hastings' authoritative Armageddon.

There were lots of small insights, like the shocking fact that an American commander flattened the ancient French village of Mortain in pique because they had had a hard fight with the Germans round it. Apparently, the Americans treated France like a conquered,

backward territory, not expecting to even find a cine-
ma! They've just done it in Iraq too, digging trenches
through Babylon, and knocking that ancient city about
in the name of military necessity.

I couldn't help contrasting this with Colonel Tim
Collins' pep-talk to his regiment, the 1st Battalion of
the Royal Irish before they went into Iraq, when
amongst other inspiring things he told them: 'Iraq is
steeped in history. It is the site of the Garden of Eden,
of the Great Flood, and the birthplace of Abraham.
Tread lightly there... you will have to go a long way to
find a more decent, generous and upright people than
the Iraqis...' I had always wondered why only the
French and Americans liberated Paris, but according
to Beevor, the infuriating Monty had turned down the
invitation to join the Allies for the symbolic entry into
the capital, for no apparent reason. As a very young
captain in the army in 1962, I remember having to go
to an officers' lecture at the Officers' Library at Aldershot. Unusually, all our names had to be submitted and
approved beforehand, and once there, the grounds and
parking area were crawling with military police, and
our identity was checked before we were allowed to
enter the hall. No one had any idea what the lecture
was going to be about, so it was a complete surprise
when Montgomery was ushered onto the stage and giv-
en a great welcome.

Valerie Davies

I remember little of his talk; it seemed to be mostly showing off, and getting cheap laughs from the audience at the expense of the kilt-wearing Highland officers down in the front. I sat there priggish and poker-faced, all of twenty-three, refusing to laugh. He just seemed a tiny little exhibitionist, strutting about the stage wangling good-mannered or sycophantic laughter. My father, who had been a genuine Desert Rat in the famous 7th Armoured Division, couldn't bear him either. Churchill reputedly described him as: *'In war unbeatable. In peace unbearable.'*

Perhaps the most interesting thing about Beevor's book for me, was his description of the hour before midnight on 5 June 1944, when '...the roar of hundreds of aircraft engines in a constant stream could be heard over villages in southern and central England. People in their nightclothes went out into their gardens to stare up at the seemingly endless air armada silhouetted against the scudding clouds'.

Another piece of the jigsaw that I keep putting together of my childhood. With my father abroad throughout the war, and my mother gone, I've only had fragments of memory of those times. From reading Beevor I now know that that was the night, as a six-year-old, that I lay in bed rigid with fear, having woken to the noise, and hearing the thunder of those hundreds of planes passing over us in Weymouth. I had thought they were Hitler's planes coming for us. Since my mother was out as usual, I lay and waited for the air raid warning which never came, so as to get my fifteen-month-old brother and five-year-old sister downstairs to the air raid shelter.

It seemed even more sinister that we had no air raid warning... what had happened to the people who usually warned us? By now I had learned to make scrambled egg to feed the baby, and even today, the smell of Farley's rusks dissolved in milk for him, brings back those bleak times. Apart from Beevor, I didn't read any of my other books. After my weekend course, I lost my concentration. I found it was the same for Belinda.

I fed the birds each day before breakfast, then I could sit and watch them gather on the grass outside the French windows... a pair of blackbirds, two plump pink-breasted doves, a shower of sparrows of course, a male chaffinch with his rosy bosom and smart black and white markings, a few silvereyes, and of course, the inevitable hungry and determined starlings and my-nahs. I learned at lunch at Stella's that the mynahs were imported from India to sit on the cattle and re-move the ticks. All I can say is that they are not on the job, being far too busy marauding around the rest of the countryside, terrorising other birds, and playing chicken on country roads...

Walking Lucy in Cornwall Park or around the Epsom streets was a pleasure when I wasn't tired, or still recovering from a badly twisted ankle caused by hanging onto the lead when she took off down a slope at full pelt after a provocative yapping little dog. Scents of daphne and jasmine floating on the air, the colours of pink and white magnolias, cherry blossom, scarlet and bright pink camellias, and pale pink luculia, with clear blue sky behind, make Auckland a joy at this time of the year. On the other hand, I dislike Auckland at night; all the lights which blot out the stars, street lights shining in the windows lighting up the bedroom, the noise of ambulance and police sirens, and other people's parties.

Gracious Epsom has become a Chinese suburb, so Cornwall Park was full of dogged Chinese (or perhaps Asian would be more accurate) walkers, who all shrink away from Lucy as though she is about to spring on them and tear them apart.

The downside of this Asian settlement is that the gracious old houses get torn down and big new stucco palaces go up, while the trees and gardens of Epsom are also gradually disappearing.

I used to wait every year for one splendid, full-grown liquid amber to flaunt its autumn glory, until the day the Asian owners moved in and chopped it down... the latest is one of my favourite gardens near

Eugenie, with paths and topiary, trees and grass – a green garden.

The new Asian owners have chopped down all the trees, rooted out all the hedges, and are now erecting a high, wooden fence all around the property so that no one can see in, presumably to protect them from bandits, triad members, kidnappers and other criminals in law-abiding Epsom. I remember high-walled homes with spikes on top to keep out malefactors in Hong Kong, forty years ago. So many Chinese were fearful, probably with good reason.

Michael's malus trees are still waiting to bud up. He lives in a house a few doors from Eugenie, hidden from the road down a straight drive lined with standard malus, which arch across to meet in the middle. When they bloom, the drive is a romantic tunnel of cloudy pink and white blossom. Between the trees are camellias trimmed into pyramidal columns, and white Japanese anemones cover the ground. It makes me realise how old I am, to realise that Michael, the young black-eyed, black-haired law student with whom I used to sing songs like Where'er you Walk, while Oiroa played the piano, is now a judge, whose profoundly common-sense pronouncements from the bench give me great satisfaction.

One of the days, Charlie came home from an exam, and told me that when everyone walked out at the end, and opened their cell phones, they all found messages from their friends telling them that Michael Jackson had died. I found it very intriguing to imagine this host of youngsters peering at their text messages in a teenage reflex action, and all finding the same thing.

Stella said what I felt... that the papers and TV were full of nothing but stuff about a person in whom she hadn't the slightest interest. My real sadness came on learning that the chimp that Jackson had curled up to sleep with, who went around in nappies, has since been jettisoned, and now exists in a sanctuary for abandoned chimps.

Many comments on TV that it would be like Diana's death.

I felt like saying, not really – the acres of flowers outside Buckingham Palace, Kensington Palace, and all through Kensington Gardens, were an outpouring of genuine grief at the loss of someone who symbolised love and compassion, beauty and fun to people around the world.

The film I saw of the weekend after her funeral, as people wandered through Kensington Gardens, lighting candles, making shrines, pinning notes and cards and mementoes to the trees; the softness, the gentleness, the quiet sadness, the sense of loss, and the connection between people of all ages and nationalities, was unforgettable.

It's become fashionable since then to denigrate the wave of love and grief which swept the world, suggesting it was a hysterical mass reaction. But it wasn't. Deborah Bull, the well-known ballerina and columnist, wrote in her diary of Diana's funeral being: *'the most comprehensive and controlled display of public grief I am ever likely to witness...'* Diana had penetrated to a core of longing for goodness and compassion in many people whose hearts were open, and her death hurt those who loved her.

And they were many. Since then, her reputation has been undermined by the continuing stream of writings by people who have wanted to expose her weaknesses, and make money from the love and interest people had in her.

Part of her extraordinary attraction was that in her lifetime, she often seemed to personify all the various feminine archetypes described by Jean Bolen in her book 'The Goddesses in Everywoman.' The shy young girl who became engaged to the heir to the throne was the personification of Persephone/Proserpine. The negative aspects of Persephone include powerlessness, which results in deviousness, lying and manipulation, which supporters of her husband accused Diana of. Persephone, when she was in the underworld, became depressed and didn't eat, another famous characteristic of Diana.

She then became a doting mother like Demeter/Ceres, who rescued her daughter from the underworld. The Ceres archetype demonstrates maternal love, not just for her own children, but for all children, and one only has to remember the numerous pictures of Diana cuddling children to recognise that symbolism. Ceres is also the supportive friend, the one who, like Diana, offered support in the letters she wrote to cancer patients, spending time with her friend dying of AIDS, and making regular visits to patients and children in hospital. Volunteers who work in childcare centres, hospitals and so on are exhibiting their Ceres side, a very strong one in Diana.

As Diana's beauty blossomed, she became the archetype of Aphrodite/Venus, the goddess of love, and her spoiling of *James Hewitt*, such as buying him expensive clothes, was an aspect of the love-besotted Aphrodite. The sparkle and beauty that she developed were part of the legendary allure of the Aphrodite woman.

And when Diana began growing into her career, she displayed very impressive Athena/Minerva qualities of commitment and concentration on the details of her work so that she was always boned up and prepared for her assignments, according to her staff. Perhaps her courage in walking through a minefield was part of the Athene archetype. Her commitment to her good health and fitness was another Athene characteristic – one of Athene's minor goddess roles was as the goddess of health, Hygeia.

Diana's brother famously compared her with the goddess of the hunt, *Artemis the Greek, Diana,* the Roman name for the goddess. He described the huntress becoming the hunted, pursued by the press pack. But in her lifetime, her identification with the downtrodden and the homeless, and her concerns for victims of war, disease or landmines, were very typical of the Artemis/Diana archetype. The picture of her holding a grieving woman in a churchyard in Bosnia was a graphic illustration of this aspect of Artemis.

As Hera/Juno, wife of the king of heaven, she was perhaps most recognisable to the many women who identified with her. As the spurned wife, she revealed all the famous characteristics of the angry, jealous Hera, hurt wife of unfaithful, philandering Zeus, and, like Hera, displaying the rage and vindictiveness which caused her to name her rival 'the Rottweiler'. Classically, Diana, like Hera, felt married to her core, and was on record as saying she didn't want a divorce in spite of the troubles in her marriage. This is typical Hera, who continues to feel married even after divorce, and so continues to feel pain every time she's reminded that she's not.

Valerie Davies

Towards the end of her life, Diana seemed to be displaying some of the domestic home-loving qualities of Hestia/Vesta, the goddess of the hearth, beginning an art collection, and searching for a quieter, more private life (her brother refused her the country cottage on his estate that she wanted as a refuge). And as jealous, wounded ex-wife she was at the same time also flaunting the wilder and more negative aspects of Hera and Aphrodite by flirting with the unworthy Dodi Fayed... almost, it seemed, in wounded retaliation for Charles's public display of devotion to Camilla, when he threw a grand party for her fiftieth birthday and showered his mistress with diamonds. (Charles's behaviour had caused consternation in the army for years among those like the dyed-in-the-wool colonel friend who said to us that he couldn't condone it).

In her short flight through the imagination of the world, Diana blazed and died out like a shooting star, loved by many and despised by others. Some men and women were repelled by her... I've often wondered if, on the one hand, they unconsciously recognised their own archetypes or were dealing unwillingly with such an archetype in their own lives, as Diana mirrored each aspect of the goddesses so powerfully. She pressed people's buttons. A lot of fun and fashion and compassion disappeared when Diana left the world. 'We had become accustomed to her smile; we had become accustomed to her face...'

I used to look at the tall, young gods/teenagers I was caring for, and loved them for their sweetness, for that sense of their budding manhood. Piers was so capable when I was struggling with uncomprehending Spanish receptionists, trying to contact his parents, and took over the phone with such authority. Charlie and his friends at fifteen are teetering on the edge of young manhood, and I've never been more aware of the sensitivity and beauty of young men. When I left, I bent down to the sleeping giant, as I called Piers, stretched out, dozing on the sofa, and he put up his arms to hug me so tenderly, that I dared to kiss him goodbye (on the cheek).

I went for a weekend course with Cindy. At the end I felt I had been handed the keys of heaven. As a scientist, she was able to explain quantum physics in a way that I understood, and could see that scientists are now describing what mystics have understood for centuries. We explored higher states of consciousness and also released lots of buried childhood feelings – more of the 'unexamined' life dragged into awareness.

Both Belinda and Frances were there too, I couldn't begin to count the number of different courses I've done with both of them. It was a weekend enhanced by the elemental weather howling in across the harbour, and beating up against the windows. The house sits almost over the water, with just a few pohutukawa trees growing on the side of the cliff between it and the sea, and it felt like an ocean liner carving its way through storm-tossed seas. When the worst squalls battered against the windows and shook the house, it almost felt like connecting with great winds of the galaxy, as though our focused wills were drawing the creative forces of the cosmos towards us.

And now home, laden with Eugenie's lavish presents from France and Spain... two silk pashminas, a classic faded patchwork cushion cover from Provence, and a red crocodile Guy Laroche wallet... I shall feel rich every time I pull it out of my handbag. I drove through a storm, which had turned, into a hurricane by the time I reached the village.

The wind was screaming through the trees, huge grey swells crested with white were hurling themselves against the rocks, and the air was filled with leaves and salt spray, and thunderous noise. Exhilarating. Cold though it was, I left the window open through the night so that I could hear the continuous thunder of the waves.

Cara was a little standoffish after my absence, but at least not so angry that she spat at me, and hung onto the carpet of her cage with her claws like she did when we collected her from a cattery for the first time! Heaven to be in my own bed, in the pitch dark, and to hear nothing but the wind and the waves.

July 17

The day after I returned, I went over to Eugenie's house, and to my horror, as soon as I opened the door, I knew the deep freeze was off. The stench of rotting food was horrendous. So on with the rubber gloves, finding the bucket, detergents and disinfectants. I was just about to collapse with a cup of tea to recover from this ordeal, when the phone rang. Patrick's nephew, wife and two teenagers said they were fifteen minutes away, and would be dropping in on their way home...

Still recovering, as much from the course as the marathon stint with the boys... I find that others have also been feeling exhausted... releasing so much of the buried pain we touched into at the weekend, I suppose – in other words, a healing crisis. A great session at acupuncture, Lyn restored my twisted ankle to full mobility. I had no idea how much it still hurt until she started poking around.

On returning to the car parked outside, I found a brown paper bag stuffed under the windscreen wipers. I pulled it out with foreboding, and was right to be foreboded. A doddery old man with Parkinson's (I discovered later) had bashed into the two side doors. How, no one can visualise, since it was parked perfectly ordinarily alongside the kerb, opposite a right-hand road, with plenty of room if he had wanted to do a U-turn. Que sera, sera... but very inconvenient; half an hour's drive to a panel beater. He was unrepentant and quite tetchy.

Driving home through the grey misty morning, it was low tide at Whangateau, with the wind whipping up ribbons of steel grey water curling across the channels in the sands. The rain now is steady and heavy, but I am sitting here with the French windows open, listening to the sound of it falling, and dripping off the trees and shrubs. It's beautiful, and yet I'm conscious that it isn't for all the sodden creatures in unsheltered fields.

When the government paid a subsidy to farmers in the 1970s to fence their fields with wire and posts, they forthwith ripped out all the old hedges of hawthorn and bramble planted by the settlers, and put in their subsidised fences, thus gaining another yard of grazing land round every field. And at the same time, they destroyed homes for birds, and shelter for animals from bitter wind and rain and the blazing sun, as well as removing sustenance for man, as well as wildlife, since we can no longer go picking blackberries, nuts, and sometimes apples. It must have changed the microclimates too, with nothing to stop the wind howling across the paddocks. I'm reminded of Mao Tse-Tung's mad murder of all the sparrows in China and the resulting famine and dust bowl created by locusts eating all the grass because there were no sparrows left to eat them...

I've been pushing into the fire the last twigs and handfuls of leaves that we gathered from the eucalyptus tree, which came down in the great storm two years ago. They are dry and crackling, and the aromatic scent fills the room. I shall be sad when the last fragments have gone up in smoke.

July 20

Last night, we went for drinks with Mike and Annie. They had friends there as well, and from the moment we walked into the room, some wonderful alchemy began to manifest, and we had a rollicking laughing occasion. All too short.

The weather continues stormy and wild. Cold winds, icy rains. I enjoy it, and yet I hate to think of wet calves and lambs being born into this bitter rain and wind, with no shelter or barn like they would have in England, and no cowherd, farmer or shepherd to help either cow or ewe. Sheep take their chances and die alone on New Zealand hills.

We're burning pine logs now, and the resinous smell of pine permeates the room. When the TV crew came last week to interview Patrick for some book programme, I had a long and impassioned discussion with the soundman, who had the same type of wood burner. We agreed that it was great for boiling water, frying bacon and eggs, and heating a stew during a power cut.

Waking in the night at the height of the storm, I looked out of the window towards the sea, in the direction of the dawn. It was pitch black, and most unusually, a ship, outlined with light, was slowly moving across the bay. I watched till the trees hid it, and thought how fortunate we are today, that we don't have to worry about 'those in peril on the sea'. A hundred years ago, everyone was in peril in a storm.

Julian had his operation on Friday followed by a number of painful complications. Eugenie, of course, is rising to the occasion with her usual magnificence. But I worry about her too... her emails to me on business matters about their house next door, were timed for 6.30 a.m., and she had got up at five. Tonight, when she rang, she was cooking supper after being at the hospital most of the day, and when home, had caught up on unnecessary things like ironing; she said she felt refreshed after meditating. Thank heavens she does.

Some night birds are screeching. I wish I knew what they were. Someone told me they had come from Great Barrier Island. Patrick showed me how to Google Katie Melua, who sings the entrancing song When You Taught Me How to Dance, from the film

Miss Potter. It's been on my mind for weeks since I saw
the film again on TV. I only watched it for the song,
and the sequence where they dance to the musical box.
It has stayed with me since I first heard it a couple of
years ago, and I went back a second time to see the
film, just to hear the song.

When troubadours and minnesingers travelled
around towns and isolated villages in medieval times
they must have been welcomed with such joy, to sing
their precious songs in the halls and round the fires.
Their memories would have lingered, and people would
have tried to remember the songs and hum them, and
would have been saddened as day by day the tunes faded in their memories and they would have longed for
the troubadours to return and to hear the songs again.

I felt like that about 'When You Taught Me How to
Dance.' How can you get to hear the song from a film
track, I felt? But now I can play it at will, it has lost its
tantalising, magic pull. This is what the twentieth century has done to music. In 1953, when the music master at my boarding school in the Cameron Highlands in
Malaya acquired a copy of Beethoven's Symphony No.
9, conducted by Toscanini, we senior girls were invited
to listen to the sacred record. It was a Sunday afternoon and we sat shyly and solemnly in the staff-room
and were overwhelmed by it.

Valerie Davies

When the music master found the art master thundering out the last movement on the piano in the assembly hall, a great feud erupted between them which lasted the whole term; the art master seeing no reason for not extemporising on the piano, and the music master condemning him for bowdlerising and cheapening Beethoven's masterpiece. It seemed to matter terribly. Those who liked the art master were on his side. Those who didn't like him were for the music master. And I used to stand for hours by a crackling radio late at night in the holidays, craning to hear Tchaikovsky, Grieg, Mozart – coming faintly from far away, probably on a distant BBC World programme.

Music was hard to come by then, and so far more significant than it is today. And we made our own. Some nights we sat outside the house by the river at Kota Bharu, when a group of chaps used to come, and all the generations sat and sang to someone's flute – songs like 'The Foggy,' 'Foggy Dew,' 'Skip to My Lou,' and 'On Top of Old Smoky.'

Lots of Burl Ives. We didn't sing well, we just enjoyed singing. (Where we sat under the stars by the river, the Japanese had passed in their motor boats at dawn, twelve years before, on the morning they invaded Malaya. The line of bullet holes from their machine guns was still there in the pink stucco walls, testimony to their random brutality.)

Knowing that Renee Zellweger produced the Beatrix Potter film, I can see her fingerprints. Strange how people who speak English as their birthright also think they understand English customs – in this case imagining ridiculous afternoon teas with chinless wonders and their mothers to introduce Beatrix to a husband – the reality was that the marriage market was held at dances, and she would have learned to dance before she was out of the schoolroom.

Neither would she have dragged the old chaperone around like a drowned rat. Girls stopped being chaperoned out walking in Jane Austen's day, hence Elizabeth Bennett going for long walks, and meeting Darcy and Col Fitzwilliam in Rosings Park, as well as walking across the fields to sick Jane at Netherfield Hall, arriving with her famously muddied petticoats.

July 22

I went to see the film 'Phèdre' at Matakana. Wonderful staging and acting, and also wonderful to know we were seeing the whole play, with no cuts, sexing up for film, or otherwise tinkering with the original. By using a huge crag of rock to support the heavy slab of ceiling, along with the simple magnificence of the marble floor, the men in ordinary military fatigues or working clothes, and the women in long, flowing, timeless robes of no particular date, they somehow achieved a classical Grecian feel, and at the same time a contemporary feel. Greek pillars and classical robes would have dated it, and pushed it back in time.

And yet, powerful as it was, afterwards I drove home thinking I had just seen a collection of people feeling they were victims of the gods, instead of attempting to use some insight and help themselves. And by allowing themselves to be victims of their own passions, they brought their own disaster upon themselves. Everyone took themselves so seriously that everyone lost their sense of proportion. It brought home to me how even if one has no insight, even a sense of humour can bring sanity and normality into life. Feeling this way makes me feel like a philistine, but I didn't experience the sense of catharsis which was supposed to be the raison d'etre for Greek tragedies.

It reminded me of an essay I had to write for 'A'-level studies fifty-five years ago, discussing whether you could have a successful or great tragedy, if the people involved were not great people in themselves. And the reverse, that you can't have great tragedy if the people involved are trivial. I suppose Theseus would have been called a great king in that scenario.

But I now measure greatness so differently that I have different measurements for everything else too. Courage (he did, after all, brave the Minotaur), bravado in battle, success with women, arrogance, pride, and desire for revenge, so he cursed his son in his rage asking the gods to destroy him, all these qualities of Theseus, leave me cold.

Greatness, to me, is personified by someone like Caliph Umar, the Muslim conqueror of Jerusalem in 637 CE. The Christian and Jewish inhabitants of the city capitulated on condition the Caliph received the surrender in person. Umar entered the city dressed in tattered robes, accompanied by one slave, carrying only dates, a water skin and a sack of barley. He ruled with wisdom and mercy and preserved all the holy places in the city. The city prospered under his tolerance and clemency. No one died needlessly. Culture, religion, arts and agriculture all flourished. That's greatness to me... *'Mercy... becomes the throned monarch better than his crown...'*

The vicar has replied somewhat crisply to my long diatribe about the liturgy. I sent him what I had written, and asked if there was another view. There was. He told me the Maori Prayer was early missionary Henry William's original translation – which I would have found fascinating if I'd known at the time... why don't they tell you?

He also said the prayer I disliked was written by an English priest in the 1980s, and *'reflects both the times it was written, the theology of the 1980s and the limitations thereof. It is a prayer beloved by many here...'* I replied that the Book of Common Prayer had also been beloved, and this begged the question of when prayers become obsolete, how long they lasted, and who decided when they were outmoded.

He had suggested that the Book of Common Prayer should be banned, it does *'nothing except fossilise God'...* I learn from others that the vicar is a good man who does good works, even though I, and others, I have also learned, disagree with his literary tastes!

I've just re-read the whole of Susan Cooper's (five books) *The Dark is Rising series.* It was a strange experience. I used to be so paralysed with fear over *the battle with the Dark,* I could hardly read them before. Same with *The Lord of the Rings.* Now that I've cleared so much childhood fear I found I could read all five at one gulp, without so much as a twinge. I may never read them again; they have lost their power over me.

July 23

Dawn was calm and pink. A respite in the middle of the stormy weather. Yet it feels as though we've passed the peak of winter, and the daffodils are out under the trees, a sure sign. A rabbit bobbed into sight outside the sitting room window yesterday, but I discover from my neighbour, Kate, that he is an unloved and well-known rabbit. Poor little thing. We have so little wildlife in this country that I rather treasure what small manifestations make their presence felt... no hares or moles or badgers, no small deer, no squirrels or shrews, water voles or foxes to name a few.

I've been yearning for a good massage. I found a good woman, Danish, Kristina, and during the session, she told me about her encounter with an angel when she was at sea on a fishing trawler. She's a tiny little thing, and was doing a man's job back then, as a fisherman, and working a hundred hours a week. Her back was aching; she had toothache and was at the end of her strength. On her six-hour sleep shift, she sat on her bunk and wept, and in despair said aloud 'Help me.'

She then saw a bright light, which materialised into a figure about seven feet high, though she couldn't see the face. She felt it was female, and this great column of light said words to her which she says she's never forgotten, 'Let your mind be still.' Kristina leant against her in deep peace, and the next thing she knew, she was waking at the end of her six hours sleep, all her pains and misery gone, feeling bright and strong again. 'The angel healed me,' she said.

I've given up eating fish now that she has told me she used to dread the catch being pulled in, and how cruel it was for the fish. She confirmed what I had always feared. But my diet is becoming increasingly narrow!

Valerie Davies

Went to a preparatory meeting with eight others to discuss starting a *'Course in Miracles'* study group. It didn't appeal to me, but the idea of a group did, since there is a hole we are all feeling now that our other little group has dissolved. I've resisted the Course in Miracles for years; I've felt the people doing it have never been my sort. It seemed too doctrinaire, and I never saw any signs of change in the one person who spent most time proselytising me. Jackson persuaded me that perhaps there was a way of opening up to a wider perspective... so I went to the meeting.

To my dismay, a woman I've been running away from for some years turned up. She gives me the impression of having a completely closed mind, because she says now that she possesses the 'Peace of God', she's finished with all that growth stuff. All we need to do, she kept saying, is to read the Course. In spite of Jackson being, as it were, the convenor, she hogged the space – I have some work to do on this issue, while Jackson announced at the end of the evening he wouldn't be back!

I sat next to an intriguing man who lives in an eco-village. There are fifteen houses there, each with five acres, and a hundred acres of common land. Lots of tree planting naturally! Colin spoke fluently about the spiritual path, and we seemed to be on the same wavelength. He's lent me a good book on the Course. He

332

told me he had left South Africa in 1974. He belonged to a Jehovah's Witness family, and through his teens they had prepared him, and trained him to face what was waiting for him: conscription.

When he refused, like all Jehovah's Witnesses, at twenty he was flung into solitary confinement, with no hope of release. It was a life sentence. He was stripped to his underpants and left alone with a Bible, a bucket of water for washing and drinking, and a chamber pot. He was allowed out once a day to fill the one, and empty the other. No exercise. Bread and water. A hunk of bread about six inches by four inches daily. He crumbled it into about five hundred crumbs, and then ate it slowly, crumb by crumb, with a sip of water after each mouthful, to try to make himself feel full. He read the Bible endlessly, prayed, did exercises, and watched an ant crawl up the wall to amuse himself, and make the time pass. No visitors. Only his faith in God kept him going.

Helen Suzman and Amnesty finally got him released after a year. He was given back his clothes, and asked to sign a form saying he had not been ill-treated. He gibbed at this, saying it was not true; so they said either he signed, and re-joined his parents who were waiting for him outside, or he went back to his cell... he signed. The whole family then fled to this country. He told me how, changing planes at Sydney and walking through the airport, they passed the restaurant. There was a white man sitting at a table eating with a black person. He burst into tears. Now he knew he was in a different world.

He speaks half a dozen languages, including Maori, and is a Sinophile who does Chinese translations from his home, a tiny dwelling, he says. He is a gentle, sensitive man, who I think must have been a monk for lifetimes, and still is, working away in his anchorite's cell.

July 27

Met Belinda at the market. We had, what pre-course would have been a coffee together, but this time, was a pot of pure herbal tea each! Everything seems to have a constant ripple of pleasure these days.

I'm finishing the biography of Lydia Lopokova, 'Bloomsbury Ballerina,' at the same time as I'm reading Colin's book, 'Path of Light,' by Robert Perry. 'Path of Light' has turned all my prejudices about A Course in Miracles on their heads, and I can see me taking it very seriously.

Lydia Lopokova was delicious. She was an Imperial-trained dancer, who joined Diaghilev's Ballet Russes in Paris, and was seduced into going to America with promises of great salaries. It sounded like Irina Baronova's story all over again, with Lopokova's career too collapsing on tiny stages on one night stands through one-horse towns where no one cared a crumpet about art, and didn't want 'highbrow immorality' on stage. Her struggles to survive as a classical dancer in America in the First World War were much the same as Baronova's during the Second World War.

During the Second World War, all Lopokova's brothers and sisters were in the ballet back in Russia, but only some of them survived the Siege of Leningrad, to then be faced with persecution. Fedor, her brother, a successful choreographer and director of the Mariinsky Theatre, now renamed the Bolshoi, fell foul of the authorities with a 'witty, graceful comedy' about a collective farm! His crime was to use Shostakovich's score, criticised as *'a pretence against music,'* and to put the cast of farm-workers in ballet shoes and do pointe work!

The librettist was sent to the gulag from which he never returned, and Fedor stripped of his new promotion as director of the Bolshoi.

The end of his career.

Maynard Keynes, Lopokova's husband, was a thirty-eight-year old homosexual bachelor when she charmed him into marriage in the thirties, and they lived happily ever after. His career however, was not unalloyed happiness.

After the despair, he felt over the Versailles Settlement after the First World War, he was dispatched to

Washington in the next war to negotiate the help Britain needed to stay in the struggle against Hitler.

The stress of his battle with the Americans killed him in the end. The US used this crisis in the world's history to attempt to destroy once and for all the power of Britain. The American loans, repaid with interest, took Britain sixty years to repay. As part of the Lend-Lease deal, the Americans required Britain to limit her export trade (her only form of survival), run down her gold and dollar reserves, and liquidate all her assets in the US. They even tried to restrict Britain's trade to specialist items like whisky and Harris tweed.

Maynard's job was to try to bargain for a better deal, but Britain was in no bargaining position. He achieved a little leeway over the whisky and the tweed, and got the Americans to let Britain hold some gold reserves. Fighting and winning two world wars ruined Britain.

Known for his integrity as well as brilliance, I rather liked this gentle thoughtful man's definition of capitalism: *'the astounding belief that the most wickedest of men will do the most wickedest of things for the greater good of everyone'!*

Strange how the historic hostility from the War of Independence has never really evaporated in the States –typified by Roosevelt continually nagging Churchill over giving up the Empire, (wasn't their acquisition of

Hawaii and the Philippines empire building?) and his son Elliott rather rudely tackling Churchill at Yalta, saying, *'What are you going to do about your Indians?'* and Churchill replying, *'Well, not what you did with yours.'*

Then Roosevelt and his envoys telling Stalin that this war would finish the British, so they didn't matter in the negotiations, and trying to arrange meetings behind Churchill's back. (Stalin and Roosevelt did actually make a secret treaty at Yalta over Japan.)

I go back to my old friend U.S. Grant, who at the end of his life wrote in his 1885 memoirs:

England and the United States are natural allies and should be the best of friends. They speak one language, and are related by blood and other ties... England governs her own colonies, and particularly those embracing people of different races from her own, better than any other nation...

He valued the support England gave the North during the Civil War, recording that:

Even in Manchester, which suffered fearfully by having the cotton cut off from her mills, they had a monster demonstration in favour of the North at the very time when their workmen were almost famishing.

Another president, Eisenhower, admitted to Sir John Colville that India was better governed under Britain than after Independence, but still complained about colonialism and the Empire! He said that liberty was more important to Americans than good government! Is it possible to have liberty without good government? But is it good government to allow everyone to carry firearms, to clamp medieval chains on prisoners' wrists and ankles, and allow bear-baiting in South Carolina? Or maybe these are liberties!

I've thought a lot about the vicar and the Prayer Book fossilising God. I know the phrase 'miserable sinners' used to drive people mad, including me, and yet now, I think that many people, until they recognise their underlying childhood knocks and fears, are unconsciously miserable. The ego is all about the unresolved conflicts of the past, the hidden wounds and unfulfilled needs from early childhood. And if you believe, as one would think vicars in the Anglican Church would, that sin is being unconscious and thus separated from God, then the phrase 'miserable sinners' is perfectly accurate.

Phrases like, '*Almighty God, in whom we live and move and have our being*'... are surely genuine spiritual insight... and spiritually accurate too. Surely believers aim to feel like that? And who could quarrel with such a prayer as, *'beseeching thee to inspire continually the universal church with the spirit of truth, unity and concord'...*

And the General Thanksgiving:

We bless thee for our creation, preservation, and all the blessings of this life... for the means of grace, and for the hope of glory... And we beseech thee, give us that due sense of all thy mercies, that our hearts may be unfeignedly thankful, and that we show forth thy praise, not only with our lips, but in our lives; by giving up ourselves to thy service, and walking before thee in holiness and righteousness all our days...

Archbishop Cranmer and his colleagues seem to me to have had a deep understanding of the spiritual life... and surely, the spiritual life doesn't date?

It's like saying the Upanishads fossilise God. The perfect antidote to all this, was to read in the Listener that in a McPhail and Gadsby TV skit, McPhail was kneeling at the communion table, and after sipping the communion wine, he handed it back and asked, *'You haven't got a Chablis have you?'*

This caused a nationwide storm.

Looking through an old diary from 1997, I found a piteous little quote from Charlie, when I went to pick up Piers for his first whole weekend with me. Charlie was four, and he said: *'Grannie, can we bof stay the whole weekend with you, and Piers can be my angel and look after me?'*

They did, and it was the only time any of the grand-children ever played me up. Little Charlie did, at bed-time, and when I finally came into the bedroom, and said I wouldn't be having them again together if they didn't settle down, Charlie started to giggle. As I stalked out, I heard Piers say to his brother: *'She means it, Charlie!'* And silence fell. We've often used that phrase since... *'She means it, Charlie...'*

I wish they were still little. The day before Charlie started school; I had him for the day, and took him to the beach, as I did with each grandchild. Mocking my-self, I said to him: *'Now darling I've asked each grand-child not to grow any older, and they've completely ignored me and gone on growing. Will you make sure you don't grow any older?'* And he said to me: *'I've got to, Grannie, but I'll still be your darling.'*

The weather is calm and bright, and absolutely freezing. The sky sparkles with stars at night, and the sea is flat, like an inland lake. The Southern Cross points brightly across the water, and I long to know the other stars in the southern sky, Orion's Girdle I can make out and the Pot Handle, but the rest of the galaxies and constellations are unknown to me. This is what comes of being uprooted from one's past. One night as a sixteen-year-old, I stood on a cliff edge in Malacca with my father, and he pointed out the North Star and the Southern Cross in the same night sky, and said I'd never see them both together again.

July 28

A fat blackbird is sitting on a bending branch of the Queen of the Night, gobbling all the white berries.

And a tui was sitting on the edge of the bird bath, before taking the plunge, at just the right angle for the sun to shine on him, revealing all the glossy turquoise feathers. His little white bobble at the neck, which caused the settlers to call him the parson bird, jiggled away during the bath, drops of water flying everywhere.

I don't understand the sea!

The sky is blue, there isn't a breath of wind, and yet the sea is behaving as though we're in the middle of a storm, hurling frothy white waves onto the shore, higher than I've seen them for a long time, and the bay is a cauldron of seething white foam.

Piers has emerged from his court case with his license intact – rightly so, since he was not to blame. Charlie wanted to go to court with him.

'How lovely,' I said, *'to want to support his brother.'* *'We thought it would be a good deterrent,'* was his realistic mother's reply!

341

July 29

I went to yoga in the village last night. Hannah had told me about it. Women's Refuge had sent a teacher out to us benighted women living in the sticks. The instructor, who wasn't a bit like all the svelte yoga teachers I've experienced before, Indian or otherwise, did a grumble at the beginning about how cheap these classes were, and how yoga teachers in Auckland she'd been talking to were pretty miffed, because this devalued their expensive lessons.

After this grudging beginning, we went into a series of yoga exercises, which were not yoga as I had enjoyed it before, *but hey, you get what you pay for.* I inwardly gibbed at doing one exercise, which she later admitted was part of the belly dancing routines, which she also teaches. This surprised me even more, for the somewhat homely, stout woman confronting us didn't look a bit like the curvy, sexy women I've seen doing belly dancing! But it was good to be doing some exercise again. To my surprise Kate, who I thought was a yoga whiz, was there, and we partnered each other for one of the exercises, which again, I had never done before... and to my relief, I'm not stiff this morning.

I do understand the sea! The rough weather reached us late last night. How fascinating that storms travel faster by water, and the sea brought us early warning of the rough weather. As I write, there's a plump thrush feasting on the orange crab apples from the standard malus, planted in an old copper. A pair of tuis are chirping and clicking to each other, and doing the wild flying chases and sharp dives that seem to be part of their mating dance at this time of year, making the garden a dangerous place to be, as they plunge around the small, low-hanging trees.

According to writer Elsdon Best, *Captain Cook,* like the Maoris, thought tuis were delicious eating. Worse still, the Maoris used to catch the male birds and trim the brush-like growth at the end of their tongues so they could train them to speak. They taught tuis chants as long as fifty words, keeping them imprisoned in the dark in a tiny cage till they were trained.

Each poor prisoner, when able to do all the Maori cries and chants, was then imprisoned for the rest of his life in a cage, shaped rather like a Maori eel-pot, fifteen inches wide at the bottom, and thirteen inches high. The birdcage was often hung at the entrance to a marae. This reminds me of the old Chinese men in long grey or brown robes, in Hong Kong, who would solemnly take their caged birds for a walk in the parks, still in their cages.

August 2

Wonderful massage on Friday. Kristina really got into my sore lower back, as well as my neck. For the first time in years yesterday, instead of sitting down to put on my stockings, I found myself automatically standing on one leg like I used to when I was young! After the massage, feeling quite dopey, I met Beryl for coffee, and then home, to make a lemon and almond cake for lunch with Belinda.

She came the next day, full of cold, and I dosed her up with Stone's ginger wine in hot water, honey and orange, which never fails to make people feel better – I did the same for Hannah on Thursday. Patrick had a hearty, male, earth-type, 'blood-type O' lunch; steak pie, potatoes, kumara and carrot, before Belinda came, and pottered off to his study. We had a sensitive, pure, New Age, 'blood-type A' lunch!

I had cooked Marianne's recipe for beetroot relish on Thursday, made with orange juice, garlic, sugar and red wine vinegar (liver cleansing). We had that with courgette and feta fritters, sour cream (but no cream for me), cucumber (cleansing) and rocket salad (healthy)! Downed with peach juice, and finished off with the lemon almond cake (unvirtuously iced), and Turkish apple tea.

Belinda told me how the refugee, Coptic Christian, Iraqi girls at the school where she teaches are all just waiting to get out of school and find husbands. She told me that they all have exquisite eyebrows. In Iran where she has stayed, she said all the women have beautifully shaped eyebrows. They are even more important than the eyes, she said, gazing over the top of their face veils, and they trim and shape them with razor blades.

We both wished that western beauticians would learn the simple, painless, and very quick Middle Eastern way of removing facial hair, by twirling two long bits of cotton together, and running it over the face. It's called threading. I suppose beauty parlours wouldn't feel they could charge as much as they do for such a simple, quick process, compared with waxing and all that goes with it.

Both Piers and Annabel had their school balls this weekend. Great tension and excitement for weeks for Annabel, who was in charge of the 'after-ball' party. Their venue was flooded five days before, and so unusable. So, at short notice she had to make all the arrangements for somewhere else. The one she finally nailed took all their money, with nothing left over for drinks for 150 thirsty teenagers. Roland, bless his heart, offered to pay for the drinks, and underwrite the whole affair, knowing perfectly well it was unlikely he would see any of his money again.

So on Friday night, his darling daughter was voted best dressed, and I'm quite sure that if they'd had the

category, she would have been *'most-beautiful'.* Her
mother told me that at the pre-ball party, Annabel's
scarcely-known partner arrived, walked up to this
blue-eyed beauty with long dark tresses, dressed in a
full-length turquoise chiffon dress, took her hands, and
said: 'Oh Annabel, you are so beautiful,' and promptly
fell in love with her. But Annabel isn't interested. Oh,
the pains of youth.

Piers had his ball the next night. Eugenie sent me
the pics as soon as she returned from the pre-ball
gathering last night. So I knew what he looked like,
and his girlfriend too, almost as though I'd been at the
pre-ball event. He was standing in the picture, tall,
strong and straight, looking so proud and pleased. He
wore a black jacket and trousers, black shirt and red
tie, and Eugenie said he was thrilled with this outfit.
He had his arm round his girlfriend's waist, and they
both looked so young and sweet. The young tear your
heart.

Glancing through the gossip, violence, intrusive
stories, egotistical columns, and general mayhem that
are life, if one believes the Sunday papers, I stopped at
a story with a picture of a familiar baby.

She was the adoptive baby of a high-flying Maori
couple who was kidnapped seven years ago. Her kid-
napper has been released unrepentant, but since he had
served two-thirds of his sentence, the parole board had

to release him. I don't get it. Why sentence him to eleven years if you know he'll serve only seven, if unrepentant, and even less if he's a good boy? And if he doesn't accept that what he did was wrong, will he do it again?

But worse was the fact dropped in at the end of the story that the little girl now lives on a farm with her birth parents. I hadn't caught up with this before, and I'm told that the adoptive parents were not very happy about it. All adoptive parents except Maori and Pacific Islanders have to go through endless adoption screening procedures.

But sacred, ancient customs allow these peoples to give away babies and take them back and shift them around willy-nilly. What happens in practice is that the child grows up feeling not wanted and miserable, and angry with his birth parents – two thirds of the unhappy, angry prisoners Patrick once interviewed in Mt Eden were the products of these unofficial adoptions.

Worse still, when a mother or stepfather looks after a child they haven't bonded with, research shows that they find it very easy to be unkind or insensitive. It is also demonstrated repeatedly in the child death and abuse statistics. The children themselves, having had their early bonding broken – when farmed out, or handed back – is unable to trust or bond with anyone again. He or she grows up very often to be an adult too wounded to have a rewarding and trusting relationship with a partner, and often becomes a parent with defective parenting skills, thus continuing the cycle of misery and abuse.

So this baby was handed back like so many. Her adoptive mother had explained that after having a miscarriage, her Maori whanau had promised her the next baby born in the family. This turned out to be her sister's baby. The adoptive father, retired and in his sixties, said the new baby was a project for his retirement, all of which makes the baby sound like a brown paper parcel with no feelings or rights of her own. And how has this affected the little girl? We all know nowadays that breaking the bonds of love damages a child. So how can we allow this to go on happening? And when is someone going to grasp the nettle and stop this practice?

Why in this area alone, is there one law for Maoris and Polynesians, and another law for everyone else? It is the very area where most damage is done, and where the consequences for society are hurt, damaged children who too often become anti-social adults, who produce more damaged children, and the terrible cycle of pain, violence, prison, drunkenness, drugs and all the other ills of hurt people are perpetuated. Too many grow up feeling victimised and angry, and displace this pain on to society and history. And we all pay in every way for this damage to our community, not just Maori and Polynesian people.

I responded with deep hurt to something someone said tonight. I raged futilely around the house, and later, after restraining myself from composing a subtle but retaliatory reply, I remembered something from A Course in Miracles I'd been reading that afternoon. It worked. I stopped wanting to defend or attack, justify myself, try to make the other wrong, or keep myself in the right; stopped feeling hurt, feeling furious, feeling puzzled. It just all melted away, and I felt okay. The incident, from out of left field, turned into little insignificant local stuff, petty pace. I felt untouched by it. Miracle indeed.

August 3

I must remember that chapter heading from Too Soon Old, Too Late Smart – 'The problems of the elderly are frequently serious, but seldom interesting'. I fear my children consider me elderly but seldom interesting...

Oh, to see ourselves as others see us, especially those near and dear to us. I fear to my family I am a boring old bat, and maybe to others too.

August 4

Valerie Davies

I was just going out to my Course in Miracles meeting last night when someone rang, so angry about an innocent (I thought) message that I'd left on the answer-phone that I felt knocked off my feet. I really had to work at C in M... I'm also realising that I'm really stirring up my life to have this happen... not sure if I'm strong enough to go on if my life is going to be torn to ribbons like this. It was a good meeting. I was not the only one to have had a week of upheavals...

As I write, a little pink-breasted chaffinch with his crisp black and white markings hopped past the French windows pecking at invisible morsels... and there's a couple of blackbirds, one guzzling the white berries from the Queen of the Night, the other also pecking at invisible nourishment on the ground. I can feel another bird table coming on.

Ever since I was at Eugenie's and fed the birds, and also saw Stella's bird feeder hanging from an overhanging branch, I've been racking my brains for a suitable place.

It has to be in such a place that Cara couldn't get at them. It also has to be in a place where if they make a mess, as they do, it doesn't involve me in the perpetual cleaning up I've had to do in the past.

And it has to be somewhere where I can see them. All I need now is some wood and a handyman (willing)... small pleasures for a sore soul.

August 6

No one has any idea how upset I've been. I've recognised that I cooked it up to recognise an old habit I can do without.

As I prepared supper, trying to toss par-boiled potatoes, golden kumara, and parsnips in flour, in order to baste in hot oil and roast, and while I was also making a parsley sauce to pour over the cauliflower, I was also back and forth on the phone and email to Eugenie, helping her write and re-write advertising slogans for one of her child organisations.

She had liked what I had said the previous night when I was also cooking supper and she had rung me to help her draft a radio ad!

My multi-tasking tonight also included trying to take an interest in Patrick telling me about his research on various Japanese submarines, which had penetrated the New Zealand coast during the war, at the same time as all the other goings-on.

My reading has been desultory and self-indulgent, as I've been feeling a bit fragile with all the hard work Kristina is doing on my back.

I've only read a historical novel by Anya Seton, *Devil Water*. Interestingly, it was written nearly fifty years ago and exactly echoes the information and psychology of the cavalier and border communities in America dealt with in my birthday book, *Albion's Seed*.

Valerie Davies

Beryl lent me the novel, and I didn't think I could be bothered with it. I'm glad I opened it and got hooked on it. Raced through it in one evening. On the other hand, I've enjoyed leisurely threading my way through *The Assassin's Cloak* again, an anthology of extracts from diaries... many of which I have on my bookshelves.

Among the diarists was Louisa May Alcott. Her description of her sister's death, was exactly how she told of Beth *dying in Little Women,* with one important difference. She wrote,:

A few moments after the last breath came...I saw a light mist rise from the body, float up, and vanish in the air. Mother's eyes followed mine, and when I said 'What did you see?' she described the same light mist. Dr G said it was the life departing visibly.

I also discovered from an entry from Chips Channon's diaries, that it was he who reported (apparently without irony), Emerald Cunard's reply: *'Are they all Poles?'* to his snobbish observation: *'this is what we fought for,'* as he gazed at the jewels and white ties and tails of the other guests.

I walked out of yoga after half an hour, having just paid the full amount in advance for the term, and filled in several forms for officialdom as well. The teacher, whose name was never divulged to me, had, on the other hand, revealed that she was adding in dance and Pilates along with her other routines. Then, she described later how to do a Pilates exercise, and said she'd got it out of a book, because she never had, and never would, do a Pilates class. I wasn't sure whether this was because she felt Pilates was a bowdlerisation of yoga, or a despised middle-class fad.

I decided this was not what I wanted. I had wanted to learn a yoga routine and set of exercises I could go on doing at home every day. I didn't like the atmosphere, the lack of friendliness, good manners, or even expertise. There was also a scruffy, slightly truculent, feminist energy; an old-fashioned sort, which is often scornful about the middle class, and things like housework, grooming, and good manners. Interesting that half the people from the previous week had not returned either.

The days are bright, cold, and sunny. The nights clear, cold, and moonlit. Tonight is the full moon. I got up last night to get a drink and saw the tops of the trees shining silver in the moonlight. I put on my dressing gown and went out into the silent night, with the moon streaming across the sea, making broad avenues of light between the trees. Back inside, I pulled back all the curtains, so the moon could shine into the house.

Valerie Davies

It was another clear night for the full moon shining like herrings in the sea, to quote Dorothy Wordsworth. All the hedges and leaves were burnished with silver, and I went out with Cara to watch the path of light rippling across the black water. There was only the insistent call of a nearby morepork, the faint sound of the water lapping against the rocks, and the dying engine throbs of a returning fishing boat. When it had anchored, there was nothing but sea, bird, and silver silence. Back in the house, I went to sleep by fire-light.

Today, the sun is shining, the willow trees are covered in a green haze, cherry blossom is attracting the tuis, and lambs and tiny calves lie in the grass in the sun. And it's freezing. My feet have been cold all day. Proofread Patrick's column while I drank my early morning tea in bed.

I dreamed last night of two of our Cavalier King Charles spaniels, Rupert and Kelly. I woke up aching for them, and for all our other dearly loved dogs. Their names are a litany of love: Sheba, Shadrach, Tina, Benedick and Pelham, Bella, Beau, Anya and Amy, Bey, Barley, Kelly and Rupert, Charlotte, Honey, Jacob and Murphy. They were mostly rescued, and we usually had three at a time. Six Cavalier King Charles, in three lots of two, two Afghans, two Labradors, two salukis, a springer spaniel, a borzoi, a boxer, a boxer-mastiff cross, and a mastiff. All beloved. All missed.

Had my hair cut for the third time by my new man. It will be for the last time, unless it starts to improve in the next week, or when I've washed it. I had him cut off the thick thatch of silver hair which I had hoped we were going to be able to mould into a bob. He clearly wasn't up to it. So I showed him a photo of me taken with the boys ten years ago, with a lovely cut, and asked him to duplicate it. He hasn't.

My hair looks like it used to over fifty years ago when a Chinese hairdresser in a Malayan village had chopped at various chunks of hair with blunt, dirty scissors, and made it shorter, but not very attractive. But this man charged me $75 for this rather masculine haircut. I am trying not to stare down the barrel of yet another six weeks of bad hair days before I can find someone else... probably Beryl's hairdresser who has had the temerity to go to South Africa for a holiday for six weeks.

We had dinner at the local last night. Another pleasant occasion, with a real candlelit chandelier above our heads. The waitress had a warm, friendly energy, which made the evening. She also made a perfect coffee with Kahlú.

The departure of the strange man with the heavy energy has made the difference between enjoying going there, and only going when we were desperate for something to eat!

This morning I met Belinda at the market for coffee, or rather for Turkish apple tea, which lovely Mel has now bought for us. Had a long natter, then bought vegetables, and kanuka honey from the very tall, gentle Frenchman at the market.

Reading in bed last night, I found Helen Palmer's *The Enneagram*, to check up on my character structure and how I operate. This time of reading, I could see how as a number four in this system, the 'tragic romantic', I've allowed myself to drift in and out of depression and melancholia unconsciously. I hope this reminds me next time I start to go down. I could also see how even the way I dress and create my home is not unique, but a characteristic of this type of character structure. The book talked of my character structure as being attracted to metaphysics and psychology, and being a grief counsellor, animal rights activist, and attracted to religion, ritual and art. My life is laid out there – even to the counselling, and the animals rights activism, thirty years ago I revived SAFE (Save Animals from Experimentation) and became its president with Patrick!

Even more illuminating was to recognise one of my nearest and dearest, and to see how our two personalities react to each other. The text explained how the number four in conflict with this *character 'will either spiral into deep depression or will become caustic and embittered.'* I always chose depression. I now see the games I've been playing so clearly, and can now step back from the rackets, and not sink under the bewilderment of why it was happening, each time things went wrong. Reading this analysis of our relationship and also of my character structure has given me such peace of mind. I've stopped blaming myself and puzzling over it.

August 8

Collected the mail today from the village store, and found a letter from Inland Revenue. We were felled some weeks ago when they sent a demand for a huge sum that they called provisional tax. It was a third of our income, and on top of the tax already paid, would have been more than 50 per cent tax, and would have bankrupted us. Unlike all the other times we've sold large assets to comply with their unexpected and outrageous demands, this time we wrote querying it, with some very strong arguments.

When I picked up the mail this morning, there was another dreaded letter from them. It contained a printout of a new statement of our position, with a revised assessment, and a demand for a tiny payment in February. We had won! There was no explanation, no apology, no accompanying letter, just the anonymous print-out. I was torn between immense relief, and incredulity at their rudeness, ineptness, and high-handedness.

Mike and Annie for supper. I was disappointed with it. The chicken legs were small and scrawny instead of large and generous... I stuffed their skins with garlic and lemon, tossed them in flour and ginger, and then baked them to eat with creamy garlic potatoes. The potatoes were unsuccessful too, as the second bottle of cream turned out to be sour.

This was followed by mince apple crumble, in which I think I put too much almond into the crust, being overly conscious of Annie's gluten intolerance... and I was so disorganised by thinking I had plenty of time when I didn't, that I forgot to make some nibbles, or even offer anything until far too late... apart from that, the dining table looked very pretty! It was all white, decorated with a glass jar of white daisies. Unfortunately, you can't eat white daisies!

August 10

Busy; taking Patrick to the doctor in the morning, in the afternoon I had someone come for a counselling session, and in the evening Course in Miracles meeting. It was at Beryl's lovely old house, and we were down to six, a perfect number...I wish we could stay that way; it was a harmonious little group. And yet only one member of the group seems to be tackling the exercises, and reading the lessons consecutively. It's the difference between dabbling and taking it seriously, I feel.

I was amazed to learn that Colin feels utterly alone at his eco-village, because no one else is interested in anything but growing vegetables and planting trees. But they do have feuds, and some of them haven't spoken to each other for years, he told us... and there was me, thinking it would be a tiny microcosm of a perfect community, everyone in harmony, with beliefs in common, and loving their neighbour!

Another astonishing story was Mary-Anne's, who told us about her trip to Australia during the floods a few months ago. The chap she was staying with said he had a job to do, so they went out in his four-wheel drive, in the torrential rain. They reached a road with water flowing over it, but he thought the four-wheel drive could handle it.

The next thing, they were floating down the flooded river, and as they nudged up against a frail tea-tree, the car began to sink, and the driver seemed paralysed. With water up to his chin, Mary-Anne dragged him out through the back door, and they clung on to the tree until someone saw them and rescued them with a digger! The things that happen to elderly ladies!

August 13

Valerie Davies

A board meeting yesterday at Henderson, so when I'd dropped Patrick there, I headed off to Titirangi, meaning to do my shopping there. But parking looked as bad as ever, and failed my heart, I know not how, so I carried on to New Lynn, which also had its hazards. After driving around and around several times, trying to avoid the deep hole in which the new railway is being dug, I finally managed to park in front of the mall, and wandered in.

I was met by all my pet nightmares – miserable children crying, and being dragged along by desperate parents, morbidly obese ladies tottering along swathed in scarves, and wearing jandals for comfort on a freezing day, a teenager in a wheelchair unable to move a finger, with shades over his eyes, things on his head, gloves on his nerveless hands stuck out at right angles, and refugees looking alone and lost.

As I looked miserably at one wheelchair in the food court, and the fattest lady of all sitting with the child in the wheel chair, I saw her pop a chip in his mouth, and saw the grateful smile on his face, and it was a small comfort that they did enjoy small pleasures like anyone else...

After my food shopping, I took off to Laingholm, to see our old house there. Another mistake. It was totally neglected. My beautiful garden had been wrecked; all my trees and plantings pulled out, knee high grass, and

360

the ivy on the trellis gone mad in huge triffid-like branches. Why would you pull out a clump of silver birches, and the hydrangeas and agapanthus and michaelmas daisies around them? The daisies along the fence long gone, and the fence looking as though it was about to topple over. I hate to think what the inside of that lovely house must look like if it's anything like the outside.

Fled back to Henderson, and collected Patrick. Hurray, the new chairman doesn't see why I should always have to drive Patrick to the board, so they will supply transport. I was not elected to the board, this wonderful man rightly pointed out! My life will be transformed.

August 18

Had a deep tissue massage with Kristina on Thursday. My back has got worse than ever in the last few months. She used some marvellous Chinese treatment called a moxa stick. It felt like warm oil on all the sore places on the spine, yet she says she never touches with it. Met Belinda for our Turkish apple tea date, and she brought me a couple of rather nutty New Age magazines. Did my shopping for vegetables and tamarillo chutney, to Patrick's relish!

After discovering last week that my permanent cold was a lack of amino acids, I've been bulking up on them with meat protein and amino acid pills. Hadn't been really thinking about my diet, but by the time I took into account that I rarely, if ever, have red meat any more, no pork, given up chicken and fish, and restrict the dairy, there wasn't much protein left.

There's a limit to how many nuts, and how much goats cheese one can eat, and I've never been very fond of the pulse diet, chick peas, lentils, beans and so on, while I positively hate kidney beans. So back to some chicken and sometimes lamb in my diet, and the cold disappeared after a week. Patrick, of course, is not subjected to my dietary whims, and so continues to chomp through the sustaining earth-type red meat diet he enjoys.

I had a busy weekend writing various articles and interviews, and doing endless proofreading.

Good grist for the mill – subsidising my self-indulgent sessions with all *the 'New Age nutters,'* in Patrick's term.

Last night was the weekly Course in Miracles meeting. My last. I seem to make a career of joining groups and leaving them abruptly, but last night, I felt such a round peg in a square hole that it was utterly frustrating to be there, much as I like most members of the group. It felt as though I wanted to swim at the deep end, and everyone else was playing in the paddling pool, and not realising you have to learn how to swim if you want to go in the deep end. This is arrogant, probably...

Among other things I wrote to Colin this morning, I said:

I was quite devastated by the response of the group to the idea that 'purification' meant counselling or psychotherapy. Robert Perry stated this quite clearly in the book you lent me. When twenty-six years ago I first encountered personal growth (another name for purification), I was electrified, because I could see that this was what the churches should have been doing for centuries, instead of trying to be 'spiritual'. Certainly the monasteries, and serious mystics were committed to purification, which in the words of the Gnostics meant 'seeking the sources of anger, fear, grief, envy...' and in Carl Jung's thinking, this inner exploration is a spiritual quest.

It means actually discovering what the ancient Greek injunction: 'Know Thyself' means, and yet, without an expert counsellor, teacher, mentor, the ego can still deceive us. And as Socrates said: *the unexamined life is not worth living.*

The 'Shadow' is the stuff we are unconscious of... and these early patterns are deeply embedded, preverbal and wholly unconscious. The journey to awareness and full consciousness involves bringing this unconscious stuff into the light, and therefore becoming free of it. It is the unconscious stuff, which runs our life... what is conscious we can deal with.

In Jung's terms, this is called integration. In religious terms this process is called purification, in contemporary terms, personal growth or psychotherapy. It's about looking at compulsive and repeating patterns of behaviour which are survival mechanisms, not choices. So we go on making the same mistakes in relationships and in life.

Some people never start this journey, others start and give up, and others get stuck. This happens because the ego knows that this inner work will cause change, and the ego is comfortable with the same old things. Growth requires commitment and insight, both things the ego will resist. The world is full of egos resisting change, growth, and responsibility.

It is not an easy journey, and I've been stuck often. But I also think that since it's a spiritual journey, it will never end, until we come home, so I'm hanging in, no matter what hard yards it takes. This is the bedrock of my life, and it's on this that I see the Course in Miracles resting. I believe Principle 7: 'Miracles are everyone's right, but purification is necessary first'.

In my note to everyone else, a short one with no explanations, which could hurt or irritate, I signed off with my favourite quote from an anonymous seventh century poet, which was a much neater way of saying everything I said to Colin:

Pilgrim, remember
For all your pain
The Master you seek abroad
You will find at home
Or seek in vain.

Among the responses was a message from a member of the group who took it literally, and loved the idea of staying home! Colin sent a warm, intelligent response and I shall miss him.

August 20

It's a cold grey day, the sea pounding onto the rocks, huge white horses, and a nasty cold wind. And for all that, it still feels like spring. The cherry tree is hung with bloom along the bough, the kowhai tree is dangling yellow petals from the branches, and there are buds on the apricot crepuscule rose climber. More than time I got into the garden, to tame the ivy and the marguerite daisies, and do some topiary and planting. The malus trees are budding and the orange clivia are coming into flower. The flight paths through the garden are continually clogged with traffic... at least six tuis fluttering through, the wood pigeon couple blundering from tree to telephone wires, blackbirds and thrushes, a chaffinch, fan-tails and silvereyes, even, the other day, a couple of swallows resting momentarily on the roof of the garage.

I'm feeling too fragile to garden at the moment, the hand I crushed in the car accident thirty-three years ago has suddenly become excruciatingly painful. I've rubbed Deep Heat in, and wrapped it in a tea towel, but it doesn't seem to be particularly efficacious!

Yesterday was my last trip into Patrick's board meeting for many a day. While I waited for him, I went for a coffee after I'd done my shopping.

At the table next to me were two men in their late fifties, big paunches, hard, lined faces, tough cookies. But my heart melted as I eavesdropped on their conversation.

The biggest, toughest one was saying: *'She watches telly all the time, and I stay out of the way, then when she switches off, I come in and sit down to watch, and she screams at me, "all you ever do is watch telly." When I go past, I put a hand on her shoulder, and she screams "don't you dare touch me"...'*

His voice faded out in despair, and then the other began his tale of woe, which I couldn't hear, except to hear him end: *'So I don't know what to do.'*

These two big men sat and drank their lattes in moody silence, and then the bigger one left.

An old lady with a stick hovered uncertainly, trying to work out where to sit. The remaining man jumped up, and in the kindest voice said:

'Here, have my seat, I'm just going.' He moved out from behind the table, and helped her in. He cleared his cup away, and then gathered up all the torn bits of blue sugar packet that the other man had shredded into tiny pieces onto the table in his distress. I caught his eye, and he smiled; a smile of complicity, with such kindness, and understanding of the old lady, that it stayed with me all day... one of those tiny actions which make the world a softer place.

Hannah came today, a tonic as ever. She didn't clean Patrick's room as he was still in bed, not good today, as for several days. As Hannah and I admired a big cock pheasant that was pecking around on the bank outside the window, we talked of other birds. She told me that at her home in the South Island, there had been a lonely male paradise duck. His mate had been killed, and he remained celibate and alone for the fifteen remaining years of his life... so it isn't just big tough men who have sad lives! Hannah too has dropped out of the local yoga classes.

I took Patrick to the doctor to get his blood pressure taken. That's okay, so now we know that the problem is not blood pressure. The specialist is off to Vancouver for two weeks, but tells Patrick to ring him in Vancouver if he is in trouble, and he will ring the neurological department and get him admitted to hospital here! Sad talk with Eugenie about her woes. Annabel, on the other hand, went to see Cindy for a session, and rang to marvel, and tell me she'd never been so happy in her whole life. We talked for an hour and a half. So satisfying. Grandchildren are such a gift. We only discover this in later life, when it explodes into our life with a starburst of joy...

Not much concentration for reading at the moment so I dip into old favourites, I Heard The Owl call my Name, a poignant story about Canadian Indians, Kilvert's Diaries, and another rather delicious book about Victorian parsons, as well as, inevitably, the odd relaxing Georgette Heyer. Kilvert revels in the small things in life, the ice in his bath, the wintry pattern of the leafless trees in the sky, a sunset, and then of course, there's the girls he loved and always lost... I flinch at his description of various children beaten by their parents, and encouraged by him not to spare the Victorian rod.

August 25

The garden has a delicate atmosphere at the moment, as though some angelic presence is hovering. The plum tree was vibrating with dozens of bees the other day, all snuffling away in the blossom for honey.

Wherever a bee was feasting, single petals fell, showering the paths and the grass with round pink spots like confetti. The scent of the blossom is ravishing, and combined with the scent of the jasmine, makes the garden fragrant as well as flowery. Mutabilis and Jean Ducher are waving their blowsy blooms, and the other roses and the wisteria are beginning to bud up. The spring rain (for that is what it feels like) is causing everything to start flowering early. Even little lizards are beginning to flick around the paths, as though it's warmer than it is.

Spaghetti bolognaise with Mike and Annie on Sunday night, was preceded by Mike's delivery of more home-killed firewood, and then a stately drive back to their house in their magnificent new Cadillac. Probably the only time in my life I will ever sit in a Cadillac! It had a rare and expensive smell. I baked a coffee and Kahlúa cake to eat as pudding, but the Kahlúa cream was the best thing about it.

My reading at the moment is the 'New Age nutter' variety, books on the Pleiades, and another on pyramids and the stars. I also relaxed and laughed my way to good health reading once again, Adrian Mole and Weapons of Mass Destruction. My painful hand has recovered since I gave up eating tomatoes and potatoes. I can see I'll be down to bread (gluten-free) and water (purified) quite soon!

August 25

I picked up an old book from Patrick's shelves, German air ace Werner Baumbach's explanation of why the Luftwaffe didn't manage to beat the RAF – no acceptance of responsibility for war – instead he invented the fact that Britain and the allies were rearming at such a rate that the Germans never had a chance to catch up! And yet everyone knew that Britain was hopelessly behind in every form of defence. Ingenuously, Baumbach quoted Hitler, a few pages further on, making this very point as a good reason for attacking Poland, while the British had no means of helping the Poles.

A rather unattractive atmosphere of 'poor us.' The brave, baffled, heroic Germans; fighting the good fight, but handicapped by their leader who turned out to be mad!

I'm rather repelled by the zoo's grief drama over the death of Kashin the elephant, when they felt no qualms, a few weeks ago, about uprooting three primates who had spent their whole lives of twenty-five and twenty years at the zoo, and sending them off to an American zoo to breed.

Their acceptance of the value of animals' feelings, and their rights, is fairly selective. All of the above is judgemental, I know, and showing me how everything

IS judgement till one shifts one's perspective (but will I ever?).

The garden is accusing me, and I put off tackling it by telling myself I have to get the secateurs and the shears sharpened. It's alive with bird life, silvereyes flicking in and out of the plum tree and the bird bath, mating tuis nearly colliding with mating blackbirds, and hungry wood pigeons dropping in for a snack on the kowhai tree. Whereas the tuis suck the honey from the yellow flowers with their beaks, the pigeons seem to be ripping the flowers or something off the twigs and swallowing them. The branches shudder each time they tear whatever it is off. I wonder if that's why the tree always looks so stringy and chewed up.

August 30

Yesterday I took the ancient rusty shears and even rustier blunt secateurs to the knife sharpener in the market. He has transformed them into things of beauty with a cutting edge. He said they were beautiful quality, no wonder they were so old; they had staying power. I bought the secateurs over thirty years ago. The shears were elderly in 1990, when old Alf gave them to us, when he gave up gardening to go into a rest home. All his garden implements were ancient, and most seem to have walked away with various tradesmen who probably didn't realise how precious they were. The shears are the one thing left, and probably at least fifty years old.

So, up and out this morning, tackling the ivy and the hedge down the steps. I didn't last long. The sound of calves calling for their mothers, and their mothers bellowing back in grief, always destroys me every year. There must be a better way of farming... when I see the mothers tenderly licking their newborn calves, and know that in a few more days, or even hours, they will be parted, as happens every year to every cow, my heartaches.

Patrick is not well. Since his sudden dive a couple of weeks ago, he has suddenly seemed frail. The lack of balance is constant, and he reluctantly uses a stick now. Yet he is on the ball at board meetings and full of ideas for his column every week. He also embarked on writing another book, which is giving him stimulation and enjoyment. Next week is the famous eightieth birthday party, and it feels as though he's keeping himself going for that. His eldest son's phone call from Australia the other day, saying he couldn't come after all, for completely cast-iron reasons, was a great blow.

Eugenie on the phone and email constantly, she'd been having a bad week/day... she shared this message on her email which comforted her from Neale Donald Walsch:

The Sound Of Water

On this day of your life, dear friend, I believe God wants you to know...that there is a solution to all of this- and it is right around the next corner.

A few weeks from now, you will not even be facing this problem. A few months from now, you will have forgotten you ever had it. A few years from now, you will wonder why you let yourself worry so much.

I'm not trying to make light of it here. I just want to put it in perspective.

Okay? Trust God here. Trust life. And breathe.

I suggested she send it round the family, as there were a few other members who were badly in need of it, judging from my phone calls today! I've discovered that it's the fresh shoots the wood pigeons eat on the kowhai tree.

12

Sep/Oct 2009

September 1

Eugenie and Julian came up to do a tidy-up around the pool, and had an impromptu lunch with us, like old times. It'll be sad when they no longer come this way. Mike and Annie came to measure up for the steps and railing they are creating for Patrick's birthday present. Thoughtful and generous.

Graeme dropped in with both his little dogs the next day. I ended up taking them both into the garden so he and Patrick could talk undisturbed. It felt like being a grannie again, keeping the children amused, only with dogs now. He told us that he and Joan had been driving home the day before, when the car in front had run over a mother duck. Before she died, she managed to shepherd her brood of baby ducklings back to the grass verge, and then collapsed, brave heart.

Graeme and Joan stopped and gathered up the babies and took them home, and popped them in the bath, away from the dogs. They are now safely in residence at the bird rescue refuge.

Strange day yesterday. Beryl couldn't make it for a cup of coffee, I arrived at the wrong time for my massage, so Kristina was busy with another body, went to the upholsterer to organise Patrick's chair to be re-*sprung* for his birthday, and the business was just closing down, went to the baker for a loaf of Vienna, but none left, so I decided to have a decent cup of coffee made by Angela, who is a coffee genius. It was cold.

Angela was rightly preoccupied with an old German shepherd who was sitting anxiously outside the bakery door, and had been for nearly an hour. Finally, its owners arrived. They had forgotten they'd told her to stay, and they'd gone off to visit friends. The relief in the poor old thing was quite heart*breaking*.

A Course in Miracles seems to be affecting me markedly. I can only *put it down to* my lack of concentration. I can't read any history or other books as I used to. Just the Course book, and related books, and when I want a change, something light and un*emotional*, like Jane Austen, or Alan Bennett, to name two I've read in the last few days. Thomas Hardy, I toyed with, but even my favourites, *The Woodlanders*, *Tess of the d'Urbervilles*, and *Far from the Madding Crowd* seemed too fraught with anguish, much as I love the atmosphere of a way of life now gone.

Probably my favourite passage in all literature is the description of the dairy farm at Talbothays where Angel Clare and Tess fall in love. Hardy writes of water meadows, purple dusks and misty dawns, hot silent summer afternoons, the smells, the sounds, the colours, thick forests, old byways, moss growing on ancient tiled roofs, barn doors and posts polished by sheep rubbing against them in that dreaming Dorset countryside – the old 'Summerlands' – before pollution and technology.

On the school bus to Swanage when I was a girl, we were always conscious of Hardy. It was as though the mark he had laid on that countryside was there for us all to see, and it was always part of our understanding of the scenery we travelled through each day. Every day when we passed Woolbridge Manor, the Elizabethan farmhouse where Tess and Angel Clare spent their honeymoon, and where my parents did also, I thought of them, and wondered if the unpleasant portraits on the stairs, which had unnerved Tess and Angel, were still there.

Looking up at the grassy ridges around Corfe Castle, I used to wonder where Sergeant Troy teased and terrorised and entrapped Bathsheba with his sword play, and I wanted to explore the lane at Wool, when I heard the senior girls talking on the bus about the Cistercian Abbey down there, where Angel had sleep-walked, carrying Tess.

But Hardy hurts too much to qualify for a light read, which is all I'm up for at the moment. The Course book was quite impenetrable to me twenty-five years ago, when I first bought it. But in the years since, whenever I've seen it in the bookcase, I've decided not to throw it away in case I ever wanted it.

Now, every page is as clear as glass – totally logical, and blessedly free from Christian masochism, martyrdom, and misery. The message or at least, my interpretation so far, seems to be: trust, be happy, be harmless and unafraid.

There's no guilt, no mortifying of the body, mind or spirit, no blame, no shame, but a rigorous and regular routine of inner exercise and a reorganisation of one's thinking...

The mental exercises which will be the means of getting to the destination – peace of mind, among other things – seemed easy, and somewhat pointless, and then I realised they were turning my thinking upside down. 'Know thyself,' said the oracle.

And I thought I did, up to a point. I know now that I am a totally unknown quantity to myself. The exercises have exposed me to myself, and I'm only on the twenty-first; there are 344 to go!

For starters, I had no idea how intolerant and judgemental I am.

I judge everything and everyone, from George Bush to Robert Mugabe; the CIA to wife-beaters; Inland Revenue to fundamentalists of whatever hue, Christian, Muslim, Jewish, Hindu; big-spending on the taxpayer by ex-Governor Generals or politicians, to Japanese whale hunters; *everyone* who oppresses women, beats children or ill-uses animals; Spanish Conquistadores and bull fighters; Nazis, militant Israelis and the Taliban; people who chop down trees and drop litter, to mention just a few of my bêtes *noires...*

It's a horrifying list, and doesn't include various individuals from my past, on whom I am now doing my best to suspend judgement!

I have always been a fierce partisan, and now I am seeing that the only way to have no judgement is to have no opinions, which is rather what Marcus Aurelius said.

Where this is taking me, I don't know. I just know I'm on a journey. But the journey is a mystery.

I Ching says:

You have just been plunged onto a new ...path... there is no question that the strength with which this spiritual system has gripped you is an indication of that path's correctness for you...

Well, there you go, as they say in this neck of the woods.

The title, *A Course in Miracles*, has made me think about s*ome of the miracles in my life*–just ordinary ones–if there is such a thing as an ordinary miracle! Three come to mind straight away, and funnily enough, all connected with cars! The first, in the depths of our setbacks after the Thomas case, financial as well as everything else, was when I had parked on a hill, outside a very snooty antique shop which we'd often patronised in our palmy days. The car was a battered Morris Minor with a handbrake, which had just packed up, and this was the only parking space I could find. It had to be as close to the shop I was going to as possible, as the chronic fatigue was at its very worst, and this was a bad day. I jammed the car against the kerb at the top of the steep hill.

Returning to it, I found someone had parked so close in front of me that I had to reverse in order to ease my way out, but I knew I didn't have the skills to do it with a broken handbrake. In total despair, I shut my eyes, and groaned with no real hope of any succour, 'Oh God, help me.' When I opened them, there was a backpacker rather cheekily using my bonnet on which to spread out his map to read it! I leapt out of the car, and explained my predicament. No worries, he was used to coping with old cars in various stages of break-down! He eased himself into the driver's seat, and the thing was done.

Some years later, in somewhat better financial shape, and driving a good, reliable car, I was shepherd-ing some visiting English friends around the Auckland sights. When we returned to the car, there was a psy-chedelically painted van sitting next door, bonnet up, and loud, raucous music emanating from it. In my normal intolerant fashion, I inwardly judged the owner with his head in the engine, as a hoon. Maybe as judgement, the good reliable car refused to start.

John, friend of my youth, claimed complete incom-petence, and I sat there in blank panic wondering what on earth to do. The boy came out of the engine of the van next door, and said: 'Can I help you, I'm a mechan-ic.' He did a few fiddles, and the car jumped back into life. A bit further down the road, as we passed Auck-land Grammar School, I said: 'That was a miracle,' and John and Jane both replied, 'Oh I've put that behind us long ago,' and the other, 'Oh, that's behind us now, I'd forgotten all about it.' Miracles, I realised, are in the eye of the beholder.

The third miracle was during a garden safari in Kerikeri. As I was driving up a steep, winding drive, someone was coming down, so I reversed. But I hadn't seen a three foot deep drain on the last bend, and tipped over into it. Patrick, who was in a very delicate state, nearly did have a heart attack, as it was his office car, and I felt terrible.

As we climbed painfully out, a four-wheel drive drew up on the road, and out jumped two competent locals, the husband delving into the boot for some boards to insert under the car wheels to drive it out. The elderly driver of the oncoming car had stopped, and he got out and said, 'I used to be a Monte Carlo rally driver, I'll get it out for you.' It took less than five minutes before we were back on the road, and all the guardian angels had driven off. God and her angels work in mysterious ways... and they are, I discovered from this, available for help in mundane matters as well as big crises.

September 2

Complete meltdown today.

Cried for most of the afternoon. Can't remember the last time I had a good cry, and I didn't enjoy it. Old patterns that have to be dealt with surfaced, and with it the old despair. No good wanting to blame the people who pressed my buttons. And I hate feeling victim to it. And realising that I haven't dealt with it after all these years of trying to clear the misery of my child-hood makes me angry and despairing... self-examination requires such down-to-earth hard labour!

Later, I rang a friend. We had a laugh about it and I feel a lot better. Now I have to clear this unwanted drama from my life.

In the agony of mind I had felt, once more I turned to I Ching, and felt quite calm after I read:

Whatever material problems you have are only shadows of your spiritual struggle. If you perceive a problem, then your problem is that you perceive it as a problem in the first place: you know better...

Then I remembered the Enneagram character structures, and realised this was the same old stuff, and so I could step back and move on.

I took Cara for a walk round the cemetery in the moonlight. It was clear and cold, and the moon not yet full, but lighting a wide path across the sea. I sent an email to Belinda, who's dropping in for a cup of tea on Saturday, suggesting instead, 'a flask of wine (not communion), a loaf of bread (not gluten free), thou, and some cheese (not hard).' Her answer cheered me up. As did P.G. Wodehouse, with whom I went to bed.

I was particularly tickled with Wooster's prep school take on one of the great moments in English history,

I remember the Rev. Aubrey giving the late Sir Philip Sidney a big build-up because, when wounded at the battle of somewhere and offered a quick one by a companion in arms, he told the chap who was setting them up to leave him out of that round and slip his spot to a nearby stretcher-case, whose need was greater than his...'

I woke (briefly) in the night to hear Cara purring loudly as she lay on the mohair and possum wrap (for my use) on the pillow by my head on one side, and the sea roaring outside the window on the other side. Two rather blissful sounds. I went back to sleep with the sound of the water. Now the bay is filled with bright blue rollers and swirling, glacial, white foam in the sunshine and a bitter wind is blowing hard. Apparently, we are expecting stiff easterly swells. They seem to have arrived.

As I look out of the window there is a large bronze, green and white woodpigeon rocking in the wind at the end of a branch of the golden kowhai tree.

Yesterday, I looked out, and on the bank, pecking at unseen morsels in the grass, were two birds the size of a thrush, with bright yellow heads the same yellow as the nasturtiums growing on the bank. If they hadn't been moving, it would have been impossible to distinguish them from the flowers.

I have no idea what they were, too big for yellow heads, which move in flocks, not pairs...I also heard a kookaburra cackling down near Kate... haven't heard them for a while.

September 8

Belinda came for the bread and the wine! It was Il Rosso Sangiovese, delicious; drunk with warm, crusty artisan bread and Danish butter, a ripe Castello cheese, camembert, olives and tomatoes. Followed by coffee and choc fudge. We had a good natter, ranging over things spiritual to things temporal, from the Lords of the Seven Rays, and St Germain, to the Shah of Persia's jewellery collection in Teheran, and the Wallace Collection in London. I lent her a book on the Windsors' jewels.

Among other things, Belinda told me the story of a nearly blind Polynesian girl she is coaching for her fifth form exams. She isn't getting her homework done, and Belinda finally discovered that her older sister has gone back to Samoa to pick up a baby to adopt and bring here, leaving her existing eighteen-month-old son here, in the schoolgirl's charge. This baby is so upset at the absence of his mother in Samoa that the schoolgirl is up till the small hours with him.

Her mother, the grandmother, and the only worker in the house, refuses to help and refuses to meet social workers to try to iron the thing out. The story had every element that upsets me the most; the unofficial casual adoptions, which so often come to grief, the ignorance of bonding so that the eighteen-month-old is subjected to damaging emotional trauma, and the exploitation of younger members of the family. Then there was the bloody-mindedness, refusal to cooperate, and dishonest exploitation of New Zealand immigration laws.

I told Belinda how when Eugenie was at school, she agonised about a Maori girl on the school bus, who had no school uniform and seemed so depressed and wretched. We contacted the school, and they organised a maths class in which the girls all measured each other.

Equipped with these measurements, we bought every item of school uniform, and delivered them to the school, where the girl was given a gift from an anonymous person. She was beside herself. On the bus, she was radiant wearing it all. And within three weeks it had all gone.

Her granny wanted the parka and thick socks for working in the fields digging potatoes, and every other item had been picked off by other family members.

Belinda said that was what happened all the time, even with the free specs they got for shortsighted children, and which were then appropriated by older members of the family who the family elders said needed them more.

These spectacles are supplied by a trust, free of charge, except for a $25 examination fee, which Belinda said many families try every which way to dodge paying.

When does accepting charity become trying to rip off the rich Palagis?

We also discussed Ramadan, apropos an Indian woman with a migraine by 9.30 in the morning, which she said she knew was dehydration. So, she had to suffer for the whole day, working in a busy dairy, and then had to prepare a feast for the family to eat after sundown. I've always worried how bus drivers and surgeons, to name a few, cope with the rigours of Ramadan, how desperate parents deal with their children, and how hungry husbands, short-tempered with anger during the fasting, respond to their exhausted, fasting wives.

I wonder about those desperate bus drivers, or doctors working long shifts in hospital, and nurses and teachers, and wonder how they manage to do their jobs under such stress.

I wouldn't want a diagnosis or an operation from a Muslim doctor during Ramadan. Not prejudice, just enough knowledge to know how fasting, falling sugar levels, and dehydration affect concentration levels and even eyesight. Has there been any research into the effect of Ramadan on working patterns, one wonders.

It would of course be considered racist, and therefore rejected...

Hunger and stress seem to bring up such anger in some Muslim men during this period, and it doesn't seem to dissipate very quickly when things are back to normal.

And how tragic to see human beings flagellating themselves with starvation, thirst and all the attendant ills, because they think God wants them to.

Why would God want his creation to be miserable? As if God would. Why would He/She?

The next day, Sunday, was Patrick's eightieth birthday party with children, grandchildren, nephews, and even his eighty-six-year-old sister up from Taranaki, gathering at Eugenie's house. She and Julian created a gracious, friendly atmosphere, and everyone seemed to enjoy it.

Patrick's second son, Mark, also brought wit and gaiety to the occasion.

My particular four grandchildren, all lanky teenagers now, coalesced, and every now and then disappeared for a joy ride in Piers' new car.

The weather continues to be bright and sunny, and so dry that already we want rain for the garden.

The moon in the clear sky shines brilliantly every night. The full moon of Saturday rose bright orange above the horizon.

The Sound Of Water

I waited and watched in the bitter wind looking out to sea for its appearance, and then stood and watched while the orange pumpkin moved slowly up the sky, and turned first to a gold ball, and then a silver disc, shining across the black water.

September 13

After damp days with some rain, all the liquid ambers are leafing up, nasturtiums flowering along paths, and the wisteria beginning to green... the tuis are indefatigable and very tame. As I walked up the footpath, there was a tui on the plum tree branch overhead, continuing to warble though I was only three feet away, his pristine white necktie bobbing away with the throbbing from his throat.

I stood on the veranda last night in the inky darkness, soft rain falling, and listened to the sound of the sea on the rocks below. There was a lovely fragrance which I couldn't place... too early for Queen of the Night or star jasmine... perhaps it was the kowhai, or maybe the cabbage tree blossom. I thought how lucky I was to be able to stand outside, breathing sweet air, no sound but the sea, just the black night and the peace.

My brain is still as addled as ever. I do blame the Course, and I blame it too for the various dramas, which keep ricocheting, into my life, disturbing old friendships and relationships. I have to keep asking

389

myself: does this feel right/good for me? This is a question, which I have never asked before, if it meant severing old ties and relationships. But for too long I've used words like loyalty and faithfulness and patience and tolerance to ride rough-shod over my own feelings, and make it right for others, to keep relationships going, and make excuses for others. Now, I have to face the fact that if it doesn't feel good for me, then I have to be honest with myself. I don't feel like 'putting up' with things anymore. It's not so much assertiveness, but giving myself the same consideration that I've always given others. Loving myself as much as my neighbour!

I also have the same problem, which Elizabeth Bennett faced, of 'uniting truth and civility in the same sentence,' because I have to reply to someone's gift of their book. I read it with distaste; it could have been a glorious life of opportunities few people ever enjoy. Instead, it united inverted snobbery with joylessness. Somehow, I have to be grateful and say 'thank you'. In this instance, it is not my soul at risk, but someone else's self-esteem, so my perverted sense of morality allows me to try to lie graciously

Patrick's actual eightieth birthday at last on Wednesday. He spent it at a board meeting where he was feted, and I had the chance to bake a coffee and walnut birthday cake and wrap all his presents. Books, inevitably, plus a very good Japanese woodblock of a snow scene (by the Master Hiroshige) bought for $4 at a car boot sale, and a charming carving of a sparrow in some heavy bronze-coloured substance.

The next day we had lunch at Pigeon's Perch and a mooch round the Red Barn, where I found a good copy of Dorothy Wordsworth's Journals for $1. The one I had already was a tattered mess. On Friday, I did a dash into Auckland, delivering my second copy of Greek Myths to Annabel. She says she loves them and is studying Troy and The Aeneid. I then dropped in flowers, wine, and thanks to Eugenie and Julian for Patrick's party, and followed this by a session with Belinda's chiropractor, who hardly touched me, but works with the same energy as Cindy.

Time will tell.

It is called NSA – neuro-spinal adjustment, a mysterious experience.

Saturday brought a rendezvous with Belinda. It was freezing at the market, but I found a turquoise necklace for Annabel to wear with her turquoise graduation dress, did my vegetable shopping, and came home satisfied.

A poignant card arrived from a friend whose son had died suddenly. It read:

"I do not like the way the cards are shuffled
And yet I like the game and want to play

Valerie Davies

*So through the long, long night with brow unruf-
fled I play what I get until the break of day.''*

Anon

September 15

Peace of mind. Vanity satisfied. No more bad hair
days! Beryl's hairdresser is magic, and cheap. Less than
half the price of the expensive man who's *butchered my
hair for the last few months.*

An easy cooking day. I defrosted some lentil soup
for lunch, and frozen chicken for supper. I had thought
I'd defrosted the soup last week, but I never label, so
what I found last week when it had melted was not lentil soup, but half a Christmas pudding. Since it
couldn't be refrozen, we had Christmas pudding for
supper, Patrick with ice-cream, me with rum butter –
no way was I going to waste a good Christmas pudding
with inferior trimmings!

The weather feels like high summer. I took Cara
over to the cemetery for a walk, and we sat on the
green marble sun-warmed bench and watched the
smart, big game boats coming home to harbour, and
the shabby, chippy, little fishing boats chugging out to
sea.

As the first ones left, the smooth waters of the harbour suddenly came alive, throbbing with fish jumping,
presumably, to escape big fish below. It seemed strange

that the fishermen should carry on sailing out to sea, instead of casting their nets over the side for a huge miraculous catch... I thought about this, and decided that unlike Galilee, these fishermen probably had quotas, and would have to throw this catch back because the fish were too small. This is where huge populations and over-fishing have led us.

The air was sweet with perfume. It must have come from the tiny wild freesias growing in the grass among daisies and small pink trumpet-shaped flowers. I hope the grass is not due to be cut for a while. The yellow birds were back in the garden today – I think they're goldfinches – and also the resident chaffinch. Swallows also swooping round the garden. A mackerel sky tonight, pink ridge of cloud like the furrows of a ploughed field, sprawling across a pale turquoise sky.

September 16

The days are like summer; warm, blue and sparkling. I went to Matheson's Bay, only visited once before at high tide, when it didn't appeal. At low tide today, it was beautiful. I looked at the semi-circle of the bay and visualised the dozens of whales basking there in the early morning, fifty years ago, as a friend had described it. Those were the days when the sea was teeming with life, and old photographs show beaming fishermen holding handfuls of huge, waving-legged lobsters.

I walked out to the flat rocks from where the sea had receded, and gazed into the rock pools. They were a world of colour, yellow sands, green and khaki seaweed, black and brown kina or sea urchins, spiked with pink, mother of pearl sparkling on the sides of tiny shells.

And they were alive with subterranean life... tiny fish darting round the rocks, their shadows reflecting in the sandy bottom, prickly kina nestled into crevices, some even camouflaged with little heaps of stones over them, pink and cream-tipped prickles showing through.

Moving shells of different sizes too, home to little hermit crabs, and one large crab, five inches across, but so camouflaged with fronds of seaweed growing on its back and off its legs, that it could hardly be seen. Tiny trees and shrubs of different coloured seaweed swaying in the imperceptibly moving water made the little pools look like miniature landscapes, as well as microcosms of the ocean.

Beyond these flat tables of rock intersected with deep crevices and pools, the waves were surging in, breaking over the outer rocks.

A canoeist made his way in, grumbling about the unexpected swell. He had caught two big snapper, bright orange with turquoise spots on their gleaming silver sides.

The notice on the beach stipulating how many fish per person depressed me. Kina were open slather, fifty per person, and yet I only saw a few dozen left. Maori and Island gatherers come down to our beach, and clamber back up the cliff with sack-fulls. They tear them open and eat them raw down on the beach. I would have thought they were still alive.

I went early to bed last night after my second painless NSA session. But my neck was red-hot and sore by nightfall, and I slept round the clock from eight to eight, accompanied by my faithful black familiar, Cara. Dreams, like the previous nights, were vivid, and architectural. I can still see the lanes, alleys, and rooftops of all the villages I visited last night, recognisably English. Nowhere that I knew, but charming and nostalgic.

September 20

The unexpected joy of Piers arriving in his new car on Thursday. After a chat, covering history in his imminent exam, he went to explore Pakiri, more for the pleasure of driving over the steep, challenging and winding dirt road than anything else.

He then returned and lay sprawled along the sofa for a couple of hours in the sun, while I sat at the computer.

Then he staggered over to the other house and slept for a bit. After which, he drove back to Auckland, for a joyful reunion with his parents, I presumed!

A rendezvous with Belinda at the market. We both agreed that our weekly meeting has become important, and not to be missed. She suggested meeting for lunch after the market next week.

I've finally finished reading the book on the battle on the Imjin River, Korea, which my brother Derek had sent to Patrick for his birthday. The story of the Glorious Gloucesters, the Northumberland Fusiliers and the Royal Ulster Rifles, my brother's regiment, was sometimes too painful to read. I could only manage small bursts. The people, or rather, the types, from those regiments were so familiar to me, the decent, kind, brave men my father soldiered with.

The heroism, gallantry, and selflessness of them all, a few thousand men against an invisible and unexpected army of 300,000, was humbling. They were in a situation that few in the two world wars had experienced. Most battles then took place between two sides, and they clashed and then retreated. But these men were ambushed, suddenly surrounded, fighting with no food or water for days, running out of ammunition, and never faltering or complaining. General Ridgway's comments after the Gloucesters had been captured, and the other regiments badly mauled, made it sound as though the American commanders had left the British in the lurch, and there was certainly a complete lack of communication.

The sufferings of the prisoners in Chinese camps sounded as bad as, or worse than, the Japanese POW camps, the same sadism and starvation. The British were shocked by the state of the forgotten and demoralised American prisoners who were already there. Humour, and the refusal to be brainwashed, kept up the British morale.

The officers were separated from the men, but the men rose to the challenge and produced their own leaders.

I laughed out loud at the description of the classic attempts at brainwashing on the impervious British Tommies, with each unrepentant soldier standing up for his public confession and beginning, 'I've been a very naughty boy,' to cheers and catcalls and whistles, completely mystifying their stern, unsmiling Chinese instructors/brainwashers.

I remember as a girl, hearing about Colonel Carne's seventeen months in solitary confinement because the Chinese were retaliating over some derisory verses about Mao sung at a camp concert.

When my parents met him at lunch some years after he had been released, they put his silence and reclusiveness down to his imprisonment.

But reading this book, I see now he was always a taciturn man.

I looked up the battle on Google, wanting to put it into the context of the Korean War.

It had no context! The British and the battle weren't mentioned!

Presumably, it's like the American view of World War Two, which didn't start until 1941, after Pearl Harbour, according to their memorials. The previous, perilous two years of backs against the wall have no existence in American history!

This may be the last book on the wars I shall read. Something has changed. It's an effort to read these things any more.

Instead, I've been going back to Ken Wilber, who always enlightens and inspires, whatever book or page of his I open.

In an essay Jane once sent me, he wrote:

The Brilliant Clarity of Ever-Present Awareness, about the Great Search: 'the loveless contraction hidden in the heart of the separate–self sense, a contraction that drives intense yearning for a tomorrow in which salvation will finally arrive, but during which time, thank God, I can continue to be myself. The greater the Great Search, the more I can deny God... The Great Search is the great enemy of what is'.

A few pages later, after discussing the ever-present Spirit, the simple ever-present Witness, Wilber writes:

When I rest as the timeless Witness, the Great Search is undone. The great Search is the enemy of the ever-present Spirit, a brutal lie in the face of a gentle infinity. The Great Search is the search for the ultimate experience, a fabulous vision, a paradise of pleasure, an unendingly good time, a powerful insight – a search for God, a search for Goddess, a search for Spirit – but Spirit is not an object. Spirit cannot be grasped, reached, sought, or seen; it is the ever-present Seer. To search for the Seer is to miss the point...How could you possibly search for that which is right now aware of this page. YOU ARE THAT. You cannot go out looking for that which is the Looker...

Today, it was lesson 41 from the Course (I sometimes repeat a lesson). It was quite different to the preceding ones. Using the phrase for today, we merely had to drop down into inner space for five minutes. 'Merely,' did I say? I did as instructed, and thirty-five minutes later came to.

I had found something. What I first felt was a sense of recognition or familiarity. It felt like a knowing, which was also a seeing. I felt I understood Meister Eckhart's words, the 'Ground of Being'. It was a very simple thing. It also felt like a river of being, running through everything, running behind everything, never ending, eternally present. I returned to a sense of absolute peace and the calm, contented feeling of knowing that 'that' is always there. I can return.

September 23

Patrick went to an early emergency meeting of his board this morning. I've always loved having the house to myself – the solitude I've always wanted. In his early diaries, Thomas Merton moaned on about not having solitude and silence. I know how he feels, but how could these things be missing in a Trappist monastery? And it's a lot easier to be alone in a crowd surely, than in a one-on-one relationship! Silence is easier than solitude. I never have the radio on, rarely the TV, and sometimes go for months without playing any music. Patrick listens to music and radio through his headphones.

The days after contacting that silent river of being seemed calm and beautiful. Ken Wilber's understanding of how to ground the insights of the spiritual life took me back to Brother Lawrence's practise of the Presence of God.

Every page of Brother Lawrence's letters breathe both common sense and holiness. 'The time of business,' he said, 'does not with me differ from the time of prayer, and in the noise and clatter of my kitchen, while several persons are at the same time calling for different things, I possess God in as great tranquillity as if I were upon my knees ...'

It was reported of him that:

In the greatest hurry of business in the kitchen, *he still preserved his recollections and heavenly-mindedness. He was never hasty not loitering, but did each thing in its season, with an even uninterrupted composure and tranquillity of spirit...*

Julian and Eugenie came up at the weekend for a scrub and polish of the house before putting it on the market. Eugenie was in a state of desperation.

Despair looked at me from her blank eyes, sometimes so large and lustrous; but today, pebbles of despair as she thrashed around doing the work of ten men, which it would have been easier to pay for.

I made a cake from a recipe on the last page of Nigella Lawson's book Feasts.

This was a funeral cake, but the beautiful loaf in its tin with a long sprig of rosemary for remembrance on top inspired me. It was absolutely delicious, and has entered my repertoire with a fanfare. On Monday, I got up in good time to make another rosemary cake for morning tea with Kate and Jocelyn. This time I used twice the amount of cooked apple and lemon, more sugar and added vanilla.

It was a triumph. The big, tender, golden loaf with a sugary top, infused with the taste of lemon and rosemary, and with the rosemary sprig down the centre, was a culinary poem just to look at. It had a pure, classic feeling, qualities which can be applied to things other than music or sculpture! We all felt it was a work of art, which didn't stop us devouring it in large moist chunks, and Jocelyn took the recipe.

Both girls very pure, so we had apple tea instead of coffee, and we talked for hours, until nearly one o'clock. Jocelyn brought a jar of her fig and ginger jam, Kate, a fragrant bouquet of herbs and pink and violet flowers. I had laid a table with a linen cloth with a heavy crochet lace border, and with the curving Regency-style silver teapot, the bone china rosebud sprigged cups and saucers edged with gold, silver king's pattern cake-knives, white lace and linen napkins; it looked like one of those romantic magazine photographs. I left it, cake, crumbs, rosemary sprigs and all, untouched all day long to savour.

Yesterday, I fell off the wagon. Went shopping and doing errands with Patrick in town, and I never seemed to get into my stride. Going over to the other house to work out where I would start doing Eugenie's paint touch-ups, I found a book there, Alexander

McCall Smith's, 'The Sunday Philosophy Club,' which I read till I had finished it. Charming, erudite and civilised – art, music, ethics – all merging seamlessly. But apart from meditating, I hadn't been present all day, just for the sake of blobbing out with a book, going absent without leave as it were.

Thank heavens for Rumi, who I turned to this morning and his wonderful:

> *Come, come, come, whoever you are! Wanderer,*
> *Worshipper, lover of learning*
> *This is not a caravan of despair.*
> *It doesn't matter if you've*
> *Broken your vow a thousand times*
> *Still and yet again*
> *Come!*

As I copied this poem, I became aware of people outside.

There was a veritable regiment of Jehovah's Witnesses milling about, come to capture or rescue the erring souls of this village of roughly 400 people.

Since Julian and Eugenie are not here, the neighbours are away in Brisbane, and the weekenders, as they're known in the village, in both the other nearby houses are not here, it being mid-week, my soul was the only one up for grabs in this street.

The nice young man who made the attempt was obviously working a new technique, approaching the subject of God obliquely, beginning with a suggestion that we talk about families today, and the terrible rates of divorce and unhappiness.

He came at it from several angles, but I repelled him each time, kindly, I hope, but I wanted to actually get on with my own thoughts.

I reassured him that he was preaching to the converted, and that I prayed for the suffering, and he finally accepted the brush-off.

The friendly missionary last year, who assaulted this citadel of non-religion, when I said I had my own deeply held beliefs, shot back at me, 'But do you read your Bible?' I was able to answer evasively, but truthfully, 'My Bible is by my bed.' He accepted this as the answer to his question, and went off to harvest what he probably hoped were richer pastures, but what I feared would be deserts of disbelief. I can't imagine anything more demoralising than the constant rebuffs they must endure.

On the way through Whangateau, I saw a mother duck shepherding her family of tiny brown fluffy babies along the footpath, while she calmly brought up the rear.

There must have been at least a dozen, and one hadn't managed to make it up onto the low step-up of the pavement, and was now trying to keep up, anxiously scurrying along in the gutter!

Cara is still asleep on the unmade bed, a flat, black semi-circle. She slept all night stretched up against me, seeming to be purring every time I awoke. Maybe she was making amends for a dreadful incident last night in the cemetery.

As I strolled towards the look-out where I habitually inspect the flat rock far below with waves splashing over it at high tide, a cock pheasant ran across and into the undergrowth on the edge of the cliff.

Cara was a long way behind, and hadn't seen it, so I thought all was well. But when she reached me, she stood and sensed the area. She could have been a pointer, the way she sussed out the presence of the bird. Ignoring my peremptory calls, she purposefully plunged down the cliff. I attempted to grab her, but it was too dangerous. Occasionally, as I peered into the undergrowth, I would catch sight of her blackness skulking through the bushes. I went home with my arms full of pohutukawa twigs as usual, to use as firewood, and then came back in the hope of tracking her.

She turned out to be sitting behind a gravestone, and when she attempted to escape me again I grabbed her by a foreleg, and carried her firmly home, where we made sure she stayed. I hope it's not the breeding season. Once before at Kerikeri, she came home with a baby pheasant in her mouth half the size that she was. The distraught parents were actually chasing her. (The baby escaped, and was reunited with them)

September 26

The days go by so quickly, and yet each week seems to last ten years. Thursday suddenly turned into a day from hell.

First thing in the morning, I discovered that thanks to Eugenie helpfully giving me a password, which she thought, would remove an annoying message on my computer screen, all her emails were coming through to me. All of them since the beginning of the year! This meant that 6,792 messages were on their way into my computer. I switched off in panic, and illogically wrenched out the plug at the wall, but not before 396 had gate crashed their way into my system. This also told me something about her hectic work life.

While I was wrestling with this, and trying to get the computer man out here, Hannah arrived early, before I had done a tidy-up so she could actually clean. The computer man bustled in, Derek rang on Skype from England, and I had to ask him to ring back later, the local Derek, our indispensable handyman, arrived to help Patrick split the remaining logs in the garage, and a man from the electricity company arrived to sort out the problem of the meter in the garage.

The computer problem dominated my life all day, because hundreds of them had infiltrated not just into the inbox, but the out box, and the delete box... and then I'd find more...they felt like the maggots which once invaded the kitchen in Coromandel, and I kept finding them days later, even in the fold of my wallet! The level of stress I felt was ridiculous.

When Derek rang back from Plymouth after all the drama was over, he told me some fascinating things apropos of the Korean War book he'd sent Patrick for his birthday. His regiment, which had fought so bravely with the Gloucesters, at Imjin, but never got the same credit, was stationed in Hong Kong when the prisoners of war were finally released, after several years of near-starvation, torture and every form of deprivation. But back then, over fifty years ago, no one took any of this into account, and the poor wretches were sent straight back to their regiment in Hong Kong.

When Derek was posted to the regiment in 1967, they were in Germany. Reporting to the adjutant for his first Orderly Officer duty, he was told that the seventeen ex-POW's who were still serving with the regiment, would all be locked in Hut 23, and left there for the weekend. To Derek's astonishment, in they all filed, and with them, loads of food and crates and crates of beer, and there they all stayed for the whole *weekend, getting drunker and drunker, talking,* laughing, weeping. It was the regiment's well-meaning and ham-fisted way of dealing with post-traumatic shock, something no one even acknowledged in those days. A MASH type response...Hawkeye would have understood!

Today, they'd all be given post-traumatic counselling, and psychiatric care. After my father's war, everyone just went back to their homes, and jobs, in the army or out of it, and pretended no one was any different. But I remember my father and his friends all had flashbacks and nightmares for years.

I wake at night, hearing a possum huffing and puffing in the loquat tree outside my window, where he is chewing through the just-ripened fruit. The first time I heard a possum doing this in the darkness, I thought we had a python breathing by the window, regardless of the fact that there are no snakes in this country. I hope he leaves enough fruit to properly ripen for the wood pigeons. The loquats have turned their lovely apricot colour at least a month earlier than usual this year.

September 27

A tough few days. After the drama of yesterday, we spent all day Friday waiting to go to the hospital for Patrick's 4.30 appointment. When they'd finished with him it was dark, so back out into blackness, dazzling lights, rain and the Friday-night-first-day-of-the-holidays traffic. Julian and Eugenie are up here tidying with a big bin which we are also helping to fill, meaning we too are tidying up – a harrowing task.

Saturday lunch with Belinda at one of our favourite cafés, looking out at the overflowing waterfall in the rain, brought some surprises. When she said she had something amazing to tell me, I had thought it was about Cindy's course, which we start at the end of next week. But it was much more earth-shaking. In the space of a week, she had applied for a teaching job in Qatar, filled in the application forms, completed the interview, and is probably off in a few weeks. I thought I would feel sad. But I totally accept that it's the perfect thing for her. I let my good friend go without a pang, but I will still miss her.

September 30

Monday was another day of chaos, with Mike, Annie, George, the village handyman, Christopher (son) and Maria (girlfriend), arriving to dig out the steep front path and put in steps and a rail for Patrick's birthday present. It turned out to be a huge project, and what with delivering drinks, freshly-baked cake, morning and afternoon tea to the workers, who included Jim working next door at Eugenie's and the computer man coming out to eliminate another three thousand Eugenian files I had found dotted through the computer, it turned into another frantic day.

And the next day, the same. However, the finished product is very fine, adding to the feel of the entrance to the house, and much easier than the slippery bricks. Everyone marvelled at the bird life in the garden. I can stand under the plum tree, or by the bottlebrush, and a tui will sit in the branches, a few feet away and sing. His head goes from side to side, as he warbles variations on his theme. And it isn't just a one-off, he sings all day.

The regime Patrick and I started about six weeks ago is showing great dividends. We meditate for half an hour every night at seven o'clock. I still struggle with repeating everything constantly, and saying something, and then having to shout... C'est la vie, and we have another MRI scan next week.

Last night, now that daylight saving means it's light when we begin, I simply lit a candle and some tea-lights when we started. When we opened our eyes half an hour later, it was dark, and the room was lit by the flames of the fire and the candles. The silver candlesticks, and the glass jars and vases holding a collection of orchid blooms and camellias were gleaming in the candle-light. It felt so beautiful that we couldn't bear to move. Apart from making up the fire, I stayed there, after Patrick went to bed, savouring it, for another two hours.

Amongst other things, I thought about my children's childhood, when, although I struggled as a solo mother, and we went through some incredibly hard times after the Arthur Thomas case, not knowing if Patrick would have a job the next week, I didn't feel we had a hard life.

I had grown up with not much money, but we had a different measurement of well-being then. I thought back to my late childhood with my stepmother, and the criteria was 'good'. The list of necessities began with good manners, and went on with good food, good beds, good books, good clothes, good company. It was an experience of quality, and discrimination, rather than quantity or fashion. Good rugs were valued more than fitted carpet, good humour mattered more than plumbing.

So because I managed to supply these things in my children's childhood, and always managed to find lovely places to live, paid for ballet and concerts rather than holidays; and since, thanks to grandparents, the children were often dressed with parcels from Harrods or Liberty, I hadn't felt that we were deprived. Later, with Patrick, the children had good musical instruments, piano, clarinet and flute, and went to good schools. But we didn't have flash cars, and our home was an ode to Bloomsbury, with worn rugs, battered antiques, faded colours and lots of books, rather than a jingle to New York with fitted carpet, smart sofas and up-market fittings.

Now Patrick and I live what some might think was a very simple life, with an old car, an ancient TV, and a little cottage. But with all the 'goods' in place, no TV (we never switch it on), with hardly any other people near, no noise or pollution from traffic, aeroplanes, or any other technology –just fresh, fragrant air, bird song, the sound of the wind and the waves, starry skies at night and silence – our life seems utter luxury.

October 2

A few weeks ago, one of the Maori women on Patrick's board offered to give Patrick a lift home, dropping him at Warkworth, since she was going up to Whangarei. I misunderstood the timing of our rendezvous at Warkworth, and arrived twenty minutes late. This gracious, generous woman had sat in the car park, refusing to leave Patrick until I arrived, in spite of the long journey ahead of her.

This week, Patrick was waiting outside the board building for his taxi, which was late. A Maori member of a board committee came out, and seeing him there, insisted on getting a chair from a nearby café for Patrick to sit on, and refused to leave until the taxi came, and he could return the chair. For each of these people, time was no object, but courtesy and generosity were. Qualities which the western world in general seems to have forgotten, though obviously there are exceptions. I fear there are many occasions in my past when I would have thought time was more important than anything else, alas.

When I was trimming the miniature-variegated ivy round the birdbath yesterday morning, I kept hearing a surprising amount of traffic driving up our quiet cul-de-sac, eventually turning round and driving off. Even the local fishery's truck chugged up and parked for a while. A little later, I was quite touched to see four people standing on the picnic table looking out to sea. How sweet that they're enjoying the view, I thought to myself. Then Jim, who was still working on Eugenie's house, came over for a cup of tea, full of derision for the sightseers ... waiting for the tsunami, he laughed. I hadn't heard the news! So all the traffic and gazing was good old schadenfreude! The tsunami never arrived, to my disappointment too.

In spite of being exhausted, I went to Helena's in the evening, as I thought Rachel and Jackson were off overseas the next day. They weren't. But it turned out to be one of the happiest meetings I've experienced there. I talked to people I had always avoided, and enjoyed unexpected pleasure, and was approached by several people I've always longed to talk to, but who I felt before didn't have anything to say to me. I felt something had changed in me, thanks to a session with Cindy.

October 3

I went over to Eugenie's house today to check the chlorine tablets for the pool, and was dismayed to find a couple of swallows swooping over the pool, and dipping in *as they went past. Which means that they're drinking chlorinated water... unless they were snatching insects. Hope that was the reason, but doubt it.*

A hoolie has been going on at the cemetery by the grave of the boy who was killed in an accident three years ago. I wonder whether it was his twenty-first birthday, or the date he died. Anyway, a little crowd came and stood in the rain under umbrellas, with music blaring from a speaker in one of the cars parked outside the gates. They were there for over two hours in the rain, and came away rather the worse for wear, driving off with screeching of brakes, wheelies and much noise. No one expects to get picked up for merry driving out here...

Cooked a refreshing supper using a recipe from the paper; hard-boiled eggs in a caper and olive vinaigrette over steamed leeks. With warm crusty bread it was delicious, what I call a fragrant dish.

October 5

Spent most of the weekend working on Patrick's timeline of sixty years work in journalism and other achievements for Eugenie. It was surprisingly tiring, trying to bring order out of chaos, and it took every ounce of concentration wringing the facts out of Patrick, and checking his wonky chronology.

It made me think about my forty-three years in journalism...and the relationships with readers, which often evolved...particularly when I was writing for solo parents who felt there was no one else who understood, thirty-five years ago and more. Reviewing the interviews I did, which were mostly for entertainment value, with people like Iris Murdoch, and Dr Spock, Barbara Cartland and Robert Helpmann, Dr Seuss, and other then famous, and now forgotten people, there is one that I treasure.

It was an interview for the *Auckland Star* with a yachtsman called David McTaggart down at the Westhaven Marina. He had just created an organization called Greenpeace, and was off to Mururoa to protest against French nuclear testing. Greenpeace's first protest was in 1972. Quakers, as part of the peace movement, had been involved in the protests, and as I was an 'attender' at Quakers, they had asked me to go and interview this unknown Canadian who had started this new environmental organization. Neither Quakers, nor I, had any idea how far he and his organization would go. At the time, it seemed a brave and forlorn hope.

I'm also proud that Dr Christian Barnard tried to sue me over an article I wrote about vivisection, and about the cruelty to animals involved in his often needless experiments – like, for example, his boast on New Zealand television of making 'a two-headed dog to match the Russians' horrible experiment.

A bullying letter arrived from a top Auckland barrister, demanding an apology, a retraction, all my notes, and threatening a suit for major damages; demanding a reply within forty-eight hours (only the Rural Delivery didn't deliver it until several days later).

It felt as though the world was falling in when I read this. I'd have to do prison, rather than pay him money we didn't have.

I also felt prison would be preferable to paying him money even if we did have it.

When my solicitor wrote telling him what I would be saying in court to bring animal experimentation and exploitation out in the open, Barnard dropped the case. But a year or so later, he announced that he no longer used animals, saying there were some limits beyond which no civilised person would go. I've always wondered if it had anything to do with my article and letter.

My most worthwhile achievement was writing a story in order to set up a branch of Alcoholics Anonymous in Hong Kong. I went to several meetings of the handful of people the organiser had collected, and then wrote a story in the South China Morning Post. A.A. then took off, and the organiser, whose pseudonym was Margaret, became a dear friend. Staying with me recently, she told me there are now seventeen branches in Hong Kong, fourteen of them for Chinese, with the literature translated into Cantonese.

The weather is freezing, wet and wintry, with snow trapping people in their cars on the Desert Road. So back to roaring fires, hot soup, and comforting fish pie for lunch. We had soup and rolls for supper, lovely crunchy-crusted sourdough, heated up in the oven. Patrick asked me what was in the soup, since I pride myself on conjuring up soups out of nothing. This one was made from half a leek, in lieu of onion, a dollop of left over mashed kumara from yesterday, stock made from soaking some old dried-up mushrooms in boiling water, a chicken Oxo cube, some ginger, coriander, a dash of curry powder, and a quick whiz in the blender. Plenty of chopped parsley. Not bad.

Every night after supper and our meditation (good for our blood pressure amongst other things) we now listen to some music. Tonight we had Purcell, a medley of songs and orchestra, Alfred Deller, Kathleen Ferrier, Heather Harper, Janet Baker, each voice so unique and instantly recognisable. I love Purcell's trumpets, his drums, and the soul in his songs.

October 6

Still freezing, though at least the sun shines intermittently. Thank heavens it's the holidays, so that school children can stay warm at home, instead of fighting their way onto buses with heavy bags to get to school. In spite of the wintry weather, a pair of thrushes is building a nest in the camellia tree. I had planned to trim it back severely, as has been done before, and to topiary it. But those plans are now on hold, and I intend to drape the base in chicken wire to deter any cats: one in particular! When two blackbirds were feeding their nestlings a couple of years ago, a nearby Siamese climbed in one night and ravaged the nest. Luckily that cat is no longer around.

I've finished re-reading Evelyn Underhill's classic, 'Mysticism.' My friend Oiroa gave it to me over thirty years ago, when she felt she no longer needed it. It has been like a Bible to me, the last word on the spiritual life. Now, it feels rather dry, and sometimes even dogmatic in its thinking. Though she mentions eastern mystics, Underhill is biased towards the Christian mystics, but also makes, it seems to me, astounding judgements and categories among them.

She seemed stuck in that old feminine deference to masculine thinking. Male ideas of ascetism, and rigid rules and a hierarchy for the spiritual life were accepted without question, and so of course she seemed to agree with the church's traditional model of continual self-denial, abstinence and misery as a necessary path to spiritual maturity. Give me Quaker George Fox's sane, common sense attitude. When cavalier William Penn asked his advice about continuing to wear his sword, Fox is reputed to have said, 'I advise thee to wear it as long thou canst.' Penn soon found he couldn't, and didn't want to, wear it.

This re-reading has shown me how far I have moved away from the way I used to think. I met Oiroa, or Oi as she was known, at Quaker meetings, and we became close friends in spite of the forty years between us. Talking to a mutual friend who had no idea of Oi's hidden life; he said she was the most 'whole' person he had ever known. This delighted me, since this is what holiness means; he had unwittingly defined exactly what she was.

Went for a walk in the cold afternoon, cuddled the various dogs who came to greet me, and returned to afternoon tea of fragrant lapsang souchong, freshly baked scones, and Jocelyn's 'ruby jewel fig and ginger conserve', by the fire. Cara joined in this unbridled hedonism, leaping off the most comfortable chair (mine) in the house, to demand some milk. I give her a tiny dish, to try to limit her milk consumption, but she goes on demanding more until I refill it.

Officially, she shouldn't have milk at all, but since she has put herself on a very pure diet of expensive biscuits for fussy cats, and fresh roast chicken or fresh salmon, it has worked for her, and she now seems to be able to digest and slurp down as much milk as she fancies. I am forever trying to find things for her to eat, but she will only accept tinned salmon or tuna occasionally, and when she goes off fresh chicken or fish, I am at a standstill. All the dogs gratefully ate whatever *they were given*. But this self-invited and self-willed little cat, who ran away from home to join us, has laid down her own rules from the beginning. Patrick missed our little orgy of self–indulgence because he was struggling with a board conference call.

October 8

On Wednesday, I awoke knowing I had dry cleaning to pick up in Warkworth. So I rang Jackson to see if he was free for coffee and to lend me the Ken Robinson book.

We had a full-on New Age natter, from the benefits of the amino acids in millet, and how civilizations which switched from millet to wheat declined, to Karen Armstrong and the Dalai Lama, religious fanaticism and Ramadan, the wisdom and compassion of animals, to Victor Frankl and Fritz Perls.

Ironically, at the next table, a couple of fundamental Christians were also having a lovely heart to heart. I listened in, while Jackson got the coffee, being intrigued by the rough builder's gear of one, shorts and boots, and the rather prissy, patchwork knitted jumper worn by the other with a mismatching tartan scarf and John Lennon specs, somewhat at odds with his balding hair.

I heard the name Solomon, and followed a disjointed discussion, which went:

'It was his leadership...'

'Yes, and what a builder...'

'He built true...'

'It was his wisdom as well...'

'I used to think leadership was waiting for everyone to get it. Now, if someone's in my way, I just bowl 'em over.'

Hearty laughter... sycophantic from patchwork jumper...

'That's the way... leadership...'

'But what about all those women...'

'Oh, he needed their energy...'

Jumper said something inaudible and faintly embarrassed to this, and I was left tantalized, as Jackson returned with the coffee.

I followed this up by dropping into Salamander Books to say hello to Sally. She told me how ill Mary-Anne had been, and how her son had come to look after her. As she lay on her bed feeling shocking, after a couple of days vomiting, she suddenly became aware of white light just to the right of her. Hoping this meant she was passing over into the next world, she waited, but instead she began to feel better! After a while she got up, went into her son in the next room, and told him about this experience. He said 'Mum, I was visualising you having two angels standing to the right of your bed, and sending you healing!' This lovely man works with autistic children.

The morning was not yet over.

I stopped at Pigeon's Perch to pick up their delicious olive oil, bottled in chunky little green glass flagons with a handle, and had a stimulating chat with Andy and Janet.

At Matakana, I got them to put aside the Frances Partridge biography that Patrick is giving me for our wedding anniversary.

In the evening, I went to see 'The Young Victoria,' sumptuously produced, but as usual, the historical facts distorted to make a better story – or so it felt. So people who do not know will think that Melbourne was a selfish rake who Victoria was in love with, instead of being an elderly father figure. It was a much more interesting relationship than that. Greville, the famous diarist wrote rather movingly:

I have no doubt he is passionately fond of her as he might be of his daughter if he had one: and the more because he is a man with a capacity for loving without having anything in the world to love. It became his province to educate, instruct and form the most interesting mind and character in the world.

The worst thing, as I wrote to Belinda, another aficionado of royal jewellery, was that in the last lingering shot of Victoria in all her regal finery, they dressed her in the Russian Fringe tiara, which did not come into the Royal family until Queen Alexandra was on the throne! Tut tut! I wish I didn't have such a passion for accuracy. It often spoils a good story.

The thrushes nesting in the camellia tree have given up, since they saw Cara hiding in the ivy at the base of the tree, personifying nature red in tooth and claw. Wretch. In the last few weeks I've got to know two nearby neighbours, one a few years older than me, the other nearly thirty years younger, both promising to become good friends, and social occasions are suddenly sprouting like my green beans.

October 10

Yesterday I took a chocolate birthday cake and a magnificent book on the history of architecture, which I coveted for myself, into Piers. His eighteenth birthday today. It doesn't seem very long ago since I held him in my arms in the hospital while Eugenie had a shower after the birth. And then followed the weeks that Eugenie described rightly as a battlefield, saying men had their war stories, but childbirth was a woman's battlefield. We were all coping with the aftermath of her long exhausting labour, getting used to the new baby, still traumatised from his difficult birth, keeping her business going from home, with me answering the phone and relaying messages, and finding vases for the unending stream of flowers, which were constantly arriving. All my blouses and t-shirts were ruined with indelible mustard-coloured pollen from the lily stamens in every opulent hothouse bouquet!

I was also delivering endless jugs of water to Eugenie, while she struggled with a steel contraption called a breast pump, working to put supplies of mother's milk in the deep freeze for her nanny to give to the baby when she was back at work. And then, the day I was leaving when the baby was three weeks old, Eugenie fell downstairs, and hobbled around on crutches for the next month or so, unable to hold the baby and crutches at the same time, so there I was, back again. Happy, like all mothers, because I was needed!

Yesterday, after I left them, the baby, now eighteen, jumped into his car and drove up to Kerikeri. He told me later that he went to the places I'd taken him to when he was little... the stream that disappeared into the ravine sixty feet below, the Puketi Forest and the giant kauris, and eventually Pagoda Lodge where he and Charlie had stayed with their parents after they had been with me. This was almost next door, still within easy reach of Grannie for pancakes with brown sugar and lemon, dozens of hot buttered rolls, and the river for their endless games with pooh sticks, home-made boats and dams.

Today was my first day of Cindy's six-month course on exploring consciousness, and, I suspect, more delving into unexamined corners of our elusive psyches. To my relief I don't have to be gifted, I just have to carry out her instructions. That's the good part. The down-side is that I'm the oldest person there by more than twenty years, and I'm also well out of my comfort zone getting up early to drive into Auckland on a Saturday morning.

Nil desperandum. Spring is here, the sun is shining. A pair of blackbirds is making a nest in the plum tree, and I shall guard it with my life – and chicken wire round the trunk. When Hannah came to clean today she told me that her landlady had been walking round the bay yesterday, when she saw a pod of dolphins quite close in. Envy didn't begin to describe my feelings when I heard this. Fully clothed, she waded straight into the ice- cold sea to swim with the dolphins.

BIBLIOGRAPHY

These are some of the books which have given me not just enjoyment, but also fascinating facts and information during the writing of this journal, with grateful thanks and acknowledgement to every writer.

Gail Anderson-Dargatz: *A Recipe for Bees* (Virago, 1999)

Jane Austen: *Mansfield Park* (Penguin Books, 1966)
        Pride and Prejudice (Penguin Books, 1966)
        Sanditon, (Peter Davies Ltd, 1975)

Jean H. Baker: *Mary Todd Lincoln: A Biography* (Penguin Book, 1987)

Coleman Barks: *The Illuminated Rumi* (Broadway Books, 1997)

Irina Baronova: *Irina: Ballet, Life and Love* (Viking, 2005)

James Barr: *Setting the Desert on Fire* (Norton, 2008)

Werner Baumbach: *Broken Swastika* (Robert Hale Limited, 1960)

Antony Beevor: *D-Day: The Battle for Normandy* (Viking, 2009)

Major-General David Belchem: *All in the Day's March* (Collins, 1978)

Joe Bennett: *Mustn't Grumble, In Search of England and the English* (Simon & Schuster, 2006)

Elsdon Best: *Forest Lore of the Maori* (Te Papa Press, 2005)

Benson Bobrick: *The Making of the English Bible* (Phoenix, 2003)

Jean Bolen: *Goddesses in Everywoman: A New Psychology of Women* (Harper and Row Publishers Inc, 1985)

Arthur Bryant: *Turn of the Tide 1939-1943* (Collins, 1957)   *Triumph in the West 1943-1946* (Collins, 1959)

Kenneth Burns, Richard Burns and Geoffrey C. Ward: *The Civil War* (The Bodley Head, 1991)

Robert Byron: *The Road to Oxiania* (Picador, 1981)

Walter Lawry Buller: *Buller's Birds of New Zealand* (Whitcoulls Publishers, 1967)

David Cannadine: *The Decline and Fall of the British Aristocracy* (Papermac, 1996)

Bruce Catton: *U.S. Grant and the American Military Tradition* (Little, Brown and Co, 1954)

This Hallowed Ground (Wordsworth Editions, 1998)

A Stillness at Appomattox 3vols. (Doubleday & Co.Inc, 1962)

Deepak Chopra: *Why is God Laughing?* (Harmony Books, 2003)

Synchrodestiny (Harmony Books, 2003)

Ch'u Ta–Kao: *Tao Te Ching* (A Mandala Book, 1976)

Count Galeazzo Ciano: *The Ciano Diaries 1939 – 1943* (Simon Publications, 2001)

Richard Collier: *Duce! The Rise and Fall of Benito Mussolini* (Collins, 1971)

Avery Craven: *The Coming of the Civil War* (University of Chicago Press, 1966)

David Hackett Fischer: *Albion's Seed* Oxford University Press, 1989)

Shelby Foote: *The Civil War 3 Vols.* (Vintage Books, 1974)

Peter France: *Hermits: Insights of Solitude* (Griffin, 1998)

Iain Gale: *Four Days in June* (HarperCollins Publishers, 2006)

G.M. Gilbert: *Nuremberg Diary* (Da Capo Press, 1995)

Malcolm Gladwell: *The Tipping Point* (Abacus, 2000)

Charles Glass: *The Tribes Triumphant* (Harper Perennial, 2007)

President U.S. Grant: *The Complete Personal Memoirs of Ulysses S. Grant* (Cosimo Inc, 2006)

Charles C.F. Greville: *Greville Memoirs* (Edited by Henry Reeve Longmans, Green and Co, 1913)

H.A. Guerber: *The Myths of Greece and Rome* (George G. Harrap and Company, 1910)

David Hamilton-Williams: *Waterloo: New Perspectives* (Arms and Armour Press, 1995)

Valerie Davies

Thomas Hardy: *Tess of the d'Urbervilles* (Heron Books, 1970)

Rupert Hart-Davies and George Lyttelton: *The Lyttelton Hart/Davies Letters* 6Vols (John Murray Publishers 1985, 1986, 1987)

Georgette Heyer: *The Spanish Bride* (William Heinemann Ltd, 1940)

An Infamous Army (Arrow Books, 2004)

The Masqueraders (Pan Books Ltd, 1965)

Christopher Hibbert: *Wellington A Personal History* (HarperCollins Publishers, 1997)

Waterloo (Wordsworth Editions, 1998)

Rev Francis Kilvert: *Kilvert's Diary* (Jonathan Cape Ltd, 1944)

Rom Landau: *Islam and the Arabs* (George Allen & Unwin Ltd, 1958)

Brother Lawrence: *The Practice of the Presence of God* (Peter Pauper Press, 1963)

Nigella Lawson: *Feast* (Chatto & Windus, 2004)

James Lees-Milne: *Caves of Ice* (Michael Russell Publishing Ltd, 1983)

Holy Dread (John Murray Ltd, 2001)

Kenneth W. Leish: *The White House* (The Reader's Digest Association Limited London, 1972)

Prince Lichnowsky: *Prince Lichnowsky's Memoirs, My Mission to London* (Cassell & Company Ltd, 1918)

The Guilt of Germany for the War of German Aggression (G.P. Putnam's Sons, 1918)

Gordon Livingston: *Too Soon Old, Too Late Smart* (Hachette Australia, 2005)

Kate Llewellyn: *Burning* (Hudson Publishing, 1997)

Elisabeth Luard, *Family Life: Birth, Death and the Whole Damn Thing* (Corgi Books, 1996)

Judith Mackrell: *Bloomsbury Ballerina* (Phoenix, 2009)

Fitzroy Maclean: *Eastern Approaches* (Reprint Society, 1951)

Robert K. Massie: *Dreadnought* (Pimlico, 2004)

Somerset Maugham: *The Painted Veil* (Penguin Books, 1952)

Suzy Menkes: *The Royal Jewels* (Grafton Books, 1985)

Thomas Merton: *Thomas Merton Journals* (Harper, 1998)

Clara Milburn: *Mrs Milburn's Diaries* (Harrap London, 1979)

Nancy Mitford: *Frederick the Great* (Penguin Books, 1973)

H.V. Morton: *In Search of England* (Methuen & Co Ltd London, 1927)

Ray Moseley: *Mussolini's Shadow* (Yale University Press, 1999)

Airey Neave: *Nuremberg* (Hodder and Stoughton Ltd, 1978)

Valerie Davies

Wilfred Owen: *First World War Poetry* (Edited by Jon Silkin Allen Lane, 1979)

Helen Palmer: *The Enneagram* (Harper San Francisco, 1991)

Frances Partridge: *A Pacifist's War* (Phoenix Paperback, 1999)

Everything to Lose (Phoenix Paperback, 1999)

Marguerite Patten: *Cookery in Colour* (Paul Hamlyn, 1960)

Robert Perry: *Path of Light* (Circle Publishing, 2004)

Sam Reifler: *I Ching: A New Interpretation for Modern Times* (Bantam Books, 1974)

Norman Rose: *Harold Nicolson* (Pimlico, 2006)

Andrew Salmon: *To the Last Round* (Aurum Press Ltd, 2009)

William Shirer: *The Rise and Fall of the Third Reich* (Secker and Warburg, 1962)

Berlin Diary (Tess Press, 1941)

End of a Berlin Diary (Alfred A. Knopf, 1947)

Gitta Sereny: *Albert Speer: His Battle With Truth* (Picador, 1996)

Sir John Sinclair: *The Alice Bailey Inheritance* (Turnstone Press Ltd, 1984)

Alexander McCall Smith: *The Sunday Philosophy Club* (Pantheon Books, 2004)

Rabindranath Tagore: *Gitanjali* (MacMillan and Co Ltd, 1917)

Edmond Taylor: *The Fall of the Dynasties* (Dorset Press, 1963)

Awakening from History (Gambit, 1969)

Irene and Alan Taylor: *The Assassin's Cloak* (Canongate Books, 2000)

Barbara Tuchman, *The Zimmerman Telegram* (Papermac, 1981)

The Guns of August (Bonanza Books, 1982)

Alex Von Tunzelmann: *Indian Summer* (Simon & Schuster, UK Ltd, 2007)

Evelyn Underhill: *Mysticism* (Methuen & Co Ltd, 1911)

Elfrida Vipont: *George Fox and the Valiant Sixty* (Hamish Hamilton Ltd, 1975)

Helen Waddell: *The Desert Fathers* (Vintage Spiritual Classics Original, 1998)

Lyall Watson: *Heaven's Breath* (Hodder & Stoughton, 1984)

Richard M. Watt: *The Kings Depart* (Phoenix Press, 1968)

Ken Wilber: *A Brief History of Everything* (Hill of Content Publishing, 1996)

Essay: *The Brilliant Clarity of Ever-Present Awareness*

P.G. Wodehouse: *The Mating Season* (Penguin Books, 1957)

Rev James Woodforde: *The Diary of a Country Parson 1758 -1802* (Oxford University Press, 1978)

Jesse Bowman Young: *The Battle of Gettysburg* (John Kallmann Publishers, 1996)

A Course in Miracles, Foundation for Inner Peace (1985)

The King James Bible, Oxford University Press (1929)

The Book of Common Prayer, Oxford (1767)

The I AM Discourses, Saint Germain Press Inc (1976)

Christian faith and practice in the experience of the Society of Friends, published by London Yearly Meeting of the Religious Society of Friends (1960)

Acknowledgements

While every effort has been made to contact various writers who have been quoted, my queries have been unanswered in several cases.

I would be grateful to hear from authors or publishers who feel that they have not been properly credited.

THE AUTHOR

Valerie Davies was the Woman's Editor of *The South China Morning Post* in Hong Kong for several years. She moved to New Zealand, became a writer at the Auckland Star, and was a columnist for several years before becoming the Woman's Editor. At the same time, she wrote a column for families and children in New Zealand's *Woman's Weekly* for fifteen years.

Valerie is married to Pat Booth and they now live in Northland, New Zealand.